Eternity
and
Time's *Flow*

D1563476

SUNY Series in Philosophy
George R. Lucas, Jr., editor

AND

SUNY Series in Religion
Harold Coward, editor

Eternity
and
Time's Flow

Robert Cummings Neville

Illustrations and Cover Design by Beth Neville

STATE UNIVERSITY OF NEW YORK PRESS

Published by
State University of New York Press, Albany

For information, address State University of New York Press,
State University Plaza, Albany, N.Y., 12246

Production by Marilyn P. Semerad
Marketing by Fran Keneston

Library of Congress Cataloging-in-Publication Data

Neville, Robert C.
    Eternity and time's flow / Robert Cummings Neville.
        p.   cm. — (SUNY series in philosophy) (SUNY series in
    religion)
    Includes bibliographical references and index.
    ISBN 0-7914-1599-6. — ISBN 0-7914-1600-3 (pbk.)
    1. Eternity.   2. Time—Religious aspects—Christianity.
3. Immortality.   I. Title.   II. Series.   III. Series: SUNY series
in religion.
BT912.N48   1993
115—dc20   92-27081
                                                         CIP

10 9 8 7 6 5 4 3 2 1

For Leonora Alice Neville

Contents

Author's Preface

Eternity is the symbol of the deepest longing of the civilized human spirit. Many other symbols parse it: Union with an eternal being, Nirvana or blowing out the flame of cycling lives, Transcendence of death and limitation, Immersion in nature or the Tao that overflows all finite identities, Identification with the All, Indelibility in perfect memory, Confrontation of the wholly other of time, Enlightened realization of inexpressible truth. Entire religious traditions have been built around each one, and yet there is common recognition in religions that each is but a selective approach to a deeper goal and reality. Each of these parsings has some special relation to time and can be rejected as illusory, as by modern secularists, through a special emphasis on time and temporal limitation. Nevertheless, a realistic grasp of time opens onto the longing for eternity. If time is not to be misunderstood as a fake substitute for eternity, a sequence of static Nows bumping along, time's flow should be understood as eternity's child. My purpose here is to make that case.

This book has been a very long time in gestation, and its two central ideas, eternity and time, have developed along different routes in my thinking. In the hypothesis about creation *ex nihilo* that I developed first in a dissertation and then expanded more fully in *God the Creator* (1992a; orig. 1968), the claim was made that time is created, and therefore the act of creation must be eternal. Furthermore, it was apparent in those early essays that *how* time begins, for instance with a Big Bang or always in a Steady State, is something internal to the creative act. Therefore, questions of physical cosmogony of the sort pursued by astrophysicists are all of an empirical nature to be settled without specific reference to eternal creation *ex nihilo* but set within its context. Because eternal ontological creation is of the whole of time, inclusive of absolutely everything determinate (so I argued), the theory of creation is compatible with any possible results of scientific investigation. Whatever there is, in and about time, it is created. *Any* physical science, therefore, is compatible with the metaphysics of creation *ex nihilo*.

But in what does the eternity of the creative act consist? That it is "not temporal" is uninformative. The "character" of eternity can be known only from what is involved in the ontological act of creation and from what is created. That point serves as a reference for pursuing the topic of eternity from the many directions in which it is of interest.

This book picks up the pursuit of eternity from the standpoint of practical religion, at which it appears as the topic of eternal life or immortality. It also explores eternity from the standpoint of theology, at which the question is the eternity or temporality of God. Temporality itself, at its most dynamic, symbolized in the phrase "time's flow," reveals itself to be possible only because the past, present, and future are together eternally. That is, they are not together temporally, with one coming before another—temporal *things* are together temporally but not the modes of time themselves. Rather, the modes of time come together to form the possibility of temporal things and time's flow in the very ontological constitution of temporal things; that is, in the eternity of the creation of time. More, this book comes at eternity from the standpoint of understanding moral responsibility, which I believe is impossible without acknowledging an eternal togetherness, in addition to temporal togetherness, of a moral agent's past, present, and future.

Many people regard the religious quest for immortality as mere superstition, and the theological inquiry into God's nature as the search for a ghost, and so these readers might not be impressed with an interest in eternity deriving from these standpoints. But most people do accept the idea of moral responsibility, or at least presuppose it if they deny the validity of the idea.[1] This book argues first for eternity in personal moral identity, then for eternity in divine creation, and finally for eternal life in the religious sense.

The idea of time, in contrast to eternity, had somewhat formal antecedents in my early reflections on creation *ex nihilo* but took on positive dimensions in discussions of process philosophy in *The Cosmology of Freedom* (1974). That book was written to demonstrate that temporal human freedom is not compromised by a theory of eternal creation. Process philosophy is particularly interesting for its technical representation of free, decisive action in the becoming of a moment of "present" time. The arguments in the present book adopt much of Whitehead's theory of present emergence and presuppose the success of much of his technical analysis. As my own cosmological speculations came to be more and more independent of Whitehead's, however, I came to see his preoccupation with *present* time as a mistake, moreover a mistake in which process philosophy is joined by much of the modern philosophic tradition in Europe from Descartes and Kant on down.

This book, therefore, expresses a negative polemic against the modern preoccupation, indeed obsession, with present time. It positively develops an alternative theory of time that emphasizes the equal but different and related reality of the three modes of time: past, present, and future. Only the nontemporal or eternal togetherness of the different temporal modes allows for the understanding of time's flow, I argue. Hence the conception of time to be advocated here is of its flow as set in the context of eternity. Eternity comes to be understood positively as the context within which past, present, and future are together with the internal dynamism of time's flow. The eternal act of creation thus is to be conceived as eternally dynamic or living: God. This is a Western, theistic, representation that has counterparts, though without the typical theistic connotation of personal agency, in some other religions. The partly polemical orientation of this book leads me to represent other thinkers sometimes in terms of their common reception rather than their own nuanced texts. Novice readers should consult original texts and commentaries while partisans should see my more scholarly works which are already too frequently cited.

For many years Beth Neville, my most intimate critic, has argued that the chief virtue of my metaphysical ideas is that they are entirely hospitable to the changing ideas of contemporary science. Furthermore, by transposing certain of the crucial questions of religion and morals to the metaphysical level, it is possible to dismiss many of the modern objections to religion and morals that arise from scientific methodological commitments to determinism and a closed system for the conservation of energy. God should not be conceived as a being who has to be somewhere and somewhen before creation, any more than God should be conceived as an extraterrestrial being whom the astronauts ought to be able to find. Similarly, the indeterminacy of the future required to locate responsibility in individual agents rather than in their background of antecedents need not conflict with those regularities that science discovers in actual observation and testing. So, a theme of this book is how recent advances in physical cosmology relate to the conceptions of time and eternity. In keeping with this theme, Beth Neville argues that the ancient illustration of eternity as "two people and a ham" should be replaced by the scientific ambiance of "economy class from New York to Hong Kong." Both illustrations, however, confuse eternity with everlastingness, which surely *is* boring.

The argument of this book is more eclectic than is comfortable for me. Its center is philosophical, even metaphysical. Yet the strands that provide both its orientation and its strength come from science, ethics, social analysis, cultural criticism, religion, and theology. This presents an interesting rhetorical challenge. Each of these domains, especially in its academic development, has linguistic peculiarities and quasi-technical jargon known to everyone in that field but not known to specialists in other fields. Thus every physical scientist knows what the issue of the Friedmann equation is and how it relates to Big Bang cosmologies, and every theologian knows what kenosis is about, although each is likely to be mystified by the other's "natural language" and react according to his or her own discipline's habits concerning mystification.

The rhetorical problem is whether to eliminate all specialized language and write in the lowest common denominator of the television vocabulary or to give readers credit for the ability to expand their vocabularies, and consequently their understanding of the habits of thought in specialized disciplines. I am inspired by Alfred North Whitehead to do the latter. In books such as *Science and the Modern World* he combined intellectual history, scientific analysis, cultural criticism, and moral admonition with some of the most abstract, original, and speculative metaphysics since Leibniz's *Monadology*. Furthermore, as a teacher I deplore the reduction of language to what "communicates" without effort and would not be able to limit myself to a television vocabulary even lacking Whitehead's example. Finally, a crucial intellectual and cultural issue is at stake. The exciting complexity of the contemporary world consists in part in the plurality of habits of thought enshrined in specialties: either the common person dismisses all specialties as alien, incomprehensible, and ungovernable or the common person stretches common language to include special fields. The former way leads to enslavement by experts and the latter to liberal education. How could there be a choice? So the reader should take warning, after due apologies have been received, that the writing here is maximilist rather than minimalist in its demands to learn what is mere background assumption for some specialist but that might be entirely new, even barbarous, to the novice at that specialty.

Not only style but the structure of the argument is affected by the plurality of disciplines involved. Good style is sometimes thought to consist in a clear treatment of one topic that leads to the treatment of the adjacent topic and so on to build an edifice with blocks of analysis. This style makes it possible for a reader to turn to a specific chapter or section to ascertain the book's position on its topic. But better style has to acknowledge that, because of the plurality of approaches and angles of inquiry, no consistently written chapter can be more than a partial statement. Better style returns to the material again and again, treating it from one perspective and then the next, revising the early statements in light of the latter, like a complex musical composition. Plato in the cumulative dialogues had a better style, more realistic to genuine thinking, than Aristotle in the little definitional essays.

So this book runs at time and eternity again and again, developing many lines of questioning and a complex philosophical vocabulary. The metaphysical terms are defined repeatedly, each time with additions that have accrued through the argument since the previous definition. Again and again, time and eternity will be described in philosophical and theological terms, and in ethical and religious terms; this is not mere repetition, but repetitions with a difference. Major summaries and previews are given at the end of Chapter 1 and at the beginning of Chapter 16; minor reviews and reformulations of anticipations are given in every chapter, nearly in every section.

With reference to the theological elements of the argument it should be noted at the outset that my own background is Christian, that the historical origin of some of the main metaphors, for instance, creation *ex nihilo*, comes from that tradition, and that I have a special interest in relating the argument here to Christian themes and symbols. It is always a fair criticism to say that my claims to universality are compromised or biased by my historical origin and that certain major notions are similarly biased. Yet it should also be acknowledged that a conscious effort has been made, and sometimes appears in the text, to treat theological ideas in a comparative fashion.

Finally, the argument for the use of the theological ideas, even those relating to religious practice that occur frequently in Part Four, derives from dialectical philosophical considerations and should be judged in that context. Indeed, this book reflects a formal methodological claim for theology, that it necessarily requires three genres of argument, each as a corrective of the others. One is theological writing that analyzes, reconstructs, and justifies the theological symbols of specific communities of religious faith, particularly those of its primary and secondary scriptures; if one's theology cannot do this, its applicability is severely put in doubt, and the more communities of faith it can articulate the better. Another genre of theological argument is comparative theology, the formulation of comparative categories for relating religious ideas and the careful rearticulation of those ideas in comparison with one another; only in this way will it be possible to tell whether ideas, for instance of ultimacy, are the same among religions, only similar, complementary, contradictory, or wholly irrelevant. The third theological genre is philosophical theology, the development and criticism of divine matters through philosophical argument.[2] Philosophical argument in the West has until very recently meant only philosophical argument of the Western sort. Now we know that the philosophical public includes motifs, themes, ideas, and thinkers from other traditions, although commitment to that conviction is honored more often in the breach than in regular practice. This book, in the vain pursuit of brevity, neglects even important recent Western arguments such as J. E. McTaggart's (1927), Brumbaugh's (1984), and Harris' (1988) on the metaphysics of time, Sherover's (1989) on time in politics and culture, and Vaught's (1982) on human time. The neglect of recent arguments about eternity is less serious because there are so few: Stephen Crites's Kierkegaard Study (1993) and Ray Hart's Eckhart study are gems and Lewis S. Ford's forthcoming *Transforming Theism* brings process theology into the discussion of eternity.

My debts for contributions to this book are unusually far-flung. The first and oldest is to Roy C. Dripps, my sophomore high school English teacher, who one day while walking down the hall with me said, "You know, Bob, God is not in time." I understood clearly what he meant and from that time on, because of that fact, knew that I think differently from most people. I still do not quite understand why so many people have difficulty with the idea of eternity, except that their imagination must be glued to temporal analogies. How else can we understand time except in contrast with eternity? Could it be that most people do not get time's flow? The whole point is really much more obvious than the cumbersome metaphysics developed here would suggest.

A second debt is to others during my high school years who engaged my imagination about theological matters, including two ministers, Raymond R. Sturgis and Andrew B. Smither, my friend and Sunday School teacher Helen I. Baldwin, and my very first and continuing real friend, Raymond T. Shepherd. In college and graduate school I was privileged to study philosophy and philosophical theology with many fine teachers who treated of time and eternity, including Brand Blanshard, Charles Hendel, Rulon Wells, Robert S. Brumbaugh, Paul Weiss, Richard Bernstein, and most especially John E. Smith who directed my dissertation. As to philosophy of science, I was fortunate to study with Wilfrid Sellars and F. S. C. Northrop, the latter of whom used to tell stories of his own graduate student days when he commuted between Harvard and Princeton to interpret Whitehead and Einstein to one another.

As everyone knows, the real intermixture of philosophy, science, and religion does not take place in courses on those subjects, nor in specializations that define professional careers. Rather it takes place in meal talk, late night conversations, and learning to live with people whose approaches differ from one's own. Perhaps my greatest fortune was to be tempered into a thinker who has to respect and move in all these realms before I could be disciplined into a specialist. The undergraduate and graduate friends who did this include Richard Beals, Edmund Leites, Jonathan Weiss, George Smith, David Krantz, Dennis Longwell, William Derveniotes, Gary Knoble, Jeremy Sprung, Gordon Mork, Alexander Lukens, Peter Kirschner, Edward Carleton, William Wiebenga, Robert Ehmann, Stephen Erickson, and Carl Vaught. Since that time I have carried on extended conversations on these topics with many others, including William Sullivan, Joseph Grange, Robert Mulvaney, Alexander von Schoenborn, Elizabeth M. Kraus, William Richardson, S.J., Quentin Lauer, S.J., Norris Clarke, S.J., Steve Odin, Jay Schulkin, Warren Frisina, John Berthrong, David Hall, Roger Ames, Rodney Taylor, Judith Berling, Thomas J. J. Altizer, Peter Manchester, Sung-bae Park, Edward Casey, David Weissman, Patrick Heelan, S.J., William Eastman, Joseph Hallman, Alan Olson, Robert Morrison, Curtis Daugaard, Loye Brad Ashton, John John, Sean Recroft, John B. Cobb, Jr., David Griffin, Marjorie Suchocki, Paul Sampley, Simon Parker, Horace Allen, Ray Hart, Imani-Sheila Newsome, and Harold Oliver. My thanks go to all of these, each of whom can find material in this book against which he or she warned me. Lewis S. Ford, a friend and conversation partner since graduate school, read and commented extensively on the penultimate draft of the entire book; many of his suggestions have been incorporated, and his forthcoming *Transforming Theism* is the next move in an ongoing debate. I thank Jay Schulkin for telling me, after much confusion on my part, for what audience to write this book: for Paul Tillich.

Biblical quotations are taken from the New Revised Standard Version of the Bible, copyright 1989, by the Division of Christian Education of the National Council of Churches of Christ in the United States of America.

Leonora Alice Neville, my daughter, is now a graduate student in Byzantine history, preoccupied with time and eternity in very special senses. I am proud to honor her in the dedication of this book.

Artist's Preface

For the first time in 30 years of marriage, my husband and I are both dealing with problems of eternity and time although from the different perspectives of philosophy and art. My latest drawings attempt to transcend traditional notions of time and space, both in terms of their format and their content. Scientific images revealed by recent space exploration are the basis for ink drawings which are montaged together and subsequently photocopied onto a 55 foot long unrolling scroll titled *"Toward Enlightenment."*

When I was five years old growing up on a remote apple farm, my mother and I looked up into a bright night sky undiminished by city lights. She pointed out the thick Milky Way, the aurora borealis, a constellation or two, and made me promise I would study the sky and its mysteries when I grew up. I've not become an astronomer, but amateur reading about space has revealed a diverse new world of luminous beauty which is the cosmos.

Recent scientific discoveries about the universe have not only expanded our notions of the origin of the cosmos, of eternity and time's flow, but have given us a spectacular new visual world to explore. This world is revealed in photographs of vivid colors swirling in abstract arabesques, and in equally exotic black and white diagrams, such as the computer generated "Velocity Map" of the Milky Way. According to some astrophysicists' theories, the Milky Way and thousands of other galaxies are flowing like a river across the heavens at a furious rate. The Velocity Map's arrows, generated by Avashai Dekel and Edmund Bertschinger (see *Science News*, 12/12/1992, Vol. 142, p. 408–410), have provided me with a basic pattern for brush strokes used on the cover of *Eternity and*

Time's Flow. Other images of space revealed by the Hubble Space Telescope, the NASA Infrared Telescope Facility, the Gamma Ray Observatory, the Cosmic Microwave Background Explorer and similar sources, open the artists' imaging eye to colors, textures, patterns, and shapes of extraordinary novelty. These images provide the basis for the illustrations accompanying Robert's text.

Many artists are painting accurate, large, colorful, but symbolically empty works which competently replicate photographs of space. However, for me, the greater opportunity is to alter, recombine and juxtapose this abundant wealth of visual information. The glowing beauty of the cosmic images does not need enhancement, but rather an interpretative context dealing with ancient problems of space, time, history and creativity. Thus the realm of cosmological knowledge may be used to bring humans new meaning and emotional insight about life on planet Earth.

The illustrations for *Eternity and Time's Flow* trace the development of human knowledge from Earth's dark interior recesses, then travel outward in space and backward in time to an ever expanding beginning moment. The illustrations, in order, are: 1.) ancient cave pictographs and fertility sculptures, humans' earliest attempts to control and demarcate knowledge, page 3; 2.) Garden of Eden, a glimpse of early agricultural civilization, page 15; 3.) God's rainbow promise and pulsating energy waves, page 29; 4.) Earth as both Sol's planet and a political/cultural unit, the two images fused, page 45; 5.) tripartite vision of Milky Way's map, page 65; 6.) mapping of gamma rays of Milky Way, page 77; 7.) exploding "Star 1987A", page 93; 8.) black hole, page 107; and 9.) microwave radiation fluctuations left over from the universe's explosive birth; now humans' latest attempt to demarcate their knowledge, page 123.

BETH NEVILLE, 1/3/1993

Part One

*Eternity and the Time Passion of
the Modern World*

"Ancient Cave Pictographs and Fertility Sculptures"
Neville 1993

Chapter One

A TIME TO RETHINK ETERNITY

Science

Nothing in the ancient speculations about eternity and time is as wild and improbable to common sense as the current speculation of scientific physical cosmologists. How can the ancient Indian theories of kalpas or world cycles compare with recent theories of the Big Bang or of the possible return of presently expanding matter to an infinitely dense atom? The Mahayana Buddhist theory of worlds within worlds within worlds looks like a child's analogy compared to contemporary depictions of galaxies, molecules, atoms, photons, and quarks. Hellenistic theories of eons arching over eons is nothing compared to current speculations about antimatter, dark matter, black holes, and the fifth dimension.

At the time of this writing, scientists have claimed to have found nearly persuasive evidence of a Big Bang origin of the universe some 15 to 20 billion years ago.[1] Time began, the theory asserts, when a mass so small as not to have a right side and a left side, so dense as not to have an inside relative to an outside, began to expand. Time thus began with movement, and space was created by the internal trajectory of the expanding mass's internally differentiating parts. Traces of this expansion, according to one interpretation of the observations, have been identified as early as within 300,000 years of the Bang, when background microwave radiation shows differential massing of what before had been an undifferentiated soup of matter and radiation.

At the beginning of the twentieth century, and for most people up until the last twenty years, this situation of unpicturable speculations would have been incomprehensible. After the first shocks of the "modern" cosmology of the European renaissance to the medieval worldview, the representation of the physical world has been resolutely tame. From Galileo, Descartes, and Newton down to the startling upsets of Clerk Maxwell in the nineteenth century, physical reality had been modeled on physical objects of common sense, such as billiard balls, behaving in ways that could be described and illustrated, such as movement, direction, attraction, weight, and force (see the accounts of Burtt 1932 and d'Abro 1950, as well as Silk 1989). Nothing physical could fail to have right and left sides. In a comparative sense, biological sciences, even more than physics, have been oriented to the themes, metaphors, and models of the ordinary world of experience. Although contemporary biology is based on genetics and the chemical components of genetics, its intellectual and technical popularity rests in large part on the fact that its basic elements, for instance the double helix, can be pictured.

The reasons for this domesticated imagination have included many things, but central was a penchant for reductionism. Whereas Aristotelian science had thought that classes should be multiplied to match all possible discriminations, renaissance science thought that explanation was best with the fewest considerations. This was the result of the Occamist principle that one should not multiply entities beyond necessity. What does *the fewest considerations* mean? For a long time it meant the simplest things that conform to imaginable common sense. Descartes gave the classic modern statement of this principle in his theory of understanding as analysis: analyze things down to the simplest parts that can be understood each completely in itself and then imaginatively reassemble the whole, noting what you do to put the parts back together. The Cartesian project is reflected in our practice of building theoretical models, with the exception that the parts of the models do not have to be intuitively comprehensible simples.[2] The American scientist and philosopher Charles Peirce reinterpreted Occam's principle to mean the things in which we most naturally or easily believe, especially those things belief in which comes easily with sophisticated mathematical understanding.[3] Recent physical speculations have moved into the realm of the "unbelievable" to make sense of data that do not themselves make sense without wild interpretation. The wildest of contemporary speculations seek to be tamed by observations, of course, if not by conformity to old images. But with the twentieth century's abandonment of modernity's preference for physics within the limits of the picturable, science once again joins with religion to articulate ultimate realities.

Religion

Religion in the West has had a hard time since the European renaissance because its treatments of ultimate limits and meanings are really a little silly if they have to be mapped onto a literal picturable frame. Modern physics until the twentieth century has said that time and space constitute an infinitely extended container within which events take place, as Fenway Park constitutes a playing field for baseball games (though with the exception that all the stands are infinitely far from the pitcher's mound). On the modern container theory, the creation of the world as theologically articulated would have to be represented as an event within time. What did God do before creation? Nothing? Love the divine essense? Twiddle thumbs without moving? Silly! What can eternal life (or Enlightenment or Nirvana) mean if everything is an event within the playing field and yet these events are not within the horizon of our observation? Eternal life would have to be more time later, or elsewhere, again something a bit silly and not to the religious point. If contemporary science has broken the stranglehold of the insistence that ultimate things must be picturable in terms that apply *within* the world, then perhaps religion can recover a voice of its own.

If religion does not seek its own voice in the current situation, then physics will give it to her. In his extraordinarily popular book, *A Brief History of Time* (1988), Stephen Hawking, the Lucasian Professor of Mathematics at Cambridge University, repeatedly raises the question of whether the new physics calls for or excludes a divine creator. Are the laws of the universe arbitrary, or can there be only one consistent set? If arbitrary, then there must be a creator to select them, according to Hawking. Is there an arbitrary set of initial conditions for the world? If so, he sees the need for a creator God. He presses his theological speculation:

> Even if there is only one possible unified theory, it is just a set of rules and equations. What is it that breathes fire into the equations and makes a universe for them to describe? The usual approach of science of constructing a mathematical model cannot answer the questions of why there should be a universe for the model to describe. Why does the universe go to all the bother of existing? Is the unified theory so compelling that it brings about its own existence? Or does it need a Creator, and, if so, does he have any other effect on the universe? And who created him? (1988, p. 174)

Fred Hoyle and Chandra Wickramasinghe conclude their *Cosmic Life-Force* with a chapter entitled "The Concept of a Creator" whose last paragraph reads as follows:

> The Creator has been given many shapes and names in the diverse cultures throughout the world. He has been called Jehovah, Brahma, Allah, Father in Heaven, God, in different religions, but the underlying concept has been the same. The general belief that is common to all religions is that the Universe, particularly the world of life, was created by a 'being' of incomprehensibly magnified human-type intelligence. It would be fair to say that the overwhelming majority of humans who have ever lived on this planet would have instinctively accepted this point of view in some form, totally and without reservation. In view of the thesis of this book, it would seem to be almost in the nature of our genes to be able to evolve a consciousness of precisely this kind, almost as if we are creatures destined to perceive the truth relating to our origins in an instinctive way. (1988, p. 144)

Many critical questions might be raised about both of these statements from the standpoint of the contemporary study of religion. There is far greater diversity among the world's religious conceptions of the ultimate than these scientists acknowledge. Nevertheless, the questions to which the theistic religions offer the conception of a creator God as an answer are questions that science now demands to be answered. If Buddhism and Confucianism, for instance, offer answers that at least appear to be different, they still have addressed the questions science presses, and perhaps the theistic approach has its own merits. The discussion in this book develops a model with theistic language.

Also critical questions are to be raised about the conception of God to which Hawking, Hoyle, and Wickramasinghe refer. That Hoyle and Wickramasinghe claim that God is a 'being,' and put *being* in scare quotes, signals a problem in the conception of the divine. It is the same problem that causes Hawking to ask who created God. God can no more be pictured as a 'being' within the world than ultimate origins and destiny can be depicted as events within the space-time playing field.

Metaphysics

The proper critical study of ultimate notions such as eternity, time, and God includes a moment that is more abstract than either the cosmological theories of science or the conceptions used in religious practice, direction, and meditation. Ultimate notions have a metaphysical dimension that requires clarification on its own and that is presupposed in discussions of lesser generality.

Although certain metaphysical notions will be introduced in Chapter 5 with a more elaborate discussion of metaphysics as such, a crucial relation between metaphysics on the one hand and religion and science on the other should be introduced here. Not only are metaphysical notions more abstract than those of religion and science, they are also vague with respect to them. Vagueness is not fuzziness but rather tolerance of ambiguity, confusion, and contradiction among the less abstract notions that might specify the vague ideas.[4] A metaphysical theory of selfhood, for instance, is vague with respect to whether a Freudian or Skinnerian specification of it is true, tolerating either (and maybe both if they are in fact complementary). A metaphysical theory of space-time is vague with respect to whether our world is bounded or unbounded. A metaphysical theory of divine creation is vague with respect to whether there is a Big Bang first moment or rather an infinite Steady State.

There are some important asymmetrical truth relations among a vague metaphysical theory and the less vague theories that might specify it. That a less vague theory, such as the Big Bang, is true entails that any vaguer metaphysical theory must allow for the truth of the less vague theory; if the metaphysical theory does not allow for that truth, as Aristotle's does not, then the metaphysical theory is false. Furthermore, so long as an alternative theory to the less vague one, say the Steady State theory, has any reasonable plausibility, then the vaguer metaphysical theory ought to allow for its truth as well as that of the Big Bang. The metaphysical theory is vague precisely to allow for the truth of either. The same holds with respect to theological ideas of the divine. If the theistic hypothesis about God is true, the vaguer metaphysical hypothesis needs to allow for the possibility of that truth. But if there is plausibility in nontheistic Buddhism, then the metaphysics of the divine must allow for that as well. Obviously, the range of less-vague hypotheses to which a metaphysical theory ought to be tolerant changes with time and the conditions of plausibility.

On the other hand, if a metaphysical theory is true, or is presumed to be true, that does not entail the truth of any of the less vague theories that might make it more specific. No metaphysics can prove the Big Bang or Christian theism. Rather, the service metaphysics can render to the less vague theories is to show how they are possible, especially how they are possible in relation to something to which the less vague theories do not readily connect. For instance, a metaphysical theory of divine creation can show how something can come from nothing, whether the something is a Big Bang or a Steady State; it can address Hawking's question about why the universe exists so that physics can model it. Or a metaphysics can show how a Christian conception of God or a Buddhist conception of the Unconditioned is compatible with scientific conceptions.

Given the rapidity with which scientific conceptions are changing and the vast diversity of possibly competing or overlapping religious conceptions, wisdom stresses their status as theories. Better yet, we should conceive them as hypotheses, remembering Charles Peirce's theory of hypotheses.[5] An hypothesis, he said, is a leading principle for thought or action, and it resides in communities as an actual or potential habit for thought or action. As such, most hypotheses are assumed, not questioned, and simply acted upon. This may be especially true in religion; indeed religion often both questions and voluntarily affirms its hypotheses. Other hypotheses are held in various modes of tentativeness, sometimes being explicitly doubted or tested or held in equilibrium with alternatives. The equilibrium with which many physicists of a generation ago held the Big Bang and Steady State theories now has tilted to the greater plausibility of the former.[6]

Peirce's main point is that, as actual or potential habits of engaging the world, hypotheses are always undergoing correction, being reinforced, modified, or threatened. The advantage of science is that, by means of practised observation and controlled experiments, it puts certain habits directly in position for correction, testing them as hypotheses. Religion's habits, too, are tested by the slow evolution of the human heart and community, said Peirce, and although slower than scientific testing, religious hypotheses are far surer and more deeply corrected than scientific ones. Peirce agreed with Hoyle and Wickramasinghe that speculation in all times and cultures has led instinctively to the idea of God as creator.[7]

The inquiry here into eternity and time proceeds with a tentativeness appropriate to the preceding observations. The current theory of the Big Bang will surely be developed beyond its present state. But its successor theories must include it as a primitive statement, or at least must account better for that for which the Big Bang theory accounts. Religious conceptions are tentative in a somewhat different sense, although they too evolve in conjunction with scientific conceptions. Because religious conceptions are so tied to the specific histories of practising faith communities, it is extremely difficult to tell how the apparent parallels in different traditions relate. Some thinkers believe that all religions must be saying the same thing underneath the languages that differ for historical reasons. Other thinkers believe that religious histories are so specific as to be incomparable. Neither position is an empirical belief, however, and the question is surely an empirical one. We simply are at too primitive a stage of religious studies to suggest more than plausible hypotheses about comparative matters.[8] Perhaps it is safe to assume that there is some profound truth in all the major religious traditions, otherwise their conceptions would have been corrected in the heart long ago. Yet the formulation of those conceptions to be dialectically comprehensible and

comparable has yet to be done in most cases. Finally, the metaphysical speculations to be advanced here are themselves surely to be
treated as hypotheses whose plausibility depends in part on how
much sense they make of eternity and time's flow.

The Argument

This book has four main theses. The first is that "time and eternity
make one topic, not two," to use Peter Manchester's words (see
Chapter 2 for the full quotation). The modern world has distorted
or neglected this truth by an obsession with time alone, which in
turn has led to a diminished theory of time compared with that of
the ancients (Chapter 2). Not only popular culture, science, and
religion have participated in this obsession — Western philosophers
have too (Chapter 3). Yet basic cultural assumptions, such as that
personal identity has a moral character and that moral responsibility requires a togetherness of the temporal modes of present, past,
and future, entail that time be understood in terms of eternity
(Chapter 4).

The second thesis concerns time itself: time can be understood
to flow only as contained within the ontological context of eternity.
Without eternity, time can be conceived only as a static dimension
like space, or as form, or as a series of "presents" that bump from
one to another outside of time, but not as flowing. To show how the
temporal modes of past, present, and future relate, it is necessary to
discuss some metaphysical conceptions of connection and distinction (Chapter 5). Then it can be seen how the temporal modes are
really different from one another and yet connected so as necessarily to be interconnected (Chapter 6); a prevailing fault of most
modern approaches to time is that they take one mode or another to
be paradigmatic for all. The shifting date of the present can be
understood in connection with the temporal modes to represent
time's flow (Chapter 7). The togetherness of the temporal modes,
such that time flows, is the true meaning of eternity (Chapter 8).

The third thesis concerns God: as the context for time's flow,
eternity is to be understood according to a theory of divine
creation. That is, the togetherness of the temporal modes in which
time's flow consists is created *ex nihilo* by an eternal ontological act.
Because of a confusing and contentious theological history, partic-

ularly in light of the developments of science, several false or inadequate conceptions and images of eternity and God need to be criticized (Chapter 9). Divine eternity is itself to be conceived always in conjunction with conceptions of the created temporal world, and several representations of this conjunction need to be examined (Chapter 10). Then it is possible to indicate how eternal creation stands with regard to each of the temporal modes and with regard to them all together (Chapter 11). Finally, the contextualizing of time's flow within eternity can be represented as the internal dynamic of the divine life; God is the living dynamism of the eternal act creating time's flow (Chapter 12).

The fourth thesis, of most practical interest for the human religious sensibility, is that personal identity is eternal and participates in the divine life. But if this eternal life is natural, what difference does it make to religion? In those periods in which eternal life was conceived as more life somewhere else, the practical religious question was how to get to a comfortable place and avoid the worst options. But if eternal life is the true reality of time's flow in our historical life, in what does the religious difference consist? Personal identity is first of all to be understood to be under judgment in its eternal dimension (Chapter 13). As eternal, persons are also divine, and in this sense salvation is to be understood as redeeming the time of the person's life and community (Chapter 14). As divine and yet failing under judgment, however, persons are alienated from God the eternal creator in some sense, and creation contains within it the bridging elements that Christianity calls *grace* (Chapter 15). Finally, personal eternal life can be understood as resurrection within the glory of the divine eternal life; resurrection overcomes death as the cutoff of ultimate meaning, death both as temporal finitude and fragmentation and as sin, ignorance, and disharmony (Chapter 16). The argument thus attempts to give new meaning to the ancient representations constructed to address questions of ultimate grounds and meaning.

To use the language of science in summary, this book has four main "findings":

1. Our culture places an unbalanced, almost exclusive, emphasis on time without an appropriately rich correlative

notion of eternity. Thus its assumptions tend to undermine important cultural principles, such as moral responsibility.

2. Time can indeed be understood as flowing, with future events coming to present realization and slipping into a past that becomes ever more distant; yet this understanding is possible only when the past, present, and future are seen to be set within the context of creative eternity. Thus temporal things are caught up in time's flow, and time's flow is eternal.

3. An improved theological understanding of divinity can be attained by developing a theory of creation *ex nihilo* according to which temporal things are created, and hence time with them, to constitute an inner dynamic life of God. This conception both enriches and reconstructs ancient notions of divinity that acknowledge both "transcendent agent" and "transcendent principle" models of the ultimate.

4. Because time is in eternity, everything temporal has an eternal dimension, which is one of the things often sought in religion. But if things are "naturally" eternal, what is the religious problem? Judgment, salvation, providence, and divine glory in the finite — and the counterparts of these theological and practical religious problematics in other traditions — find new formulations in the categories of eternity and time's flow.

The discussion in this book is far too historically particular for its topic. If its second thesis is right, the only perspective for understanding time's flow is *sub specie eternitatis*. Yet this discussion takes place within a rapidly shifting situation of scientific understanding and betrays the historical roots of the author's religious thought within Christianity. So let the reader beware. Nevertheless, there is no nonhistorical standpoint from which human beings can address these or any other topics, and these are too interesting to put down.

"The Garden of Eden, a glimpse of early Agricultural Civilization"
Neville 1993.

Chapter Two

THE FALL FROM ETERNITY
TO IMMORTALITY

Temporal Obsession

One of the deepest errors of the modern world is its obsessive passion for time. "When is it possible?" "When is it coming?" "Will we have time for it?" "Can we have more time?" "What will we do with the time?" "How can we relate to the events of our time?" "When is my time up?" "Can I live forever?" "How can there be a time without me?"

These questions, playing variations on the sense of *time*, are often asked in mundane contexts. Yet obviously they also are basic questions of personal and social identity, questions with metaphysical generality and religious importance. Although most of the questions were asked in every age and culture, they are pressed with an intense passion in the culture of modernity.

Modernity, the modern world, and *modern culture,* with their cognates, denote the culture that began in Europe with its renaissance, based on the ideas of mathematical physics as it was practised by the early astronomers and physicists. The culture emphasized learning from experience, not authority, and developed what we now call the *scientific method*. Paradigmatic modern science lent itself to technology, and that technology, along with many elements of modern culture including the science, has been adopted by non-European lands under the title of *modernization*.

As noted previously, the common sense that arose early from modern science assumes that the ultimate explicanda of the world are themselves of the sort to be found within the world, perhaps very small or very large but always like the things that we can observe. Atoms or atomic particles are imagined to be like grains of sand or drops of water, only smaller. Planetary motion is like vehicles speeding around a race track. Mass, weight, force, movement, direction, velocity, and other physical properties can be observed every day and measured in the school science laboratory. Most of these assumptions have been called into question by the physics of the twentieth century, especially as applied to very small and very large things. Only within the mesoscopic world of human affairs can the old modern assumptions be trusted, and then only if one does not inquire deeply into the more advanced technologies.

Perhaps twentieth century physics ought to be called *postmodern* rather than *modern*. That is a doubtful suggestion, however, because the latest conceptions arose directly out of the trajectory of inquiry that began with Kepler, Copernicus, Galileo, Leibniz, and Newton. The interesting genius of the scientific method is that it is a self-referential corrective even of the basic concepts in which it was originally framed. It is better to say that we are in a period of "late modern" science.[1] Nevertheless, our common sense is not late modern but only modern. It has not caught up with late modern physics and is hostile to religious interests in ultimate things because religious ideas are not easily mapped onto small or large, early or late, elements of the mesoscopic human world. When *modernity, the modern world*, or *modern science* is mentioned in this book, the reference is mainly to the culture prior to serious absorption of late modern physics, a situation that obtains even now in the most scientifically advanced societies.

Because of assumptions reflected in the questions listed at the beginning of this chapter, modern culture, if not late modern physics, has an obsessive passion for and about time, a perverse and distorting passion. The passion is perverse because it assumes a narrow and simplistic notion of time itself. The passion distorts because it obscures eternity as a proper object of passion and impoverishes life of its rightful rich mix of time and eternity. The better assumption than the whole of the time consciousness of modernity is that passions for things of time take their true form within a deeper passion for eternity.[2] Instead of a passion for immortality, which is simply "more time," the heart's better longing is for eternal life, which is far more than time.

Ancient Sophistication

There was a time when people sustained more complex and sophisticated suppositions about temporality than we do in the modern age. Except for the physicists among us, we congratulate ourselves just to understand temporality with the simple figure of horizontal and vertical lines—the horizontal indicating a directional flow of time and the vertical some kind of nonflowing eternity. Eternity might mean something abstractly static, such as a number, or it might mean merely more and more time without end. Mostly, we seem satisfied to think the only contrast with time to be space, not eternity; in fact, the representation of time and eternity by horizontal and vertical lines is just a translation of the matter to spatial imagery. But the understanding of time was not always this limited, this reduced to what amounts to a popular conception of scientific time.

In ancient India the sages believed in a plethora of "ages" or "kalpas," periods when things started off from a golden egg, lasted skillians of years of ordinary time, and contracted down to the egg again. These kalpas could be successive, and they could also be coexistent. It would not be correct to say that many kalpas exist at the same time, for time is *within* the kalpas; their togetherness is something else again, some "not-time" or eternity.[3] The English word *eternity* itself derives from Latin and Greek words meaning eon, or an age within which time takes place.

Buddhists, particularly of the Hua-yen school, came to believe that there are worlds within worlds, entire universes in a speck of dust, universes such as ours within the atoms of encompassing realms. Although within a given world there might be a temporal order with a direction of before and after, the Hua-yen thinkers emphasized the composite togetherness or interpenetration of all times with each other, both within given worlds and among nested worlds.[4] Buddhist reality is an eternity of temporal worlds.

In ancient China, the classic *Tao Teh Ching* begins with these lines:

> The Tao (way) that can be told of is not the eternal Tao;
> The name that can be named is not the eternal name.
> The Nameless is the origin of Heaven and Earth;
> The Named is the mother of all things.[5]

The *mother of all things* is the Tao of movement and process, of generation and corruption. The supposition behind it is the everlasting varying alternations of yin and yang. The *origin of Heaven and Earth,* by contrast, is that which gives rise to the flow of things in which Heaven and Earth are intermixed. The true Tao underlies all changes and generates the conditions within which they take place. It is not something static, like a number, for it generates all the temporal things and their time itself. But it is not itself something that comes to be or lasts through an extent of time. The mixture of the Tao that can be named and the Tao that cannot is not simple time, but not-time: eternity.

The ancient Mediterranean world, during the Hellenistic age and the period of late antiquity, also supposed that our historical world is just an eon within a myriad of eons, our plane of existence, as it were, just one dimension among others. This is one of the few generalizations that can be made with minimal distortion about this place and period, for the ancient Mediterranean world then was a fantasmagoric combination of Egyptian, Persian, Indian, Greek, Roman, Celtic, Black African, and even Chinese influences. Peter Manchester, in the most succinct study of the subject yet, makes the basic point:

> Something simple is worth saying right away about our topic, the religious experience of time and eternity in the late classical Mediterranean world. Famous complications that have taxed the greatest philosophers cannot in the end be avoided, but a good quick insight is available from reflection on a very simple proposition: time and eternity make one topic, not two.[6]

The false assumptions about time in the modern period come from making time and eternity two topics, and then forgetting the latter because the representations from modern science do not help to understand it.

In the ancient Mediterranean the most elaborately developed theory of mixtures of time was the family of Gnostic positions (see Jonas 1963). Within early Christianity, Origen's *On First Principles* contains an elaborate theory of planes and eons. But even the New Testament discussions of Christ descending from and ascending to heaven, with the multitude of powers, suppose the general cosmology of mixed times and planes (Matthew 24:29–30, 26:64; Mark 13;24–27; Luke 21:25–28; John 3:12–15, 14:2–17:26, I Corinthians 15:35–55; Ephesians 1:7–14; Philippians 2:5–11; Colossians 2:20; I Thessalonians 4:14–17, Hebrews 2:5–9; II Peter 1:16–18).

The root of Judaism, Christianity, and Islam is the creation myth in Genesis 1. In the beginning there was a formless void likened to deep waters roiled by the wind or spirit from God. God spoke and created light, which God then saw to be good. "After" that God created a separation of light from darkness and went on to name them day and night, respectively, so that finally there was evening (darkness) and morning (light), the first day (Gen. 1:1–5). Time in the ordinary modern sense of linear, "horizontal," succession was not created until light and darkness had been created as separated and related successively as day and night (actually, the Jewish "day" begins with evening dark followed by daylight). Yet much went on in the creating of that diurnal succession, and the sense in which that creating "went on" is a richer sense of time, or time-and-eternity, than merely an earlier-later succession. Whereas this seems incomprehensible to moderns, it obviously did not to the ancients whose understanding of time was more complex and sophisticated.[7] The ancient speculations are far closer to those of contemporary astrophysics than either is to commonsense modernity. Indeed, in light of contemporary physical cosmology, many of the ancient speculations seem not quaint but prescient.

Immortality and Antireligion

Like science but in different ways, religion deals with ultimate matters and, again like science, seems to require a richer notion of time and eternity to express these than is possible with the impoverished modern conceptions. One large trend within modern culture, first in Europe and now across the globe even among societies whose ancestral tradition were Buddhist, Confucian, Taoist, Hindu, shamanist, or tribal, has been to reject religion completely as incompatible with the modern scientific worldview. The "modern scientific worldview," of course, stops short of twentieth century physics. Many factors contribute to the antireligious biases within modernity in addition to the limited modern view of time. But even religious moderns have been adversely affected by modern temporal notions. Precisely because there has been no good modern way to understand eternity, or any sense of time larger than succession within the physical world, eternity has come to be thought of simply as immortality, as going on after death in a state like life. The modern religious passion, particularly among fundamentalists who want to read their ancient scriptures straight into the modern world, is for "life without end," more life like we have now, but happier.

The idea of immortality is by no means new. The ancient Hebrews, like the Chinese, believed that the body died once and for all but that the soul lingered around for a while, perhaps slowly dissolving in hell or Gehenna. For both Hebrews and Chinese, the length of time the soul lasts after death is obscurely related to the person being remembered by the living. Certain Greek thinkers associated with mystery cults believed that the soul neither is born nor dies, but is eternal like the stars; some Gnostics thought the stars are indeed souls in an extremely purified state. Those who believe the body is born and dies, whereas the soul is wholly opposite, tend sharply to separate soul from body; many of those in the ancient world who believed this tended to depreciate the value of the body.

The early Christians, however, by and large sided with their Hebrew colleagues in positively valuing body, claiming that even God takes on a body to save the world; this is the import of the doctrine of incarnation. Thus the early Christians such as Paul had nothing to do with immortality in the sense of the soul's neither arising nor ceasing, but focused instead on resurrection of the whole person, body and soul in unity. Whereas immortality for a Gnostic meant the ability to surmount and get rid of the body, for

Paul and other early Christians resurrection meant a renovated body as well as a renewed soul. Like many first century people, Paul thought of his body as something of a burden; his solution was not Gnostic escape but rather the transformation of this world so as to have a body-soul appropriate for heaven (cf. I Corinthians 15). Subsequent thinkers, for instance Origen (225), believed that souls are mortal but that they are created beings coextensive with the universe, the whole of which is created. He thought souls were created at the first moment, live through a vast number of lives, and will be absorbed back into the creator at the last moment; as creatures, for the incarnationist Origen, souls always have bodies, differing in relative purity or coarseness from life to life, depending on the accumulated state of virtue. Earthly bodies are rather coarse and starry bodies more pure.

Indian cultures have had theories of reincarnation, according to which a soul is a subtle body that inhabits successive coarse bodies. Buddhism, in some of its forms, believes that salvation consists in an ending of the seemingly endless cycle of rebirths. Whereas some Christians long for more life after death, Buddhists pray for Not Another One, Please.

Anselm (1033–1109), the early medieval Christian thinker, believed that God created a great swarm of souls when first creating the world, but without bodies.[8] History is needed so that each soul will have a single embodied life in which to work out its salvation. After the death of the historical body, each soul will reside in the "place" of its eternal reward until the end of time. Medieval European popular religion, both Christian and Jewish, like popular Buddhism, Taoism, and most forms of popular Hinduism, represented immortality geographically, with fully depicted places for the good souls, bad souls, souls doing penance, and souls in transition. As with most *effective* popular symbologies, it is hard to know how literally the people construed them. Surely they thought of the afterlife in those terms and perhaps in no others. Yet did they also understand that the terms were limited and that the afterlife (or beforelife) is not just like this life except that the rewards are given unambiguously? Perhaps some did and others did not. Jews and Christians think of God as a rock (of salvation) without ever believing that geology is a proper part of theology. Only incipiently modern, the European medievals might very well have thought of the cosmos of immortal persons as containing times within times, worlds within worlds.

Modern people, however, quickly came to think of time in the terms of modern physics, as the succession of causally related things, unified in a single chronological sweep: time is individual, Kant said (1787, B 47–48). The moderns suddenly became worried about the "date" at which God had created the world, and if that worry did not make sense, as to many people it did not, then divine creation did not make sense. For the moderns, human time is that of the linear story, a history, in which everything has its causal place. The eternal life or immortality addressed by religion could not mean life in a different plane, in another kind of time; it could mean only life later. Even divine eternity came to mean endless time in modern culture, the continuation of things in this time without end.

Religiously, it is necessary to have an understanding of the context of time, the frame within which time takes place, the inclusive ultimate within which past, present, and future are together. When religious conservatives read the ancient scriptures into modern culture, snatching up the nearest analogues they can find without a careful process of reinterpretation, they are right in an important respect. The ancient cultures asked questions of very great importance that must be asked in any age but that do not find easy representation in a culture with such a reductive set of categories as those of modern science. The conservatives' error is not insistence on the importance of the ancient issues but rather the uncritical acceptance of modernity's setting of the terms for expression. To accept the modern definition of time as just the succession of events and then to use that to translate eternity into merely unending succession is to lose on two counts. The modern terms simply fail to come up to the level of the ancient questions and answers, and the depth of antiquity is lost. And modern culture views the attempted translation as mere superstition: people do die on specific dates and do not live forever. If ancient religious insights are to be translated into modern culture, it must be by an expansion of modern culture, not a reduction of antiquity. Anything else is silly. Contemporary astrophysics is an ally of religion in pushing modern culture beyond itself; yet up to this point astrophysics has not made much of a dent on the commonsense biases of modernity, and science as a general enterprise, especially the currently fashionable biological sciences, reinforces the Cartesian biases of modernity.[9]

The topic of this book is to understand eternity, and its relation to time, by attempting to criticize and supplement the categories of modern culture. By no means can we "return" to premodern cultures. Whatever their virtues, they have been and continue to be superseded by versions of modern culture at every choice point. Perhaps modern medicine alone is sufficient to justify modernization, and that is by no means the only justification.

Modern culture itself is not without its problems. Critics have arisen from within modernity's own development, and critics appear in each instance when a nonmodern culture is faced with modernization, as in the Third World today. Some people have proclaimed the postmodern age, although evidence for more than further developments of late modernity is hard to find. There is much to be purged from the cultural forms of modernity.

At the same time, much must be added to bring the complex and sophisticated conceptions of time and eternity from ambiguity into modern culture and to move on from there. Contemporary physical cosmology has already abandoned modernity's common sense about time. But the conceptions of time in contemporary physics are not framed to address the questions posed in religion and elsewhere. What is needed is a clearer and more capacious metaphysics than has been typical of modernity and also a reinterpretation and restructuring of those aspects of religion that have to do with time and eternity. The answer to those who say that metaphysics itself is impossible is the creation of an actual metaphysics: if something is actual it must be possible.

The answer to those who say that religion itself is only premodern superstition is more complex. Part of the answer to the antireligionists is a counterattack. Modernity itself presupposes various religious forms without being responsible to them for their religious base, for instance the myth of progress and the glorification of existential despair. These are bad religious forms, degenerate and unsophisticated; most modern people become embarrassed

about them as soon as it is realized that they are only religious forms
thinly disguised as secular.

Another part of the answer to antireligionists is to show that
there is a universal religious dimension to human life, and that
every culture needs religious forms of one sort or another; this is
why even modern secularism has alternative, if limping, religious
elements. In contrast to earlier generations of anthropologists who
contrasted modern science with premodern superstitions, contemporary anthropologists interpret cultures more nearly on their own
terms and find religion ubiquitous. The normative question is
whether a culture's religious forms are adequate, not whether the
culture could do without religion. The question for contemporary
culture is the same: do we understand and relate to time and
eternity (that *single* topic) adequately?

Yet another, and likely the most important, part of the answer
to the antireligionists is the proclamation of a positive truth about
time and eternity as a religious topic. The great religions, or at least
some of them, *know* some things about time and eternity that are
important for people to understand: that knowledge can provide
orientations and rituals of formation so as to relate us appropriately
to time and eternity. Yet it cannot do this unless theologically
reinterpreted and reenculturated in each age and place. Antireligionists can always fuel their skepticism if religion and theology
have not done their job.

Skepticism and Anxiety

Perhaps it is skepticism about time itself that makes modern
culture, even newly modernizing cultures, worship present time.
As soon as a society's economy appears to guarantee by routine a
modicum of luxury, and the desperate future orientation of the
"work ethic" is relaxed, its people become the "now generation."
Preoccupation with the present does not mean merely a desire for
instant gratification. More serious than that, "instant gratification"
is meaningful only within the mythic supposition that present time
is the only time there is. From plain common sense, any gratification at a moment both results from antecedent preparing conditions
and leads to future consequences. The reality of the gratification
includes both past and future, even though its appeal might be so

strong in the moment as to preclude prudent consideration of the larger span of time. Only by pretending, contrary to obvious experience, that past and future can safely be neglected as if unreal or unconsequential, can we think of wholly instant gratification as gratifying.

Yet modern society turns on consumerism. Consumerism is not acquisitive in the sense of laying up resources for future security and enjoyment: indeed, the lack of prudent acquisitiveness threatens the economic stability on which consumerism is based. Nor is consumerism proudly celebrative, as if we deserve current rewards for accumulated achievements: the advertisement arguing that you deserve to treat yourself to a silky expensive shampoo is quite clear in its claim that there is no reason why you deserve it. Rather, there is an advertized obligation to feel good now, regardless. A significant part of being human in modern culture is the right, even obligation, to feel good in the present. There is a truth to this: self-reflexive pleasure, pleasure at feeling pleasure, is a good. But the price of the present pleasure includes making good on real connections with past and future, and these a consumer society neglects almost pathologically.

The flaw in the popular sense of time is the inference from the fact that it flows so quickly to the moral that one should seize the moment as if it alone were real. If the moment alone be real, then the past is a dropping out of reality of what one once was, and the future is an unreality only anticipated. For practical purposes, in the popular assumptions about time, only the present is real and the past and future are not real. Because the present is moving, however, we are constantly slipping into the unreality of the past and confronting the unreality of the future. In the bowels of popular culture this leads to what Tillich and others have diagnosed as an anxiety about nonbeing. If being is only present existence, and both past and future are nonbeing, and if present time always moves from one to the other, then we are always threatened by nonbeing.

Although *anxiety about nonbeing* sounds like intellectual overkill regarding popular culture, nothing else seems to account for the pervasive longing for the immediacy of the present. When consumerism undermines itself by imprudent neglect of past and future, when the youth cult idealizes a stage in life characterized by the frenzy of sexual coming of age, when popular religions movements hark to "Eastern religions" that seem to promise meditative immediacy, what else can be the motive but a desperate clutch at being?

The cultural and philosophical anxiety about nonbeing might very well be a mistake, however, based on a spiritual and philosophical neglect of eternity. The past is not unreal, only different from present existence. To slip from the present to the past is finally to be something, not just to be in the process of becoming. The future is not unreal, only different from present time. To have an open future is not to face the maw of nothingness but to have possible structures to which one must conform, often with better or worse results. Eternity, it will be argued, is the togetherness of past, present, and future in which they are all equally real and in which each allows the others to be what they are precisely in their temporal difference. Eternity is not a temporal togetherness, however, because that would have to be present, or past, or future; eternity is an *eternal* togetherness.

"God's Rainbow Promise and Pulsating Energy Waves"
Neville 1993

Chapter Three

THE PHILOSOPHICAL PASSION
FOR PRESENT TIME

Subjectivism and Experience

Among the founding motifs of modernity is what Alfred North Whitehead called the *subjectivist bias*. Discussing Descartes, Whitehead wrote:

> He also laid down the principle, that those substances which are subjects enjoying conscious experiences provide the primary data for philosophy, namely, themselves as in the enjoyment of such experience. This is the famous subjectivist bias which entered into modern philosophy through Descartes. In this doctrine Descartes undoubtedly made the greatest philosophical discovery since the age of Plato and Aristotle. For his doctrine directly traversed the notion that the proposition, 'This stone is grey,' expresses a primary form of known fact from which metaphysics can start its generalization. If we are to go back to the subjective enjoyment of experience, the type of primary starting-point is 'my perception of this stone as grey.'[1]

Not objects, nor facts as expressions or forms of objects, but the experience of objects is the primary reality in modernity's culture.

The question of truth was radically reformed in the early modern period. From Aristotle through Aquinas truth had been thought to be some variant on the theme of "adequation of the intellect to the thing."[2] With the modern period, the theme was a proposition's proving itself true in experience. That is, something in the experience of subjective conscious thinkers is sought as the mark and even the definition of truth. Descartes's own suggestion was an intuitive perspicacity and certainty, coupled with utter clarity of inference, building to a consistency of system. Spinoza and Leibniz followed him in this with their own variations. Locke appealed to the existential presence of sensations in experience, distinguishing sensations from their copies and combinations; Hume followed Locke with his own variant. The category of experience became very important in the modern period, interpreted as consciousness. Whereas the ancient and medieval Western philosophers had thought of experience as the arena of practice from which one learns, as in becoming an experienced mother, teacher, or horserider, the moderns came to think of experience as a conscious testing ground within the subjective thinker for beliefs about reality. Only the pragmatists in the modern period have rejected the modern "subjectivist bias."[3]

Kant and the Transcendental Definition of *World*

Given the importance for modernity of the experience of thinking subjects, Kant's thesis that time is the form of inner sense was perhaps the most important part of his philosophy. It articulated the assumption that likely was present from the beginning of modernity, namely, that time is the form to which all things must conform and that, if we only understood time, we would understand something apriori about everything.

Kant's argument in the *Critique of Pure Reason* was brilliant.[4] Any knowledge that comes to us from the outside, no matter what it might be, temporal or otherwise, needs to fit the form of our own thinking, which he called *inner sense.* So, too, any thought that arises from within must fit the form of thinking. And that form is time or succession. Every thought or sensation must fill a positive moment of time in consciousness and must be in a temporal sequence with preceeding and succeeding thoughts. Regardless of whether the thoughts are true or false, realistic or fanciful, referential or wholly immediate, they at least must fit in to the time frame of consciousness. Therefore, if we understand time and how it forms succession in consciousness, then we understand something about any possible experience or object of experience.

Kant's philosophy epitomizes modernity because of its brilliant definition of objective reality, or the "world," solely in terms of the temporal form of subjective experience. In the "Second Analogy" in this *Critique,* he pointed out that there is a temporal subjective order of all "representations" in consciousness (B 232–256). But not all temporal relations within the subjective order are objective. For instance, you might look first to the left and then to the right side of the house; or you might look at the right before the left. You cannot tell whether the right causes the left or vice versa, or whether there is any causal relation between right and left at all, or even whether there is a real house you are looking at rather than a fantasy. But if you watch a ship going down a river (Kant's example), no matter how you blink, look again, or stand on your head for a different perspective, in the same passage you cannot see the ship upriver after it is already downriver. Subsequent to Kant who was concerned for individual experience, philosophers substituted the community of observers checking out the order from as many angles as possible. The empirical or objective world, Kant explained, consists in the subset of temporal orders within subjective time that have objective and irreversible sequence. The way we tell the real world from the fantasies in our experience, or from the plain errors, is by checking to see which orders are regular and irreversible, and which ones can be disconnected and rearranged.

Deterministic causality thus assumes enormous importance in the modern view, at least insofar as Kant expressed its assumptions. For, only by identifying the temporal regularities of occurrences can we distinguish objective orders from those that are merely subjective. All orders of representations are subjective, but some of them are also objective and must be recognized by any knower who attends. Strict determinism is presupposed not only as the method for sorting true from false representations of things but also as the very meaning of objectivity. Objectivity is the temporal order of representations that must be recognized by any potential knowers. Note that causality for Kant does not mean "making" but rather a temporal order of successions that can be expressed as "if a, then b." Part of Kant's brilliance lay in his careful reinterpreta-

tion (*schematism* is his technical term) of all categories of things and
knowing into the structure of time. The previous example was the
schematism of causal "if a, then b" into "a regularly before b." The
category of "substance" is schematized as that which is permanent
through change (B 225); "coexistence" is schematized as mutual
causal interaction. Kant's own philosophy is called *transcendental*
because he asserted that we have a priori knowledge of all the
(transcendental) categories that can be translated or schematized
into the structure of time as the form of inner sense. Whatever
transcends experience, and hence might not have time as its form,
cannot be known empirically or theoretically, he said. What
philosophy knows transcendentally are the conditions to which
everything must conform to be known and to which knowers must
conform to know.

In retrospect, Kant's position was not as strong as many have
taken it to be. First, the kind of knowledge involved in transcendental philosophy itself, analyzing and justifying the transcendental categories, does not fall within the kinds of knowledge Kant
allowed as legitimate; this objection was raised early on by Hegel.

Second, there is no need to give an a priori definition of *world*,
or of the nature of true as opposed to illusory knowledge, as Kant
thought. Rather, we can propose hypotheses about these and other
large-scale foundational issues and then work on comparing,
improving, and testing the hypotheses. That the topic of world and
knowledge are foundational in an architectonic sense to how other
things are to be understood does not mean that they are foundational in the sense that they need to be certain or to be known a
priori before other inquiry can start. Our habitual beliefs about
foundational things work quite well until we find some realistic
occasion for questioning them. Charles Peirce raised this objection
in the 1860s and 1870s.

Third, the fact that anything to be thought must be thinkable
within the temporal structures of thinking does not mean that those
things must be thought to have a temporal structure. Many things
can be conceived by way of inference and the elaboration of
hypotheses that extend beyond the temporal flow. Kant had an
extremely subtle discussion of mathematics in this *Critique*'s
"Transcedental Aesthetic," designed to show that even arithmetic

and geometry have an essentially temporal form that requires the direct and implicit intuition of time's form. Nevertheless he supposed this was necessary because he believed arithmetic and geometry to be true a priori, which requires that we simply find them present in the forms to which all thought must conform. But there are alternative mathematical systems that are true in one sense by definition alone and in another sense only insofar as they are empirically descriptive of the world. In fact, all Kant showed is that the subjective order of representations is temporal—we think one thing after another (actually, there is also a spacelike nesting of thoughts involved in the temporal sequence). Therefore Kant's philosophy is by no means the only show in town.

Modern Kantians

Philosophers after Kant have not kept strictly to his own system, of course. Yet to a remarkable degree, his technical arguments about time as the form of inner sense have been elaborated as motifs on a much larger scale.

Hegel

Hegel, for instance, gave a kind of metaphysical ultimacy or primacy to history in his theories of the formation of the possibilities for consciousness in the *Phenomenology of Spirit*, of the possibilities for philosophy in the *Lectures on the History of Philosophy*, and of the possibilities for culture in the *Lectures on the Philosophy of Religion*. Even more important, in his *Science of Logic* Hegel interpreted the relation between logical categories in developmental ways. Of course he did not affirm that the categories emerge from one another temporally. Yet the form of their emergence is one of succession in which the later take into themselves and transcend the earlier; without the earlier, the later would have no content.

The image of sequential development became a powerful conceptual tool for the nineteenth century in European philosophy. Physics and chemistry were taken (temporarily) into the natural history of the cosmos. Species were understood in terms of their evolution. Even contemporary historical culture was conceived in terms of its causes and prospects, and the question of progress was the most important issue for human affairs.

Modernity came to a pivotal stop with the First World War. Christendom as the culture of Europe was an obvious failure, given the fact that the enemies shared the same cultural religion. Was Western philosophy too a failure? There were many reactions to that question, but nearly all the reactions abandoned the thick historical sense of the nineteenth century for some kind or other of concentration on present time as formed by consciousness.

Husserl

Husserl's phenomenology of pure consciousness took its rise shortly before the First World War (*Ideas*, 1913), but with an appreciation of the collapse of confidence that expressed itself in the war. Whereas Kant had asked what could be known a priori, given that we know certain things in mathematics and physics a priori, Husserl asked how we could know enough of the right things a priori to build a sure and indubitable foundation for the other sciences and arts. His answer to the question was to define a project for philosophy of examining ideas completely in terms of their appearance in pure consciousness. The meaning of *pure* is that all referring aspects of ideas, all their existential commitments, and all their practical uses are to be bracketed out while the transcendental consciousness examines the idea from all sides. A philosophic truth is the understanding of an idea after it has been revolved through all possible angles of conscious intentionality. Regarding time, there is no philosophic reference to whether the idea is true of anything in the past, present, or future. Nevertheless, because the idea is examined as it is intended in consciousness, the idea has the form of present time, the time of conscious awareness. Presentness to consciousness from all possible angles of intention is thus the mark of the reality of a thing.

Heidegger

Martin Heidegger did develop his philosophy after the First World War and in full consciousness of the war's cataclysmic critique of the Western tradition. He was part of the movement, in fact one of the original inspirations, that we know as *existentialism*, emphasizing the importance of existence over essence (although rejecting

Sartre's version of that point; see Richardson 1963, pp. 390, 530–552) and of decision in the present moment. But he undertook a more radical critique of the tradition than Husserl did.

Heidegger's basic category, in his early work (*Being and Time*, 1927), was *Dasein*, which means "being there." By no means is this a simple notion to be read from the linguistic meanings in its name (although Heidegger himself employed that etymological method often enough). *Dasein* is intended to call attention to the existentially located positive actuality of the experiencer. The "there" of its being provides a locus from which appears an horizon of temporal and spatial locations, past-present-future, near and far. By insistence on the actuality of *Dasein*, Heidegger overcame the idealism of Husserl. Yet his metaphysical imagination was peculiarly limited, for *Dasein* has many of the same properties of Cartesian substances, occupied with its own existence or nonexistence; *Dasein* is characterized as being toward death. Heidegger recognized the falsity of the self-contained character of substances and sought to define them with little prepositional hooks so that *Dasein* is "with" and "for" other things and people who are "at hand," and so forth. Whitehead, by imaginatively rejecting substance in favor of a radically different alternative, found both togetherness and temporality much easier to understand.

Heidegger did, however, identify a deep error in the Western tradition that had come to a head in the twentieth century; namely, what he called the *metaphysics of presence*. This error is the view that to be is to be present to some consciousness. From the standpoint of the problematic of time, this means that to be is to be in present time. Perhaps Heidegger is not altogether convincing in his attempt to convict the entire Western tradition of the "metaphysics of presence." But it was a powerful critique of his own time. It is difficult to say that Heidegger provided much of an ontological advance beyond a metaphysics of presence. In his later work he elaborated on the Kantian idea of synthesis, which produces things that have the form of time with a past, present, and future. Even in his early book on Kant (1929), he developed a notion of temporality that is ontologically prior to the mere form of succession. Nevertheless, he remained committed to a notion of experience that takes present consciousness as its formal paradigm.

Heidegger's followers, from Sartre to Derrida, have bridled against the limitation of time to present time, but have acquiesced in the main to the identification of reality with that which shows itself in present experience. For them, consciousness is a basic category, coupled with a voluntaristic emphasis on choice as that which marks the concreteness of actuality.

Analytic Philosophy

For many analytic philosophers, by contrast, consciousness has no central role, nor does choice in the existentialists' sense. Rather, the discovery of a foundation for a new Western culture lies in recognizing the habits by which we engage reality as embodied in our common sense or in language. As Charles Peirce had pointed out in the 1880s, habits are general and are never exhausted in any present exercise. So it is with common sense and language use: what is interesting is not exactly what is supposed in a moment or said, but rather what tends to be done.

Perhaps the most important contribution of "ordinary language philosophy" to the problematic of time is the distinction, associated with J. L. Austin and John R. Searle, between the use of language to express a proposition and its many uses to perform actions of other sorts, for instance to make a contract, to entertain, or to change someone's status. Here language "does" something in present time. Because the interesting part of language as such is the set of rules according to which it does things (Searle 1969, pp. 16–50), present time is intrinsically connected to past and future in which those rules were and will be developed and otherwise exercised. There is little analysis of past and future, however, except in terms of how we talk about them. The analytic philosophers were contemptuous of metaphysics or speculative philosophy. When they did talk positively of metaphysics, as Peter Strawson did, it was not speculation they had in mind at all but rather description of basic elements of common sense or of language. Therefore they had no device for articulating past or future time in contradistinction from the emphasis on present time in their contemporaries and in common sense. Even though they often recognized the importance of habit and tendency, they had no way of representing how a togetherness of past, present, and future is required if any present exercise of a habit is to be more than a particular happening. No habit is ever only a particular happening; it is always a general tendency to happen, instanced here and there.

Whitehead and Process Philosophy

Whitehead's process philosophy is perhaps the twentieth century's most elaborate attempt to rethink the problematic of time. Whitehead's genius enjoyed several advantages. First, he was wholly nonmodernist and had no interest in either building sure foundations for science — only for understanding the implications of science for philosophy — nor in trying to be New and start philosophy over again without the encumbrances of the past. He plainly admitted to being attracted more to pre-Kantian than to Kantian modes of thought. Moreover, he did not hold anything like a deterministic view of the Western philosophic tradition. He thought some of the early ideas were very good, but not well understood, and that his contribution was to understand them better. Metaphysical imagination is far more important, to his mind, than analytic development of previous philosophers' suppositions. Finally, it did not occur to him to have to avoid metaphysics or speculative philosophy. Whereas the modernist phenomenologists and analytic philosophers were trying hard not to repeat the errors of the past by avoiding metaphysics, Whitehead simply stormed ahead to compose the greatest speculative system of modernity.

Whitehead's fundamental idea is a complex mixture of three points. First, a present moment is to be conceived as an actual occasion in which something happens.[5] The occasion itself, in its presentness, comes to be in a process of becoming that Whitehead called *concrescence,* or becoming concrete.[6] Although the present moment is present, it is not yet actual, but is in the process of becoming actual. When it is finished with its becoming and is a concrete moment, it has some spatial and temporal dimension; that is, this actual occasion has a spatial size and a temporal length. From the outside, that temporal length can be subdivided according to chronological measures. But the occasion itself comes to be as a whole, and its internal becoming does not have earlier and later parts, only logical developmental stages. Within a present actual occasion the beginning stages are not actualized earlier than the later stages: actuality comes to the whole altogether. *Actuality* or *concreteness* is defined as complete definiteness or what Duns Scotus called *haecceity*. The process of becoming internal to an occasion is not a move from earlier to later stages but from an indefiniteness of possibility to a definite actual arrangement of features. Change takes place only in the becoming of a present occasion. Change is the arising of something new. Where the potential components of an occasion allow of many different possible actualizations, the process of becoming is decisive. All the themes of will and decision in modern philosophy find explicit analysis in Whitehead's theory of the present becoming of an actual occasion.

The second point in Whitehead's theory is that the potential components for actualization in an occasion are previously finished actual occasions. A present actual occasion becomes by "prehending" the past occasions and integrating them into a new completely definite entity. Thus a present occasion does not merely represent past occasions but includes them in their very being within its own becoming, modifying them only in ways necessary for them to be integrated into the new occasion.

Whitehead (1926) criticized the common belief in modern philosophy that things are "simply located," that they are only in themselves and at best can be represented in other things. On the contrary, all the past is located as well in a present becoming occasion, except insofar as past items are deliberately excluded or modified. Therefore, although each present occasion is like an atomic drop of becoming with its own spatial and temporal dimensions, it also is continuous with its past. Each past occasion, according to Whitehead, is the object of a prehension in a becoming present occasion, and all those prehensions are integrated in the process of becoming to be one large prehension that appropriates the past in a singular definite way. The past causes the present by presenting actualized elements as potentials for present becoming.

Unlike Kant's regularity theory of causation, Whitehead's theory of causation acknowledges that decisive and creative selections and integrations might take place in a present moment and that the being of the past enters into the present so as to make it up.

Unlike the older Aristotelian theory that sees the power of causation in the already actualized, Whitehead's theory of prehension sees the power to reside in present creativity working on the potentials that past actual occasions offer. The degree to which a present moment has freedom to actualize itself in different ways depends on the different possibilities for integrating the diverse potentials provided by the past actualities.

The third point in Whitehead's theory is that a present occasion actualizes itself as a finished fact that must be taken into account by future arising occasions. Given all the actualized occasions in a present moment's past, its own completion of becoming adds yet one more occasion that requires to be integrated later on. Occasions of conscious experience, such as persons have, can anticipate the future and actualize themselves deliberately so as to provide determinative conditions that effect what they want to happen. The future is structured as the field of logical possibilities that determine within a concrescing occasion how its own potentials might variously be integrated, and also that determine how the outcome of a variety of occasions might be integrated in the distance. The process of concrescence in an actual occasion thus has actual physical past things as its elementary components to be integrated, and it finishes its integration as yet one more physical fact.

Whitehead contrasted the physical beginning and ending of a process of concresence with the decisiveness of the process itself, which he called *mentality*. Mentality, for Whitehead, exists only within the process of becoming that is not yet wholly actual. All actual things are wholly physical. The mentality in concrescence is of the interesting human type only under extraordinarily complex conditions of human biology and culture; most mentality in Whitehead's technical sense is very stupid, like that in the occasions that make up a stone.

Whitehead's theory of time is therefore very simple. The past relative to a present actualizing occasion is all the occasions it can prehend, that is, all that have been actualized and are available for prehension. The future consists of all the occasions that logically can (or will) prehend the present occasion. The present consists of all the occasions that can neither be prehended by the becoming occasion at hand nor can prehend it. The other present occasions

might be prehending the same past, and they might all be prehended by the same future occasion.

Put another way, the past relative to a present consists of all
the things that have finished their process of actualization, the
present consists of all the things that are actualizing but not
finished, and the future consists of all those occasions that will
contain the present as well as the past. The important point to
notice, however, in Whitehead's interpretation of all this, is that
past, present, and *future* are defined in terms of their causal relations
with one another. They are not separate domains of the finished,
the happening, and of the yet to happen. They rather are distinguished according to different possibilities of entering into one
another as causal prehended elements. Temporal order can be
determined for a sequence of events in the past, or in the future, or
through a temporal spread including the present, all by reference to
which occasions can prehend which others.

Whitehead's interpretation of relativity theory and quantum
mechanics makes his development of this point more complex than
common sense might suspect. Contemporary physics defines certain possibilities of causation according to properties of light.
Furthermore, causal relations among things are real only from
some perspective, perhaps the perspective of the "effect," perhaps
of an observer; the standpoint of the perspective itself must be
causally related to the causal relations it prehends, and the perspective might impose some noncommonsensical elements on causation. Items can be discriminated into past, present, and future only
from some perspective that is causally connected with the items.
Modern common sense, by contrast, supposes that the items just sit
there.

Whitehead's principle contribution is his theory of the present
moment, for which the past occasions are conditions and for which
the future occasions are perhaps anticipated possibilities. The bulk
of *Process and Reality* is his analysis of what he calls the *genesis* of a
present actual occasion, its becoming; only a small portion of the
book is devoted to the "morphological" or "coordinate" analysis of
how occasions fit together in a larger stretch of space and time. This
emphasis on the present has led some of Whitehead's followers,
such as Charles Hartshorne, to focus on Whitehead's language of

experience, where *experience* means the psychic reality of present experience. Therefore Hartshorne says that past actual occasions have no reality of their own except insofar as they are prehended in some present occasion. Likewise the future has no reality except in anticipation. Unlike Whitehead, who thought all actual things are physical, Hartshorne calls himself a panpsychist because he interprets the past only from the standpoint of its functions in some present mentality; similarly for the future. Hartshorne denies that the past and future are real on their own outside of their functions in present existence. In this respect, Hartshorne holds to what Heidegger criticized as the metaphysics of presence.

Whitehead's own texts are inconclusive on the matter of the reality of the past and future. He does say, with Hartshorne, that any occasion, as soon as it finishes and becomes past, must necessarily be taken up in a further emerging occasion. But an occasion that is finished cannot cease to exist, for that would be to make a change in something that cannot change any more. Therefore it would seem that a finished actual entity exists everafter as a past fact regardless of whether and how it is taken up in subsequent moments. The past thus has a reality that is different from the reality of becoming. Similarly, the future is a real possibility for becoming, a form that is what it is irrespective of whether it is anticipated. Its internal structures vary as present moments make different conditions to be formally integrated. Although the formal character of the future is binding on present occasions, its reality is not reducible to the existential reality of present becoming. Therefore Whitehead could very well admit that the future has a reality of its own just as do the past and present. Whitehead did not address the problem of how to understand the relations among the different kinds of reality of past, present, and future.

Close as he came to recognizing the diverse realities of the modes of time, Whitehead did not see that his emphasis on the present limited him to discussions of temporality without eternity. For him, eternity meant only formal properties, something like Plato's forms. Though modernity's most comprehensive speculative philosophy, Whitehead's was bound to temporality alone and could not formulate the problem of the joint topic of time and eternity.

The philosophers of modernity have given brilliant expression to the culture's preoccupation with time. As the twentieth century has shown, time itself has come to be shrunk to present time. The present by itself can be an emblem of eternity, as it was for Augustine; but without a serious, partly external, relation to the past and future, the present is only the present, with no need to be emblematic for anything else. Yet there are good reasons why time is more complicated than the present, and eternity more than the present's *totum simul.*

"Earth as both Sol's Planet and a Political/Cultural Unit"
Neville 1993

Chapter Four

NO TIME WITHOUT ETERNITY

Contrary to the time passion of the modern world, the truth about time is that it is incomprehensible without eternity, or so this book argues. The coimplication of time and eternity is presupposed by many things at the heart of humanity, of which one shall be treated here: personal identity. After an orienting discussion of personal identity, the problem will be raised as to how to tell one's own past from the rest of the past and one's own future from the rest of the future. Then a preliminary analysis will be given of how the past and future are contained within the present and how they are not so contained. Finally, moral responsibility will be analyzed as a special element of personal identity. If human nature itself necessarily involves personal identity and moral responsibility, then to the extent that our modern culture undermines the full-blooded sense of temporality and eternity presupposed by those two conditions, human nature is in jeopardy of being undermined. If it can be shown that an essential component of human nature such as moral responsibility involves eternity with time, then perhaps the arguments concerning eternity in time's flow, eternity in the divine, and eternity in human destiny will seem not so strange or superstitious as modern common sense suggests. The analysis of all these topics in this chapter is preliminary, and even here it will be repetitive, taking up a few topics again and again, adding new complications with each discussion.

Personal Identity

That personal identity is both temporal and eternal seems paradoxical because we usually believe that temporal things are not eternal
and vice versa, as if the temporal and eternal were two sorts of
things rather than two dimensions of things. Contrary to the
popular opinion, however, personal identity cannot be temporal
without also being eternal. This can be seen from the following
considerations about how personal temporality involves temporal
thickness.

Temporal thickness does not mean only that a thing in the
present also has a past and future but also that one's identity at any
moment in life includes then and there elements from both past and
future. One's identity at a moment is never exhausted in the
elements that are datable by that moment; at the present moment
one is also one's past and one's future. The real togetherness of
past, present, and future is eternal.

To be more specific, at any "present" time, a person's identity
is formed in part by an inherited identity of that person from the
past and also by the implications of the present for future moments
in the person's identity. It is *essential* to a person, being temporally
thick, that past and future be involved in the present; *essential* is a
heavy metaphysical word that will be discussed in more technical
detail in Chapter 5. If there were no essential inheritance of past
character and essential implication for future character, then the
present moment might be a happening, but it would not be a part of
a person's identity as a being working out a character through time.[1]

The claims about personal temporal thickness involve three
levels. The first is that present experience presupposes reference to
past and future in its own meaning. This claim is compatible with
the view that the past and future are not real in themselves but exist
only as present memories and anticipations. But these are compatible only with the consequence that memory and anticipations are
always illusions; memories cannot be right or wrong if there is no
real past, and anticipations cannot be accurate or inaccurate in
discerning structures of future possibilities if there is no real future.
The remainder of this section shall explore certain of the memorial
and anticipatory structures of present experience.

The second level of claim about temporal thickness is that the past and future are just as real as the present, although with different kinds of reality, and that temporality is defined through the causal interactions of the three temporal modes. Even the present presupposes not only memory and anticipation but real inheritance and real possibilities. By means of a discussion of the distinction of the personal from the nonpersonal past, and of the personal from the nonpersonal future, in the next section the argument shall trace out in a descriptive and preliminary way the real connections between the three temporal modes; past, present, and future. Chapters 6 and 7 will return to argue the case in more detail.

The third level of temporal thickness is the claim that one's personal identity through time is not just identity at a time but identity in eternity. That is, one's identity includes youth when options are open, maturity when decisions are hedged by responsibilities, and old age when options are few and identity is mainly fixed. This will be explored in the third section through an analysis of what is implied in the present for moral responsibility for a past deed and for a commitment regarding the future. Chapters 8, 13, and 14 shall make more specific arguments in presenting a theory of eternal identity. The fourth section shall summarize the findings of the present stage of the argument.

Many things go on in a person's present moment, but they can be associated into roughly three families of experience: action, enjoyment, and engagement. Each of these involves taking in past conditions, integrating them in decisive ways that actualize some possibilities and exclude others, and affecting future consequences by the specifics of what is actualized in the present.

The present is the temporal mode of existential change, actualization, and decision. Every present in a person's life involves some action because the future is affected, some enjoyment because there is a sense of coming to unitary resolution of what possibilities to actualize, and some engagement because the person's present is set in a larger context. But usually the focus in a present experience is oriented toward one or another of these three, so that we use the language and signs of action, or enjoyment, or engagement, even though the experience can be redescribed in terms of the other foci, perhaps even reexperienced in the other terms. Each of these three modes of present experience will be analyzed to show how it involves the past and future as well as the present.

Action

Personal action involves anticipation of the future and a calculation of the causal lines leading there from the present. To act now in order to determine a future consequence requires tying in to the causal structures of the natural, social, and personal environment. But what makes present action especially "personal" is that one is able to intend the consequence to be in part "one's own" consequence. Perhaps this means that the consequence is intended to be something that one hopes to be willing to live with in the future. Perhaps one might intend the consequence but psychologically live in denial and keep it from consciousness. Even if one's own future state is not contemplated, the future is viewed implicitly as partly determined by one's self. With regard to the past, personal action always makes reference to one's previously developed capacities and character. Sometimes the present action is intended to amend those capacities, surpassing expectations or making a moral shift. But for the action to be personal, it is framed in such a way as to be the outcome of the person's own development. In our relatively unreflective actions, this often is expressed as just a sense of style: this is the way we do things. In all cases of personal action, even when that upon which we act is impersonal, and the intended consequences quite distant from our person, and those with whom we cooperate are clearly different persons, our actions are temporally thick. They anticipate a future that is partly ours, and they stem from a character and set of capacities that constitute our developed and inherited identity.

Enjoyment

Enjoyment in experience is an ambivalent term, as John Dewey pointed out.[2] It can suggest pleasure on the one hand and suffering on the other. Dewey, in fact, often used the term *suffering* instead of enjoyment. What both signify is that quality of experience that arises in present feeling when diverse elements are integrated into harmony. There are many strains of this, some of which can be listed. Resolution is the immediate feeling of coming to a decision in a present situation where the deliberative and voluntary process is at the level of consciousness; such moments are rare, but paradigmatic of the presentness of present personal identity. Sensual enjoyment is the feeling of composing the various functions of the body into harmony, each reinforcing the others. Aesthetic enjoyment involves the feeling of acknowledging the values of things more distant than one's body and integrating that acknowledgment into the present. Artistic enjoyment is the aesthetic enjoyment of specific objects to which culture draws attention for enjoyment; cultures differ in what counts as art. On the suffering side, sometimes the harmony attained in a present moment's integration is conflictual. Physical or sensual suffering is the feeling of bodily systems broken or in conflict, as in the pain of trauma, disease, an environment too cold or hot, or a constrained position. Other forms of suffering are the unhappy integration into one's present of frustrating, limiting, overly demanding, undesired, or undesirable conditions. Yet other forms have to do with integrating into one's own experience the experience and conditions of other people, including one's own, considered over time. "Enjoyments" are not simple immediate qualities that cover the consciousness of a present moment, as some philosophers have thought. Rather, they are feelings of the process of decisive integration that takes place in the present; they are unifying, but with the form of unifying resolutions inclusive of components each of which has some claim for importance in the present.

Now all enjoyments resolve the trajectories of conditions that come from the past. Sensual pleasures or pains involve bringing bodily processes into the present and giving them singular determination: heart, lungs, posture, muscle tone, apperceptive senses—all are integrated into some specific configuration with its own quality in any present moment. All these conditions have histories, often histories together as in the case of the body. Enjoyments also compose conditions with trajectories into the future. Except in the extreme instance, the body will endure, as will most of the more external conditions enjoyed or suffered. Personal enjoyment of them in the present is always pregnant with anticipations, either because of cultural and personal good sense or because of the unconscious evolutionary adaptations of the signs by which we bind together the conditions within the present.

Yet enjoyment does have a sense of immediacy about it. Feelings, even though always mediated because of the temporal thickness of the components they harmonize, can be focused with intensity on sheer quality. Blinding pain can approximate a shrieking sense of Sheer Now. Consummate pleasure might lead Goethe's Faust to cry, "Stay the moment—you are so beautiful." The mystic's ecstasy is sometimes thought to be an immediate loss of all time and absorption into eternity. But that is precisely the point. To the extent that pleasure, pain, or mystic ecstasy becomes so immediate that all sense of continuity is lost, the moment is no longer personal. There is simply the pleasure, the pain, or the mystic One. And there is something wrong, or at least perverse, in this depersonalization. The pleasures with which Mephistopheles attempted to lure Faust into stopping time were intended to debase the responsible self. The evil in pain is not only its immediate quality but the fact that it destroys personal identity. Mystic union has not been thought to be intrinsically evil in most religious traditions, but it has always been suspect as seducing people away from their proper involvements in the world: the successful mystics whose lives are models are those who return enlightened to ordinary life. Enjoyments so immediate as to destroy personal identity are indeed threatening to human nature.

Engagement

Engagement, the third family of "present experiences" along with action and enjoyment, is clearly a mixture of those two. Its dominant focus, however, is simply being with the things in the natural and social environment, interacting with them according to previously directed trajectories, according to habits and customary expectations. Decisive actions are taken in engagement, but mostly according to habit and routine. Enjoyed feelings permeate engagement, but not usually at the tip focus of consciousness. Consciousness itself expands and contracts rapidly in engagement, shifting focus for pragmatic reasons, moving easily between foreground and background considerations.

Engagement very obviously involves the past of things with which to engage, including one's own character and body. And it equally obviously includes ongoing processes of the future. The point to stress is that engagement is a character of present personal identity. A person's past is structurally connected with other things in the past. The person's future shares a field of integrated possibilities with other things. But only in the present is there active engagement with things, engagement that involves the past and future but that takes place presently.[3]

The importance of stressing this comes from the fact that process philosophy, following from Alfred North Whitehead, has denied it. Whitehead's theory of time, as sketched in the previous chapter, very neatly distinguished past, present, and future in the following way. The past is anything that can condition a present moment. The future is any moment that can be conditioned by the present (and past). Present contemporaries are any happenings that can neither condition nor be conditioned by each other, although contemporaries generally share a common past and can be taken up by events in a common feature. The result of Whitehead's view is that contemporary things in the present do not engage one another but are each closed in on its own internal processes of integrating past conditions into its own singular actualizations. Engagement for Whitehead cannot be a present matter but only a history of causal exchanges between two or more lines of causation, that identified as the person's "society" of actualizations and that of some other "society" of actualizations; Whitehead's theory of "society" will be analyzed in the next section.

To the contrary, the very meaning of engagement is to be causally and interpretively present with things. This does require that a person engage other things by presenting them with a more-than-present personal identity and take other things to be present as temporally thick as well. The reasons why process philosophy cannot account for present engagement move all throughout the limitations of its view of time, which will be discussed at length in pages to come.

The point to summarize here is that engagement, like action and enjoyment, is present experience that intrinsically involves the past and the future. The present is not only (if at all) immediately present, but mediately past and future too. The argument has discussed three paradigmatic modes of present experience and shown each to involve all three temporal modes, past, present, and future. In each of these experiential modes, their very meaning depends on making reference to past and future as well as present. The next step in the argument is to examine the distinction between those parts of the past that are one's own and those that are not, and the distinction between those parts of the future that are one's own and those that are not.

Self and Nonself

With reference to both past and future, it is necessary to be able to discriminate those elements that are part of the person's own identity from those that are not part of the person, however influential on or influenced by the person. Some parts of the past are the person's own past, and the person's present identity consists in part in the inheritance of that past and the need to realize it one way or another. Similarly, a person's present moment is causally efficacious to affect a great many things in the future, many of which have nothing to do with the person's own identity. But some parts of the future constitute who the person will be then, up to the point of death, and the present has implications for the person's identity relative to those moments that the present does not have for others of its future consequences.

Process philosophers point out rightly that a present happening arises out of an environment of past conditions. But they do not distinguish among the past conditions those that are the person's own past from those not part of personal identity. The closest they come to this distinction is in the claim that a person is a series of present moments sharing the same character. Whitehead defined a *society* as a series of actual occasions or happenings, each one of which grasps or includes the immediately preceding one as one of its components and also passes a distinguishing character down the line. He defined a society as *personal* when it is strictly ordered in serial fashion, so that, making a cut at any one occasion, that occasion "inherits from all members on one side of the cut, and from no members on the other side of the cut" (Whitehead 1929, p. 34).

A personally ordered society is the closest thing in Whitehead's system to an enduring object. It is actually a sequence of objects with a common character inherited down the line.

Whitehead's theory of a personally ordered society is not satisfactory for distinguishing the elements of the past and future that belong intrinsically to a person from those that are simply in the person's past and future. His theory could pick out only those past and future events that have the common character, the respects in which the past, present, and future are alike. Yet for real persons, the characters change, and some of the most important elements in the person are the changes. The physical, social, intellectual, and cultural traits of a newborn are distinctly different from those of the same person as a teenager, a mature adult, or a person resting in senility. Perhaps the DNA remains the same and determines a unified trajectory of aging. But DNA has to do with impersonal chemical changes, not the personal landmarks; and people knew what persons are long before scientists discovered DNA. Most often, the decisive elements of personal identity have to do with how people change by virtue of encountering new situations and how their personalities, characteristics, capacities, cultural contributions, and social roles change cumulatively through time. Reiteration of a common trait through time is precisely what is not interesting about a person.

Whitehead did not mean his definition of personally ordered societies to account for what we ordinarily intend by the phrases *human person* or *personal identity*. Rather he had a complicated theory of a human person as a great system of subsystems of causal nexuses, some of which are personally ordered like biological organs that always transform chemicals the same way and others of which change for a variety of conditions. What makes such a complex society of subsocieties a person is hierarchical ordering. That is, by means of the nervous system the subsystems are organized according to central control, and also the stimulations of the environment are filtered and organized to provide consistently interpretable information to the central control. At the "top" of the hierarchy is a nexus or causal chain of shifting occasions that interpret input and direct things by output into the nervous system. This *regnant nexus*, as Whitehead put it (1929, p. 103), is sometimes conscious, inherits its own thoughts and intentions, and exercises a high degree of creativity in embodying novelty in its moments. The advantage of this theory of personal identity is that it ties identity to the continuities and discontinuities of the body and the body's vicissitudes within the environment. But the disadvantage is that there is no intrinsic way of distinguishing past events that are part of the person's identity from those that are not. Body alone is no sure mark of distinction, as amputees know. Also, there are metabolic processes within the food chain that are bodily close to a person without being the person's own past states; one's stomach yesterday and yesterday's live chicken combine to form a digested meal today, though yesterday's chicken is not one's past self. Similar remarks apply to the distinction of self and other in the future. One begins today to build a fence that will be finished tomorrow; tomorrow's fence and one's own identity tomorrow as happy fence builder are not equally parts of one's future self, although both are causally dependent on today's activity.

What Whitehead's system lacks is a distinction between past conditions in general and those past conditions that are essential to one's identity. The essential past conditions are the previous states of the person that contribute to ongoing personal identity. Similarly, some future states affected by one's actions are one's own self in the future, in contrast to those other things also conditioned by present action. The continuity of personal identity through time consists in the interrelations of essential conditions, in contrast to other states of affairs that merely condition the present and will be conditioned by it. How to distinguish between essential and conditional features is a major topic to be developed through the subsequent discussion. For now it should be noted that (1) the present in personal identity makes intrinsic reference to both past and future and (2) it observes a distinction between those conditions in the past and future that are the person's own past and future states and those that are not, even though involved with the person causally.

Past and Future in Present Time

Not only are past and future involved in the present in personal identity, but they are involved vis-à-vis their own character as being "present" in their own time, at the date of their own present occurrence. Here lies a dreadfully important distinction for understanding personal identity. Whitehead and others say easily that the past is involved in the present as a finished fact determining the present's parameters; they also say the future is involved as anticipated. What must also be said, which they cannot easily say, is that past and future moments must be constituents of the present in their temporal wholeness, not only as past and future relative to involvement in the present, but insofar as each moment is sometimes future, sometime present, and sometimes past. The past and future moments are not exactly *present* in the present; that is, they are not temporally present. Yet the present cannot be temporally present without the temporally different past and future moments being what they are, it shall be argued. There is thus a togetherness of past, present, and future moments, each in its temporal wholeness, that is not mere temporal togetherness.

Paradoxical as this might sound, it is an obvious part of a person's moral identity. Suppose a person today in the present is standing trial for robbing a bank and is guilty, morally responsible, and liable for punishment. The day in question was a month ago when he committed the robbery. For the person to be guilty now, he had to have actually committed the robbery on that day; this is to say, part of the robber's present identity is to be the one who a month before actually committed the deed. It is not enough to say that now it is a past fact that he robbed the bank, although that is also true. There are a great many past facts that are true and condition the present. The additional element is that today's man is the same one who a month ago was the actual robber, presently (at that date) robbing the bank. The guilty man's present identity is that he was the then present robber actually doing the deed a month ago.

For the man to be culpably responsible for robbing the bank, however, he must presently be the one who the day before the robbery could have done otherwise. That is, the day of the robbery as a future possibility in which the person could have chosen not to rob is part of the person's present identity. If robbing or not robbing the bank was never an open possibility, then the robber cannot be held responsible; the robbery would have been determined by antecedent conditions over which the robber had no control. Therefore, the person's present identity in the dock consists in part in having now a past in which the day of the robbery was a future.

Finally regarding the past, the person presently standing trial is the one for whom the robbery has been a past fact for a month. Without this, the court would be trying the wrong person. Therefore, part of his present identity is having the day of the robbery as a past determining condition. Few would dispute that the past determines the present in this way, although some would say that it does so only insofar as it is actually remembered. For the purposes of the court in determining guilt, it does not matter whether the accused remembers, only whether he is in fact the one who did the deed. For purposes of sentencing, the memory might be more important.

Without saying that the past is temporally present in the present moment, to acknowledge that the man presently in the dock is guilty it is necessary to say that constituents of his present state include

1. the day of the crime as a partly open future relative to the day before the crime,
2. the day of the crime as an actual present in which the robber actualizes the crime, and
3. the day of the crime as a past fact identifying the robber with the man in the dock.

None of these things can be a constituent of the present moment if only the present is real, for they are all past relative to the present moment of the trial. The very temporality of human life in the present thus requires a peculiar relation to the past that is not temporal but eternal. The temporal past, in these senses, is eternally present in the present moment of the trial.

Future dates are also important essential components of a person's moral identity, not only in the plain temporal sense but also insofar as those dates are eternally in the present as future, present, and past.[4] Suppose a person in the present signs a mortgage agreement to purchase a house. Part of the moral identity of the present signer is the future date at which the mortgage is promised to be paid, either by completing the monthly payments or by resale of the house, selling the mortgage or paying it early. As future, the payoff day lays a moral and legal obligation on the person between now and then. There is an obligation to come to that day ready and able to pay, and this affects many things in one's life. As present, that day which now lies in the future will be the time of the actual payment. A then present financial action will be required of the person to satisfy the mortgage note and become free of that obligation. Although the action now lies in the future, the mortgagee's personal moral identity now includes an obligation actually to pay the debt on the payoff day. Finally, part of the person's present identity is a commitment to be able to put that payoff day successfully in the past, either by actually paying the debt personally or by having an estate from which it can be paid. Some mortgage companies require life insurance to guarantee such an estate. Thus, however paradoxical it might sound, the temporally present reality of obligating oneself with a mortgage requires as nontemporal eternal constituents of the present

1. the future payoff day as an open future that one ought but also might not meet with the cash,
2. the future payoff day as an actually present day of paying or not paying, and
3. the future payoff day as actually past when it is possible to be free of the debt; because the payoff day is still future, it is not determined whether the mortgagee's debt will be paid when the day is past, although the debt cannot be contracted without the possibility of that future payoff being a past fact.

Moral Identity

To summarize, a person's present moral identity requires not only the past that responsibly conditions the present, and the future that the present will condition responsibly, but the past and future dates in all temporal modes. Without the day of the robbery as an open future, the robber cannot today be held responsible for the deed of a month ago. Nor could he be held responsible without that day as his present actual deed. Without the future payoff day as an actual present deed of finishing the mortgage, the obligation to do so is meaningless, and without the future payoff as past there never would be present hope of fulfilling the obligation.

These results are paradoxical because only the past as finished past and the future as anticipated are temporally present in the present moment. However they might be necessary for meaningful personal and moral identity in the present, that necessity cannot be met by the ways in which they are temporally present in the present. That is, past and future cannot be reduced to their present consequences and anticipations so that their only reality is in the present. If only the present is real, as many people obsessed by time believe, then neither moral guilt nor moral obligation is truly possible. If one can forget one's past so that it is not actually in the present, then one has no guilt nor any past personal identity; the therapeutic model of personal identity tends in this direction. If one can change one's intentions, then there is no obligation toward the future if it does not exist save in intentions and anticipations. The more one attempts to reduce past and future to only the ways in which they are temporally present in the present, the more personal identity becomes attenuated.

But then how can the past and future in all their temporal modes be together with the present if they are not temporally present in the present? Eternity is the context in which dates are together with all three temporal modes. Eternity is not mere static nontemporal form; nor is it the present writ large. Eternity rather is the togetherness of the modes of time—past, present, and future—so that each can be its temporal self. This is the thesis to be developed throughout this book.

One's personal identity is never only what it is at a moment. Even at a moment, one's identity includes intrinsic reference to one's other moments as they are past, present, and future, as in the case of the robber and the mortgagee. Personal identity is thus both temporal and eternal, eternal in order to be temporal.

As eternal, one's identity at any moment includes all the dates of life as future, present, and past. When one's life is over on the date with no more personal future, it still is the case that one's personal eternal identity includes being a child with an open future, being an adult with a web of responsibilities, and being an old person with more memories than opportunities. How can we understand this eternity? To answer this question we need a closer look at time and at eternity. Then we shall return to what this means for personal identity, being both temporal and eternal "at once and forever." Specifically, we need to analyze the modes of time in detail, noting their differences and their relations; we need to provide a philosophical account of the phenomena noted in the previous examples. Then we need to ask what eternity is that it provides the nontemporal context in which the modes of time are together; this will turn out to be a theological topic, as the ancients knew. Finally, we need to redescribe personal identity as eternal life, life eternal in its very temporality.

Part Two

Time's Flow within Eternity

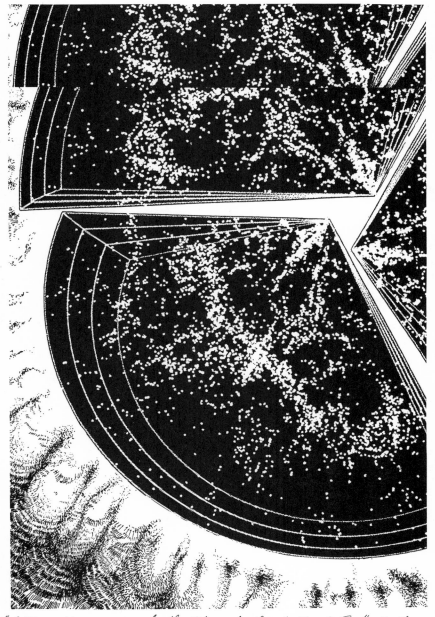

"A Tripartite vision of the Map of the Milky Way" Neville 1993

Chapter Five

A METAPHYSICS OF TIME
AND ETERNITY

This and the following three chapters constitute a formal analysis of time. The present chapter develops some metaphysical ideas crucial for understanding time's flow. The next chapter argues that time's flow requires the reality of the past and future as well as of the present, and that these are both genuinely different from one another, although necessarily related, and interdefined. Therefore the needed metaphysical ideas have to do with connection, with the integrity of those different things that are connected, and summarily with the harmony of connection and integral difference in things. These are philosophical topics as old as Plato, and yet the ideas presented here have some novelty, or at least rarity, in the current discussion.

That time and eternity constitute a metaphysical topic should not be surprising. Indeed, in the popular consciousness, East and West, they are the paradigmatic topics of metaphysics. Yet in a crucial sense they are not the most abstract metaphysical topics. Rather, they are cosmological topics, characteristic of the structures of this cosmos. Metaphysics in its most abstract sense is the study of what it means to be at all, of what the characteristics are of anything that is something, is determinate, or has identity. Metaphysics is also inclusive of ontology, the study of why there is something rather than nothing, of what it means to be rather than not to be.[1] The present chapter and the following one treat the metaphysics of time from the narrow standpoint of the investigation of determinateness. Chapter 7 treats time from the cosmological side of metaphysics, and Chapter 8 from the ontological side. But first it is necessary to introduce the metaphysical hypothesis with an apologia for metaphysics itself and to continue the discussion of metaphysics begun in Chapter 1.

Antimetaphysics

Our age is not one in which metaphysics is a popular philosophical or theological discipline. Partly for this reason, time and eternity have been neglected topics, or rather topics allowed little more than banal, unimaginative, and uncritical expression. This is particularly true of the eternity side of the topic, which most clearly has a metaphysical dimension. For the most part, the metaphysics of time and eternity has gone by default to the New Age seekers, whose seeking is rightly motivated but whose discipline and resources are thin. If the deeper philosophical dimensions of time and eternity are to be understood, then a robust discipline of metaphysics must be employed. Therefore some attention is due to the reasons why metaphysics has been in professional eclipse.

Perhaps the most pervasive cultural reason is a general loss of confidence in large ideas. Through the nineteenth century in European and American as well as in South and East Asian cultures, large ideas were the stock in trade of all educated people, especially intellectuals. For various reasons—internal collapse in the West, obsolescence relative to modernization in Asia—the grand ideas became objects of suspicion. Socialism of the Marxist variety is the last of the large ideas to capture the imagination and mold cultural senses of possibilities, and that too has been shown to be more harmful than helpful.

The answer to suspicion of large ideas should not be the flat rejection of large-scale thinking. Indeed, without large-scale thinking our cultures are moved blindly by inertial forces of economics and power. Large ideas are desperately needed to make possible the interpretation of the interdependent social and natural circumstances of the globe. Envisioning time and eternity is as important in its way for ecological management and economic planning as for religion. The fact that the traditional large ideas, and the more recent large ideas of modernity, are inadequate does not mean they are devoid of truth. Just not adequate. The answer to the suspicion of large ideas is better large ideas, not none.

A second reason for the eclipse of metaphysics is the crude empiricism of popular modernity. "If it cannot be experienced, it is not real." "If *I* cannot experience it, it is not real." Perhaps the modern (as opposed to contemporary astrophysical) idea of scientific experiment does not entail crude empiricism directly; but it does reinforce its cultural popularity. Immanuel Kant gave sophisticated expression to this empiricism with his claim, discussed in Chapter 3, that things transcending experience cannot be known. He (1787) explicitly identified metaphysics as the study of those things that transcend experience, and his "critique of pure reason" was an explicit rejection of metaphysics. A consequence of Kant's view, which but expresses a larger cultural attitude, is that, if knowledge of transcendent things is impossible, then knowledge of what experience does reveal is left to science; and philosophy concerns itself with the nature of experience itself. Much philosophy since Kant has been epistemology, the study of knowledge, and the underlying assumption has developed that what's really real is experience itself. A further implication of this that we saw previously is the assumption that only present time is real, for present time is the time of experiential consciousness.

The answer to the Kantian critique has to be many-sided, and only one side was given in Chapter 3. Another part of the answer is to point out that many people accept his conclusions without examining his argument. The argument itself is extraordinarily implausible because it asserts that we have a priori knowledge of the world in physics and mathematics (Kant 1787, "Transcendental Aesthetic"). In physics we know, said Kant, that every determination has a cause, implying that statistical causation is impossible. But statistical causation is possible. In mathematics we know, said Kant, that Euclid was right about geometry; Kant himself had attempted to construct non-Euclidian geometries and failed, concluding they were impossible. But non-Euclidian geometries are now the basis of modern physics. Kant's arguments begin with premises that cannot be sustained today.

A further response to Kant is to challenge his definition of what counts as experience. For him experience is something that can fill a temporal unit of consciousness. This is not what experience has meant in China, though perhaps it is close to its meaning in India. It surely is not what the Greeks or European medievals meant by experience, nor what we mean when we refer to an experienced mechanic, or to having experienced a year's study of French, or to what experience shows about power and corruption.[2] Hegel "refuted" Kant by showing that experience in even the narrowest sense presupposes experience in such large senses as to include all moral cultures, all religions and their history, and all philosophical speculation. Although Hegel is often taken to be the prime example of excess in metaphysics, he did it all in the name of phenomenology and logic. The basic point is that experience cannot be used in advance to declare what we can and cannot know, because its own definition or limits are set by what we in fact know. What in fact is known is controversial, but that controversy cannot be settled by an appeal to the concept of experience, for the very definition of experience awaits the outcome of the controversy.

Another response to Kant, and to the culture he represents, is to provide an alternative conception of metaphysics that does not fall prey to his criticisms. The conception advanced here is that metaphysics is the construction and examination of large-scale hypotheses about metaphysical topics. The hypotheses are not deductively certain, nor can they be built on a certain foundation. They cannot be tested against something else with absolute certainty, such as sense experience, because experience is not certain. But they can be evaluated for their inclusiveness, their adequacy to interpret everything in our world, their applicability to some dimension of life or other, their internal consistency, and their coherence.[3] Large-scale metaphysical hypotheses and systems can be evaluated vis-à-vis one another for their formal elegance and for the ease with which they translate various domains of discourse to one another. No one can say that metaphysics is impossible if there are actual examples of it and if experienced metaphysicians know how to assess their various strengths and limitations. That a metaphysical hypothesis is not certain does not mean it is mistaken or that it is not worth living with as a guide for conceiving the large-scale matters of life. Indeed, there is no way to get a grasp of the big picture without disciplined metaphysics.

With these remarks about the enterprise of metaphysics and its collateral ontology and philosophical cosmology, we can attend to the metaphysical background for the issues of time and eternity. If the hypotheses presented in these pages are unsatisfactory, it will be instructive to understand why.

What shall be presented is a metaphysical hypothesis about identity, because to be is to be something with an identity.[4] The hypothesis is that to be a thing is to be a harmony of conditional and essential features. The plausibility of this hypothesis can be seen from four considerations. The first two have to do with how things are to be connected if they are related; the second two have to do with how they are not swallowed up in their relations but have their own integrity. Conditional features constitute a thing's connections; essential ones the thing's integrity over against others.

Relation as Connection

First, to be a thing is to be related to other things. This follows from the fact that determinateness itself is relational. To be determinate is to be determinate *with respect to something*. A thing need not be determinate with respect to everything, and in those respects it is indeterminate. Yet a thing must be determinate with respect to at least something; otherwise it would not be something rather than nothing. If a thing is determinate with respect to something, then it has features that connect it with that with respect to which it is determinate. Most abstractly, these features can be called conditional because they constitute how a thing is conditioned by other things. More concretely, in this cosmos, conditional features might have to do at least with causation, with context, or with order. Causal conditions include those things in the past that constitute a thing's potentials, and the things in the future into which a thing might enter as a constituent. Contextual conditions have to do with how a thing's position in space, time, or various structured orders give it shape. Ordering conditions have to do with how, for instance, in the order of color a thing is red rather than blue, in the order of value, better or worse than some other thing, in the order of family, the niece of an uncle, and so forth. Roughly understood, causal conditions enter a present thing from the past, contextual conditions from the present, and ordering conditions from the future.

Second, philosophies that do not conceive of things metaphysically as having conditional features fall into two sorts, both inadequate. One sort is atomism that supposes that things are what they are regardless of any connections with other things. In a strict sense, atoms are not determinate with respect to one another and hence are not determinate at all. Most atomists, however, say that the atoms are related to one another externally by virtue of being in space or in space-time. What differentiates atoms and makes them determinate with respect to one another is the relative positions they occupy in the spatial (and or temporal) field. Although all atoms are indistinguishable and featureless by themselves, according to some atomists, they take on properties when clumped together as solid bodies or swirled as gases, and the rest. But this is a philosophical cheat if taken literally. How can an atom be in space unless it is already spatial? To be *in* anything is to be spatial. Spatiality must be a property of things, not a container of things that otherwise would not be spatial; this point shall be examined later. At any rate, atoms cannot relate except by bumping and sticking, and there are many kinds of connection with more complicated relations than that, for instance people knowing, animals growing.

The other sort of philosophy that denies conditional features is what Leibniz popularized as "monadology." A monad is a being that is a little world all unto itself. For Leibniz, each monad contains a perfect mirror of all the other monads, so that it seems that they communicate with, relate to, and in some cases know each other. But this is only an illusion caused by the fact that when they were originally created God structured each monad to be entertaining the perceptions of the other monads at precisely the moment those other monads were doing the things pictured. Although it seems to a monad that it is being conditioned by other things, that it can affect other things by action, and that it has a context among other things, in fact, for monadology, these seemings are wholly essential to the monad and have nothing to do with other things except insofar as the monad was made to mirror them. A simpler metaphysical hypothesis should indicate how there is real conditioning. The practical problem with both atomism and monadology is that if they are taken seriously they lead to solipsism: how do I know there is anything in addition to myself if nothing affects me and I affect nothing else?

However we proceed to account for them in detail, things must contain some conditional features to connect them to other things.

The Integrity of Relata

Third, essential features are necessary constituents of things along with conditional features because things cannot be reduced to the influences of others and their own influences on others. Things need existential identities of their own to receive and cause influences. If there were no essential features things would not have their own being but would reduce to other things. Carried out seriously, the denial of essential features would entail that nothing would have its own being and nothing could condition or be conditioned by anything else.

Essential features are no more necessary than conditional ones; both are necessary. Functionally, essential features can be understood as what the thing contributes to its conditional features to integrate them into the harmonized thing. The essential features are the principles or reasons for ordering conditional features, for selecting how to respond to conditioning things and how to condition other things. The essential features compose a thing such that its various conditions constitute its own identity. Roughly, there are three sorts of essential features: characteristic, decisive, and value-making. Characteristic essential features are those that give a thing identity over time. Decisive essential features are the ones a thing gives itself in a present moment of self-determination. Value-making essential features are those that are functions of the possibilities that a thing might have, possibilities of different worth.

Fourth, philosophies that deny essential features, in the contrast drawn between them and conditional features, fail to be able to maintain that there is a plurality of real and different things in the world. If things have no essential features over against their conditional features, they are reduced to their various relations with other things. But then it is the relations that are real, and the things are merely perspectives on the relations.[5] What provides the differences in perspectives? It could be only more relations, and then even the relations are subsumed into one highest relation whose parts are not finally distinct or distinguishable. As Bradley argued (1897, Chapter 3, for instance), following this line, in the end there is only the absolute and it is internally undifferentiated: both qualities and relations are unintelligible. Some thinkers, such as Oliver (1984), move at this point to epistemology, saying that only in experience can we preserve the impression of difference within the immediate intentional act. The difficulty with the appeal to experience is that it implies that experience lies if reality in fact is only one. The difficulty with saying reality is only one, a massive relation whose internal parts are mere abstractions (if that), is that reality has many different things in it and we experience it that way. However mistaken experience might be, it is unlikely to be mistaken in apprehending that there are differences. So there must be some essential features that allow things to be distinct from one another even while they are related.

Some people construe Buddhism as denying that things have essential features. Of course there are many kinds of Buddhism, and some do affirm that things have own-being, *svabhava*. Other Buddhists, however, do deny that things have "own-being" and interpret causation according to the doctrine of dependent coorigination, *pratitya samutpada*. To say that dependent coorigination denies essential features is a misinterpretation. Dependent coorigination says only that a thing's features come from a vast complex of past causal chains and that their conjunction in the present thing is something that will not last, given their trajectories. Dependent coorigination does not say that things do not in fact come together really and actually for their own moment; this actual coming together displays whatever is essential in the thing, however temporary. If there were no actualization or "arising and ceasing," there would be no origination, dependent or otherwise, and no "suchness." The point of the doctrine of dependent coorigination is to deny any underlying substance that serves as a substratum for qualities or that has a nature of its own outside the harmony of qualities in the moment. The doctrine of essential features entails no commitment to underlying substances.

Harmony

In sum, things are harmonies of both conditional and essential features, conditional ones in order to be determinately related to other things with respect to which they are determinate, and essential ones in order to be determinately different from those other things. Determinateness requires both connection and self-sameness. Things are both related to one another and different.

To say that things are harmonies of essential and conditional features raises the question of harmony. Two common mistakes about harmony need to be articulated and rejected immediately.

One is that a harmony is always some higher principle that integrates its components. That higher principle is supposed to be determinate itself, for without a character of its own it could do no integrating. But if it has a character of its own, it would have to be related to its own components by yet other determinate principles, ad infinitum. Sometimes, of course, higher or inclusive things relate others. But harmony in the metaphysical sense used of the conjunction of conditional and essential features in a thing is the sheer togetherness or fit of the conditional and essential features. Whitehead (1929, p. 22) termed this kind of togetherness a *contrast*. Now the features of a harmony are themselves determinate and hence are harmonies on their own, with their own components that are harmonies, and so on. So a given harmony might be extremely precarious if its component features are given to change and no longer fit. On the other hand, sometimes the fit of things reinforces the stability in the components harmonized. The metaphysical analysis of harmonies does not specify stability or change as such. To experience a thing as a harmony is to have a kind of aesthetic intuition of its hang-togetherness. To express a harmony, it is not necessary to specify any unifying principle over and above the sheer fit of the essential and conditional features.[6]

The second mistake about harmony is to suppose that it is always aesthetically pleasing. Wars and toothaches are examples of harmony, and they are not pleasant at all. In some deep metaphysical sense, a harmony is necessarily valuable because it sustains in existence the values of its components. So, a war is good insofar as the opponents are still fighting; it is evil because people get hurt and in doing so drop out of the war (perhaps out of existence). Even where bad things have some intrinsic value, it is usually misplaced, as in the example of the AIDS virus that is so subtle in its construction as to be impervious to ordinary means to cure its infection. To say that things are harmonies is to say only that they are integrations of conditional and essential features, without implying that they are stable integrations or good ones.

If every determinate thing is a harmony of essential and conditional features, then the past, present, and future too must be such harmonies. The analysis of the modes of time then can proceed by examining the various features of each. If we can see how each of the temporal modes has its own essential features, that will guard against conflating the modes to some favored one. If we can see how each must be conditioned by the other two to be itself, then it will be apparent how there cannot be the past without the present and future, or the future without the past and present, just as there cannot be a present moment without a real past and a real future that are not mere aspects of the present.

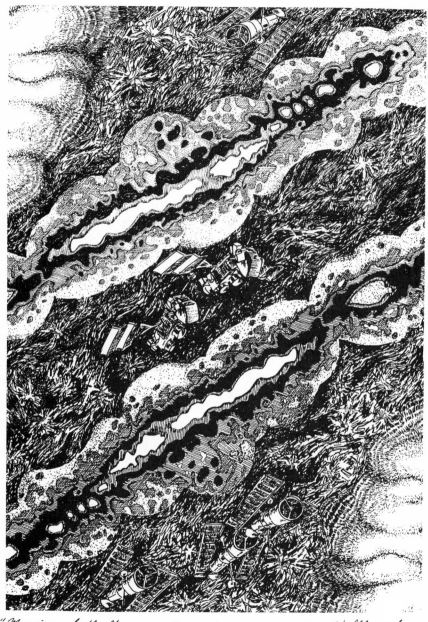

"Mapping of the Gamma Rays of the Milky Way, Hubble and
Gamma Ray Observatories"

Neville 1993

Chapter Six

TIME'S RELATIONS OF
OTHERNESS

The present, the past, and the future are essentially different from one another as temporal modes. Failure to recognize this fact accounts for much of the confusion about temporality. Too easily we have assumed that one temporal mode is paradigmatic for all the others. The thesis of this chapter is that each mode has essential features of its own that characterize the "timeliness" we associate with that mode. These will be characterized in the second section. The third section will elaborate on a peculiarly complicated part of the essential features of the future; namely, the association of value with form as such. The fourth section rehearses how the modes of time, respecting their essential features, are equally real. The first section, however, considers certain historical mistakes that have been made by taking one of the temporal modes as paradigmatic for the others. Fixation on the essential characteristics of the past has been typical of much of the modern period; a rebellion and counterfixation on the present has typified the twentieth century. Although no period has fixed on the essential characteristics of the future as paradigms for all time, there has been a certain pathology in many periods that consists in thinking all time is as open as the future.

The Present's Rebellion against Time as Past

From the early modern European period until the beginning of the twentieth century it was customary for Western thinkers to assume that all time has the character of the fixed past. The past, of course, is finished, actualized, and fixed. However it might be extended or given new meanings or unanticipatable consequences subsequently, the past is a positive fact.

The interest of modern science has been to conceive the world deterministically, as this has been expressed in the law of the conservation of energy. According to that law, the rearrangements of mass-energy can be understood if they are presumed to have a constant cumulative quantity. Therefore it is possible to think of time running in either direction, with the option of events running backward relative to their current unfolding. This deterministic assumption in Newtonian mechanics was Kant's chief motive for formulating the law of causation to say that every alteration requires a cause. Now in new sophisticated formulations it is assumed by the physics of the Big Bang.[1]

Or so many scientists have believed. Actually, the extent of determination of events by prior conditions is an empirical matter. It is obvious after five centuries of modern science that some things are highly regular. This is evident even in the social sciences. Economic connections are so tantalizingly regular that modern societies are deeply frustrated by their inability to express economic causal patterns with practical efficiency. But equally obvious is the fact that other things are not regularly connected at all. The last words your mother spoke immediately before your birth have no socially meaningful relation to the light flashing the closing price of the German mark on the Tokyo exchange on June 16, 1992. This is not to say that certain dimensions of events might not be regular whereas the events as a whole are unrelated in regular fashion. As purely physical perturbations of mass-energy, your mother's words and the flashing light surely do have regular connections in the system of the expanding universe as conceived by the physicist, although these perturbations are not socially meaningful as a social scientist would want that understood. If the example were your mother's words and the actual closing price of the mark, not a physical symbol of the price but the price itself, there would be not even the remote gravitational connections.

The socially meaningful regularities, indeed any regularities, such as they are and where they are, need to be discovered and cannot be presupposed to be ubiquitous. One of the most important questions of science is how much of the universe is regular, and in what ways, and how this relates to those aspects of the universe that are to be understood as parts of a unique story, or in some other way. Most human affairs are to be understood in terms of how people deal with the antecedent conditions and regularities of their situations, sometimes dealing with them freely so that what happens can be traced to the responsibility of particular human agents. For the most part, the real empirical regularities of the human scale of existence are not threats to human freedom but offer means of gaining some purchase on what happens; knowing how the economy works is a case in point.

A large disproportion exists between the models of the astrophysicists and the empirical work of social scientists (and most commonsense learning). Astrophysics supposes the determination of the law of the conservation of energy: this is built into physical modeling. In the nineteenth century physicists such as Laplace affirmed that celestial mechanics applied down to the details of every particle and that all events, including those of the scale of human meaning, could be reduced to those particles. Thus a Big-Bang Laplacean who accepted a model of the universe according to which it collapses after a certain extent of expansion would have to say that events in all details run backward. People would rise from their graves and regress toward childhood and birth; coal pits would turn into dinosaurs who would regurgitate great quantities of greenery every day; the imagination has a field day conjuring images of backward events, and the shape of human meaning would of course be impossible "on the way back in."

Contemporary physicists, by contrast, rarely apply their models to the human scale of things. Their laws are expressed in statistical terms. So we might imagine that within the outer limits set by the physical conditions of mass and energy, human affairs might take their particular historical way. The physical model might indeed be compatible with the human-scale indeterminations to be resolved by free responsibility, so long as the aggregate mass-energy quantities remain within the statistical determinations. The weight of cumulative evidence for responsibility in human life is far vaster and culturally richer than post-Einsteinian physical speculations. Laplace to the contrary notwithstanding, if human culture had to choose between reversible determinism and the conditions for responsibility, surely the latter would win. Perhaps the compatibility suggested here is possible and that choice can be finessed. The disproportion between the astrophysical conception of causation embodied in models of the Big Bang and the conceptions employed in affairs of human responsibility remains to be explored and resolved.

But if all time is indeed conceived deterministically in the manner of Laplace, then the present and future are just as fixed as the past. The point taken to be the present is arbitrary with regard to the determination of events, because the present and future are just as fixed as the past. Enthralled by this conception, philosophers such as Leibniz could imagine that God creates a world that begins at a point and goes on infinitely. All that happens on the first day is that things begin to unfold. But God knows as much on the first day about the end as could be known on the last day, because it is all fixed. Laplace said that if he knew the position, direction, and velocity of everything in the universe at any one time, he could determine exactly where things would be at any other time; and he boasted that because of this he did not need the explanatory hypothesis of God. Now the past might very well be wholly fixed, as we say it is, without having the kind of structure that exhibits regularities. But if the past is both fixed, as it is, and structured by absolutely regular causal laws, then those laws will force the present and future to be structured just as the past is structured.

Against this treatment of the deterministic past as the paradigm for all the temporal modes, Henri Bergson and others protested in the name of creativity and vitalism. The deterministic view spatializes time, Bergson argued, so that the earlier and later have the same structure, just like the uniform geometry of space. Time is different from space, however, precisely because each present moment adds creative increments that supplement and change the previous structure, Bergson argued. At most, the past is frozen creativity, and the future is open.

Bergson spoke for a variety of thinkers who emphasized creativity and evolution in ways not all compatible with one another. Perhaps the most sophisticated was Whitehead who elaborated an entire cosmological or metaphysical system based on the idea of process. Although he did not share the interest in evolution held by many "process" thinkers, he did present a model of creativity in the present moment that stands as a clear alternative to the metaphysical model of Aristotle, as trimmed down by modern science, that had become the common sense by his time. The present "occasion," Whitehead said, is a creative act of becoming in which past occasions function as potentials to be integrated into a new thing, and the future provides possibilities for integration. The creativity of the occasion consists in elevating some of the potentials to importance over others, patterning the components of the occasion, and eliminating the possible combinations that are excluded by the chosen comprehensive possibility that becomes actualized. Whatever Whitehead's theory fails to say about past and future, and about continuity, its imagination and analytical precision about present creativity are brilliant and true so far as they go.

Although Whitehead used anthropomorphisms such as "decision" to describe the creativity of the present moment, he was quite clear that they were intended in a wholly abstract way; *decision* means simply "cutting off possibilities that will not be actualized." European existentialists by contrast shared the focus on the present moment but sustained the anthropic shape of their metaphors. Indeed, they rejected all scientific metaphysicalizing such as Whitehead's as ready to undermine the human and insisted that philosophy deal with affairs of the human scale, particularly those of the scale of consciousness. Like Whitehead, the existentialists emphasized decision and interpreted it as will. Jean Paul Sartre's was the best known slogan: "existence precedes essence." What one chooses to make oneself determines what one is; what one is made to be by other conditions is not really oneself unless one chooses it; to fail to choose what one cannot help is to remain in bad faith.

The existentialists' insistence on decisive will was not only a protest against scientisms, although it was that too. Even more it was a reaction to the collapse of the cultural definitions of Christendom and Western culture that was perceived to occur with the First World War. European modernity thought it knew what people were and what they were supposed to be, and how to measure the distance between the two needed for progress. But Kierkegaard undermined the authority of religious knowledge with his critique of Christendom and his advocacy of the priority of will in faith. Nietzsche undermined the authority of Western "values" with his critique of deference and self-sacrifice and with his advocacy of the priority of the will to power. Marx undermined the authority of reason with his critique of ideology as expressive of material interests and his advocacy of philosophy and science as agents of change rather than cognitive disciplines. Finally Freud undermined the authority of consciousness, the bedrock of European thought since Descartes, with his critique of repression, his demonstration of an animallike unconscious, and his advocacy of the pursuit of therapeutic equilibrium rather than goodness, truth, or even beauty. The Great War confirmed the suspicions of these thinkers and left the existentialists with the conviction that people are what they make themselves. No determinative inherited essence, only willed existence with the attendant responsibilities. The present moment of will is the true mode of time. The very fixedness of the past needs to be denied its importance, however much it is honored as that which is to be transcended.

The result of the confluence of the evolutionary and process thinkers on the one hand and the existentialists on the other has been an extraordinary preoccupation with present time in the twentieth century. From the paradigmatic dominance of the past we have moved to the paradigmatic dominance of the present. This we have noticed in the previous chapter.

Few cultures have been preoccupied with future time as a model for time as a whole. But if not a preoccupation, the future as a model for all time is an aberrant temptation attendant on any culture, a kind of pathological immaturity. To confuse all time with future time is to think always that possibilities are open. Not only is the future open, but the present can be thought not to require real decisions. If decisions are accidentally made in the present, they do not really count, because there is always tomorrow in which things will be open again. Nor is the past fixed for this attitude. Rather, the past can be willed away. One never is responsible for something if one repudiates it. Children sometimes live as if always in future time. Their futures seem open even when adults know their limitations. Their present actions are protected from being consequential and usually are in fact of no great moment. And their past is like a dream world that could be dreamed otherwise. Whereas playing in the open future is appropriate in young childhood, by adolescence there are important consequences of present choice, and the past cannot always be erased: some play leads to pregnancy, the paradigmatic "responsibility for another."

The attempts to employ the features of one mode of time to cover all the modes are always seductive. They promise not only a simplification but also the specially sought advantages of the dominant temporal mode in question. Deterministic scientists want all time to be like the past because it means everything must fit their form of understanding. Vitalists, process thinkers, and existentialists want all time to be like the present because then everything is self-determined. Childish people want all time to be like the open future because then nothing ever counts and everything remains possible. None of these attempts to render all time as if it had the character of only one mode can succeed.

After this excursis into recent historical attempts to reduce away the different realities of past, present, and future, the discussion can now turn to the analysis of those differences.

The Differences between Past, Present, and Future

Past, present, and future are fundamentally different. They are other to one another. Each has essential features peculiar to itself and not shared by the others. Each has conditional features from the others, and contributes conditional features; the result is a different set of conditions in each case. Without recognizing the otherness between the temporal modes, it is impossible to accept the passage of time in its wholeness.

The analysis of the differences among the temporal modes can take advantage of the theory of essential and conditional features developed in the previous chapter. Each mode has its essential features that constitute the characteristic timeliness of the mode. But no mode could be what it is without conditional features from the other modes. The temporality of the modes, in contrast perhaps to the characteristic timeliness, is the harmony of all the modes in their essential and conditional features so as to constitute time's flow. The analysis will start with a brief sketch of the essential features of the present, the past, and the future, in that order. It should be remembered that what is presented is an hypothesis employed to make good sense of time.

The essential features of the present, in this hypothesis, are those having to do with decision and spontaneous creativity, as existentialists and process philosophers have emphasized. The present is the temporal mode in which change takes place. The present is the moment of actualization, in which each present moment creates an actual state of affairs out of mere potentials. The essential features of the present have to do with new actuality, with changing given patterns, and with deciding among possibilities for actualization. Although the present also has conditional features in its potentialities from the past and possibilities from the future that vary in value, its essential features are those that make for change, spontaneity, creativity, and actualization. If the essential features of a temporal mode are to be called its *timeliness,* the timeliness of the present is spontaneous creativity, change, and actualization. On the human scale, the "present moment" part of personal identity has to do with intention in mind and will in action.

The hypothesis that the essential features of the present have to do with change and actualization is compatible with the human emphasis on freedom and responsibility. But it is also compatible with the physicists' deterministic claim that, on the scale of events they measure, there is no change that does not fall within the limits of predictability. All that an astrophysical model such as that of the Big Bang requires is that actualized changes fall within the boundaries of the predictable.

The essential features of the past are those having to do with fixed, objective everlastingness. When a present moment finishes its becoming, it is past; what it decided and actualized is what is there. The past has no more spontaneous creativity; it is what happened. That structure is wholly factual. It cannot be changed, although subsequent events can alter or add to its meaning. The past is everlasting in the sense that ever after it will have the character of its objective nature; it is not everlasting in the sense of the hills that endure or are reiterated into each successive present moment. The difference between everlastingness and endurance is that the former is merely a fixed objective fact and may be limited to the proper dates of the past; the latter is the successive occupation of present times by a thing, an insistence on extending the proper dates of its existence from one present moment to the next, for a while.

The continual accretions to the past by present happenings provide a constantly shifting meaning to the past; that is a kind of conditional feature the past enjoys from the present. Similarly, each thing in the past has a value dependent on the possibilities actualized there, a function of conditional features from the future. But the past itself cannot change.

Some philosophers say that the past passes away and no longer exists. Yet this is impossible because the past cannot change, not into anything else nor into nothing. Of course the past no longer exists in the mode of present temporality, with the immediacy of spontaneous creativity. But the existence of the present is only a "becoming existent" existence. The existence of the past is to be actual fact. The timeliness of the past is objective everlastingness.

The essential features of the future have to do with pure form and value. Whereas the timeliness of the present and past are somewhat obvious when pointed out, the timeliness of the future as pure form and value sounds strange. This is in part because our sense of the future comes from its anticipation. We anticipate the future as a kind of extrapolation of our sense of present happenings and the remembered past, projecting a kind of field in which different things are imagined to be realized. But this is the future as a conditional feature of present experience. What is essential about the future is that it is pure normative form.

The essential features of the future cannot be well understood apart from its conditional features, precisely because we imagine the future as an extrapolation of the present. The past provides many different potentials for selective integration in the present, and what the future forms is the diversity of things to be integrated. Form means what would integrate the potentials and decisions contributed to the future by the past and present. If there were no past or present to contribute the plurality to be integrated, pure form would be wholly empty and indeterminate. There is no form of forms. The future is the harmony of what essentially makes form formal with the conditional elements to be formed.

Value and Time

A special discussion of value is important here because to identify form with value is not obvious. The tradition to do so stems from Plato and Mencius. Plato in the Republic, for instance, called that which gives form to things the *Form of the Good.* Wherever there is form, for Plato, there is something good, although perhaps not the right good in the right place. In his late dialogue, the Philebus, Plato distinguished between form as limit and the Good as the Cause of Mixture. That discussion shall be analyzed in Chapter 11. With the distinction between limit and Cause of Mixture Plato recognized that the real good is to have the right form in the right place at the right time. Aristotle and most "Platonists," including Whitehead, have interpreted Plato's theory of forms to refer to structures, some of which are structures of ideals or goods. These interpretations blatantly ignore the conjunctions and interdefinitions of form and value in both the Republic and Philebus. Furthermore, they give rise to intolerable philosophical problems in accounting for both form and value. Value usually is thought to be arbitrary because only some structural forms have it and others do not; in the mathematical Platonizing of modern physics, value is dropped out of all objective accounts completely and handed over to subjectivity as a matter of projection.

Form itself, if only structure, has no comprehensible ontological standing. If it is thought to be free-standing, like a Platonic heaven of forms, it has no relation to the temporal world nor can it be conceived by temporal creatures.[2] If form is thought to be required to stand in actual substances, either as actualized, as Aristotle thought, or as contemplated, as Whitehead thought, then no novel possibilities can be realized in the first case, or God would have to be posited as a kind of everlasting holding substance for eternal objects in the second. There may be other good reasons to believe in a God whose contemplative gaze gives form someplace to light, and so the argument is not a reductio ad absurdum. Nevertheless, the general position that form must have residence in actuality to have being does not easily acknowledge the equality of ontological status between form and actuality. Far better to say that form is the essential feature of the future and that determinate forms are the ways the future is made determinate by concrete actuality in the past and by the shifting decisions of present moments.

That form is value, as Plato believed, can be explicated by a theory that addresses the question why form is as it is (see Neville 1981, Part II). Plain formal structures are the characters embodied in things to make them what they are. The formal characters can be viewed in conjunction or isolated or analyzed into smaller formal elements. They also can be compared with other forms that are not in the things, but perhaps could be, or ought to be, or ought not to be, or would be if other things were different, and so on. Now the things in the world are valuable (or disvaluable) in various ways. They attract or repel us in our experience and give experience the rich coloration that shapes intentionality, enjoyment, suffering, and purpose. Only a position blinded by a modern fact *versus* value distinction could dispute this characterization of the world, a point to which the discussion shall return later. Things are also valuable in causal ways, as food is good for living organisms, hot sun for corn in July, and knowledge for the advancement of civilization. It is the forms in things that make the difference in value. If the forms were different, the values of things would be different. What is form in this context? Form is the ways the components of things can be together; without the form, the components could not be together. Perhaps there are different forms according to which the components can be together, perhaps not. By putting the components together with this form rather than that, or not at all, the value is achieved of having these components together just so. Put the other way around, from the standpoint of the Form of the Good, a form is a way of achieving a certain value by putting potential components together in the form's way. So forms can be conceived as ways of schematizing value to components to be unified. Different forms that all equally would unify a given set of potential components do so in ways that achieve different values. Such forms vary in their complexity and their simplicity and are better bearers of value to the degree they maximize both. But sometimes gains in simplicity are not comparable with gains in complexity, and different forms would achieve merely different values. Stated most generally, this hypothesis is that form is what would achieve value by unifying potential components of things; different forms are different ways of unifying things, applicable perhaps to different sets of things to be unified, achieving different values.

Now it is apparent, at least on this hypothesis, why pure form is neatly conceived as the essence of the future. The future is what would integrate and give value to all the present points of decision, which in turn are structured by the potentials from the past actualities. The structures of the future are the different forms of unification that might apply in various places and across the board, each a possibility of achieving a certain value. The relations among forms are logical ones and are extraordinarily nuanced from the standpoint of our usual way of imagining alternative scenarios. Each form would achieve a value if it were actualized. Each form gives value to actualization when embraced in a present moment of becoming. And each past thing has the values it does precisely because of the forms that have become embodied in it. This theory of form as value runs directly counter to modern common sense and requires considerable justification. It is not terribly important for the theory that the essential features of the future have to do with form, and the theory identifying form with value will recur in this discussion only with respect to the topics of religious worth in Part Four.

Suffice it for now to notice that different possibilities often have different values and that to realize one is to achieve that value rather than the others. The very meaning of integration in form is that holding the integrated things together achieves their combined value; sometimes the combined value is worth more than their values separately.

One of the most important strands in European modernity has conceived form and facts to be distinct from value.[3] This is not because things are experienced as valueless, but because the characters of things are confused with the characters of certain specific ways of knowing them, the ways expressible in mathematical terms. If things truly are, and are only, what mathematical physics expresses, then their worths do not register. Because we experience things as having various values, it is necessary in the scientific model to say that values are imputed to things by the experiencer. But the fact that mathematical physics does not register the beauty of a sunrise or the dignity of a human being does not mean the beauty and dignity are fictions imposed by an experiencer. It means only they do not register in the language of mathematics. This is no denegration of mathematics, only of scientistic exclusivism. A deep irony in the reduction of values from facts and form is that Platonists from Plato to Whitehead have held the hope of expressing goodness in the mathematical terms of ratio and proportion. A good case can be made for understanding form in terms of value rather than the other way around.[4]

The Equal Necessity of the Temporal Modes

The thesis proposed here is that a proper account of temporality should acknowledge three temporal modes, each with its own essential features. The essential features of the present are those having to do with spontaneous creativity actualizing changes; those of the past have to do with objective everlastingness; those of the future have to do with normative form. Each set of essential features constitutes the timeliness of each temporal mode.

None of the modes of time is real with only its essential features. Each is a harmony of essential and conditional features. Indeed, the essential features are truly indeterminate without the conditional ones. We have already seen the difficulty of expressing the nature of normative form without mentioning the conditional things to be formed. Similarly, spontaneous creativity cannot be described without potentials and possibilities, and objective everlastingness cannot be described without reference to the finishing (factum) and the actualizing of value-laden possibilities. In the next chapter the argument will fill out the connections among the temporal modes with their conditional features.

For the moment it is worth noting that sometimes the essential features of the idiosyncratic timeliness of the temporal modes have been taken to stand by themselves. When they do, paradoxically, they are images not of time but of eternity, poor images of eternity. The creative immediacy of present spontaneous creativity is sometimes taken to be the *totum simul,* the All At Once, of the divine mind. Just as a present moment embraces the before of unintegrated potentials with the after of actualized possibilities without a temporal passage from earlier to later, so divine eternity can embrace the whole within one vision. The objective everlastingness of the past has been taken to be the eternity of the determined world, always fixed and unrolling with a moving present only as a kind of show that makes no difference. The normative formality of the future is very often taken to be the static eternity of that which does not change, structure itself. All these are bad images of eternity, it will be shown later in Chapter 9. Furthermore, although they are what make each temporal mode timely, contributing its unique element to temporal passage, they are not by themselves temporal. But then, they are not by themselves. The analysis must proceed to the integration of essential and conditional features, as demanded by the metaphysics of identity.

The moral to be gained from this stage of the argument is that the temporal modes are truly different from one another. Even if they are what they are only in conjunction, by giving each other conditional features that make them together constitute time, they are not swallowed up in some super temporal mode that is "really" time. Time is their conjunction. The argument of the next chapter is to explore the connections among the modes of temporality and analyze their harmonies of conditional and essential features to be able to understand time's flow.

"Exploding Star '1987 A'"   Neville 1993

Chapter Seven

TIME'S FLOW

As the ancient hills are icons of eternity, the river is the icon of time. Time flows and, as Heraclitus said (Fragment 218), you cannot step into the same river twice. Later commentators have noted that you cannot step into the *same* river even once if the stepping takes time. But what does the metaphor of flowing mean? Augustine said (*Confessions,* Book 11, Chapter 14) of the question what is time? "If no one asks me, I know what it is. If I wish to explain it to him who asks me, I do not know." We all know what time is and that it "flows," but cannot explain what that means.

Before and After, Earlier and Later, and When

Part of the problem with the metaphor of flowing is that it suggests that time is itself a kind of substance, an independent container within which temporal things find location. In this suggestion, part of the container locates past time, another part present time, and yet another part future time; and things move from one to the other. The perplexity consists in the fact that the "location" of the present is constantly shifting. The metaphor of a time line sometimes supplements the container image, with segments or points on the line representing successive dates at which the present can be located. But the line is all at once, as is the container, and nothing directly represents the flowing. As Bergson would complain, spatial symbols cannot represent what is most interesting about time, its flow.

The present moment is the key to understanding time's flow, but not by itself. At bare minimum, time's flow is a matter of change, like Heraclitus' moving river. To understand both the logic and the experiential sense of change, we may try several candidate representations.

In one sense, change requires reference to only two units of time, the "before" unit and the "after" unit. Change is the difference between them. As a sheer measure of difference, before and after are more like logical than temporal notions. We can speak of mathematical operations in terms of before and after; before there is a sum of 12 and after adding 3 to it the sum is 15. The relations in before and after can be reversed; subtract 3 from 15 and the sum is 12. In each case the relations of before and after hold regardless of whether any time elapses between them. Before and after do not connote any passage of time at all, only differences in states that are ordered. The positive point is that before and after denote sequential order. If we can discover what makes a sequence temporal, and not merely logical or arithmetical, before and after will mark out an important element of temporal order and allow dating. Dating is naming the units in the order of before and after.

Earlier and *later* denote relations between two happenings, each of which has its own time. In the sequence of before and after, the earlier happening is finished when the later event occurs. Earlier and later do not overlap in time, although they are times with some dimension and with dates.

"When" does change take place? We would think that change takes place in present time; the past is when the change is over and the future is when the change has not begun. Augustine (*Confessions*, Book 11, Chapter 15) thought that the present has no extension whatsoever, for if it did then it would have to contain a little of the past and a little of the future. If the present is extended, then one part of the present is earlier than the later part, he thought. If that were the case, then change indeed takes place in the present, moving in the present from the earlier to the later state of affairs. But this cannot be, thought Augustine, because the past is precisely what is not present, and the same is true of the future. Therefore, he concluded, the present is like an infinitessimally thin knife edge between the future and the past in which nothing takes place, and time's flow remains a mystery.

Two things can be learned from Augustine's quandary. One is that change itself cannot be a couple of earlier and later moments, because earlier and later mark different times: when one is present the other is past or not yet. Yet change does have an order of before and after. Before things were this way and after they are another way. A complex change might have an extremely complicated set of internally nested befores and afters. In fact, a change can be analyzed structurally into the sequence of least alterations made to the initial state to get, stage by stage, to the later state, each "least alteration" marking a before and after order. Within a present moment of change, however, there is no order of earlier and later; no "before" state is earlier than a relative "after" state. This sounds paradoxical but it is the key to understanding the present moment.

Alfred North Whitehead was the one who realized that the present is a moment of change with an internal order of before and after but no internal order of earlier and later.[1] He provided the crucial model to understand this. Rather than conceiving the present as a moment that endures through its change, the present is a moment that becomes or comes into being as a whole unit. A thing in the present is not enduring through that present, but is coming to be as that present existent. After the present has become (past), it has a fulfilled temporal dimension (and spatial and perhaps other dimensions), say, a minute. While present, however, that happening did not endure its first thirty seconds before a later thirty seconds. The distinction between the seconds is made after the fact, based on an arbitrary time measure that perhaps can be correlated to the logic of before and after in the minute-long present. Whitehead picked up another image of Augustine's (*Confessions*, Book 11, Chapter 2) to express this; namely, that present time comes in "drops." There is a least unit of time in a thing's temporal flow.

Temporally Biased Representations of Time

Notice now that there are three ways of representing time, according to the temporal modes. These are functions of their essential features or unique senses of timeliness. The past is an order of actual earlier and later moments. Any past moment can itself be analyzed into internal earlier and later moments *ad indefinitum.* While each moment was in its "present" moment of becoming, it had a wholeness in coming to be that could not be existentially divided as earlier and later, only logically divided as before and after. After it is actualized and part of the past, it fits into the structures of previous, concurrent, and subsequent actualized things, and those structures allow of any sort of analysis that can be applied. Enduring things are those with a past. Viewing all time from the mode of actualized structure, we can imagine the future stretching out as a series of earlier and later moments.

The timeliness of the future is mere logical or formal order. Thus the future can be conceived as the series of before and after changes that would have to be run through to get from a specified state to a subsequent state. The logical order is wholly subjunctive with regard to actualization; that is, *if* state M is to be actualized in the future, states G, H, and I will have to be actualized before that.

The timeliness of the present is exactly to become a new thing that is a change from the past. By itself, this can be characterized as spontaneous creativity or actualization. But change is never sheer change or by itself. It is a change from something to something. That from which change takes place is the finished past, which is part of the present, not in an early part of the present but only as a logical "before." That to which the change is made is the finished present, at which point it has become a past extended happening. The changing is the coming to be of that which, when it has come to be, is an actual past fact. Thus present time is not mere change, but a change that requires a connection between the past that is its source and the future that is its outcome made past.

To sort out all these points we may recur to the distinction between essential and conditional features and detail now the conditional features that connect the temporal modes, giving them their character precisely as temporal.

The Necessary Mutual Conditioning of Time's Modes

We have already noted that the present requires conditional features from both past and future. From the past, the present requires finished actualities as potentials for its coming to be. From the future the present requires formal possibilities for combining the actual potentials into a consistent and singular actualization of the present moment. These should be examined in turn.

A present happening takes its rise from the past. Part of Whitehead's great genius was to see that past events are not only in the past but also can function in events subsequent to themselves. In fact, Whitehead criticized (1926) the main part of the modern European tradition for the mistaken doctrine he called *simple location*. The doctrine of simple location says that a thing is only when and where it comes to be. But if this is so then nothing can enter into anything else. Particularly, things cannot enter into the minds of knowers to be known. Nor can there be any continuity of things through time because each time has its own new thing that would have to be exclusive of the things in the previous times. Whitehead's alternative can be called *multiple location* (Neville 1989, pp. 149–164), and it involves distinguishing an occasion's "proper" location from its "component" locations. The proper location of an occasion is when and where it comes to be, or came to be, or will come to be; as to time, this is its proper date. The component locations are the various other occasions in which it subsequently enters as a component; what these are depends on many factors in the subsequent occasions that might include them. If an occasion whose proper location is in the past enters into a subsequent occasion, it does so as a potential for contributing to the actuality of the subsequent occasion. A present occasion thus has a variety of potentials from the past that constitute the material for its actualization.

The many potentials in a present moment are not compatible as a singular entity without integration. Some potentials must be dismissed, and the others altered and combined in various ways to constitute a singular, wholly determinate occasion. The future contributes the real possibilities for elimination, alteration, and combination of the potentials. These possibilities must be in the present, and they can function at any logical stage in the change from the initial potentials to final fact.

A distinction needs to be drawn between pure formal possibilities and real possibilities. Real possibilities are those for which the potential for actualization exists. Only real possibilities function in a present moment, and they arise in the present either by being formal structures already actualized among the potentials or by spontaneous generation in the present itself. The real possibilities in an occasion must conform to the more general traits of formal possibilities, and must as formal possibilities unite all real possibilities in all occasions to constitute a field. The real possibilities in one occasion must be compatible with the real possibilities in its neighbors.

For experiential occasions within the life of a human being or other rational creature, the ways of integrating potentials into singular moments can include intentional fields of consciousness, wherein past, contemporary, and future matters are imagined as spread out. Representations are used to pick out actual structures and anticipate the future consequences of present happenings. For pragmatic and evolutionary reasons, our representations are more or less accurate about the things that generally matter on the human scale of life. Only in the last few hundred years have we devised representations for micro and macro structures whose variables are not readily differential within the human sphere. Customarily we represent the future, which is itself a set of possibilities arranged algorithmically, as a set of imaginary events using the same kind of representations we do for actuality and the processes of actualization. Both the imaginative structure of intentionality and its truth commitments are subjects of great complexity beyond the scope of the present essay.[2]

The timeliness of the past as objective everlastingness is temporal because of conditional features deriving from the present and future. Because the present is a process of actualization, the past has the character of actuality. Actuality is existential thisness. The existential part means that the actual thing has a wholly definite spatial and temporal structure, occupying or moving through definite positive locations in space and time. These locations are its "proper" locations, and remain so everlastingly, long after the date has past and the place been occupied and transformed by other things. The proper locations are not separate containers that things occupy, but rather the existential character of the things themselves. Things are defined in large measure by the ways they occupy and structure their proper locations. That the actual past has the character of thisness (the technical Latin word is *haecceity*) means that it is utterly and completely concrete. Concreteness means complete determinateness and more. Determinateness in this regard means that each possibility is either affirmed or denied: red or not-red, the better or the worse, John's or not-John's, and so forth. Part of concreteness is that an actual thing exhibits a decision regarding every possibility. As formal, possibilities are always universal or vague; that is, they are characters that could be instantiated in any number of things: many things could be red, the better, or John's. To be actualized, any possibility still needs to be filled in with specializing decision: if red, of what value, hue, and intensity? In an actual, concrete "this," all those decisions are made. The present moment of actualization is the process of deciding all these things. The result, however, is not to be understood merely as a list of all the possibilities and subpossibilities chosen. There could be no such list because it would be infinitely long: every possibility has further components requiring decision. Rather, actuality is qualitatively different from an assemblage of possibilities in its infinite complexity and density. There is no structural possibility that is not determined about actuality, and hence there is no limit to the formal representation of actuality. But actuality is the infinitely dense "thisness" properly located in space and time, which is "more" than the determinateness of the universal forms involved.

As just indicated, from the future by way of present processes of actualization, the past has a structure. The structure not only has the formal properties of universals but constitutes matrices of togetherness among the elements of the past and in projective relation of them to the present and future. Whereas present moments of actualization have an internal integrity and "droplike" character, the actuality of the past has integrated these into larger structured elements. For the past, the internal processes of decision making are irrelevant. What is relevant is how each bit of actualization structurally fits in with the larger careers, trajectories, material, social, and cultural configurations that have been, are being, and will be actualized. The past of a person is not the set of individual decision points but the history of deeds and accumulated character of the individual in context. The past is usually understood most relevantly by its causal structures. But from an appreciative point of view, the past is most relevantly understood by the values it embodies, and how those values are causally connected.

The future is essentially pure normative form but conditionally has features from the past and present. From the past's diverse actualities, the future has the plurality-to-be-formed such that formal possibilities are real possibilities. Pure form is wholly subjunctive: it is what would integrate a certain manifold if there were such a manifold. The future, however, is determinate in some respects; it is the future of the actual world. Only by relation to actuality does pure form become temporal. Some Platonists, although probably not Plato himself as argued in the previous chapter, have believed that there exists a realm of determinate universals, what Whitehead called *eternal objects*. This view treats the subjunctive character of form as if it were actual. Imaginatively, of course, we can create pluralities and examine their formal possibilities; this is to bring the pure subjunctivity of form into relation with at least an imagined actual plurality. Kant correctly saw that mathematics involves imaginative operations that reveal the structures form might have if it were related to this or that actual potential. But the Platonists are mistaken to believe that there exists a realm of separate determinate forms with no relation to the actual world. Pure form is merely the essential part of the future that is necessarily related to the conditional parts of the future providing an actual plurality that makes structured real possibilities. Because we can imagine other actual cuts, we can imagine unreal possibilities and can make it seem as if we are investigating pure form without any relation to actuality. In fact, our imagination, in saying "draw a straight line between two points" or "consider a succession of counts, 1, 2, 3," is supplying a hypothetical set of actual conditions that provides determinate structure to form. Form is what would integrate a plurality, real or subjunctive.

From the present temporal mode, the future takes on its dynamic character. That is, by virtue of decisions that take place in successive present moments, what is really possible changes. Sometimes possibilities are excluded, sometimes new ones introduced, sometimes new conditions added for the actualization of possibilities, and so forth. Although the future itself is a set of logical possibilities really relevant to the world, it can be imagined projectively as a set of prospective dates, with decisions in each date resting on what will have been decided in earlier dates. The possibilities at any future date constitute a field for the various decisive present occasions that approach it. That is, the possibilities for any one present occasion must be compatible with the possibilities for all other present occasions. The outcome of the various lines of structured decision making, in various persons, institutions, and natural processes, might be highly conflictual, explosive, and unfortunate. But all of those are compatible in the bare minimal sense of being part of a unified singular future. Relative to the depth of the future, that is, to a succession of dates, the field of possibilities is in constant dynamic shift. The possibilities for persons and institutions are constantly shifting as decisions are made. Whereas the past is fixed and the present is the actualization of a change, the future is in a constant state of change, modified by every present decision that takes place.

How Time Flows

That time flows may now be understood in terms of the mutual conditioning of the temporal modes. No one mode by itself constitutes temporal flow, not the coming-into-being of present timeliness, nor the objective fixity of the past, nor the subjunctive formal patterns of the future. Rather, the flow of time is the actualizing of possibilities and the putting into the past of that actuality. This adds to the previous past. The actualizing changes the future possibilities so that no other actualization could be exactly like the one that flowed. And the immediacy of the present vanishes as soon as it is accomplished. Without the immediacy of actualization, nothing would happen and nothing would be actual. Without the putting of the actualization into the past, again nothing would have been accomplished. Without changing the future, it would be as if the happening made no difference to anything.

Time's flow needs the essential features, the timeliness, of all modes of temporality, as well as their mutual conditioning. (Of course the conditional features could not exist without the respective essential ones.) The essential features of the present are necessary for change to take place at all. The essential features of the past are necessary for that change to be actual. The essential features of the future are necessary for that change to be possible, and for the differences it also makes possible. If the past were not real, there would be no flow, only a single real becoming with no temporal endurance through change. If the future were not real the flow would make no difference to anything, and there would be no sense to saying it is repeatable or unrepeatable. If the dynamic moving present were not real, there would be no flow, only arbitrary stopping points on a cinema film of states of actuality or possibility.

Because time is not a container but a characteristic of temporal things, it is a bit misleading to say that *time* flows. Rather, temporal things have a flowing character such that each of their dates is future to antecedents, past to consequents, and present to contemporaries. The implications of this will be brought out in the discussion of the temporal and eternal character of individuals in Chapter 13 and 14.

If we assume for the moment that the Big Bang theory is true, then time did not flow—there was no time—until the unexploded dense core had been put into the past by a present that actualized it as a burst of energy. We should not imagine the unexploded core to have remained quiescent for eons, awaiting its date of explosion. There was no passage of time, no endurance of things, until the changes began of the Bang. Indeed, we should not even say that the unexploded core was real or actual, because it was not the past of any previous actual event. The only reality of the unexploded core is as the imagined object of the mathematical model. There is no early moment of the explosion that did not have earlier antecedents. Like Zeno's Bisection Paradox run backward, the antecedents regress toward the infinitessimally short as measured by standard units, which marks regression toward the infinitely hot and fast. With the coming to be of any early motion, there is a past from which it has changed and a future for its possibilities. There is no time without temporal things, and temporal things are in motion. Only the explosion, now perhaps so spread out as to seem the very model of the everlasting heavens, exists in time. If it turns out in physical cosmology that some Steady State theory is true, then obviously there never was a first moment.

Physical cosmology is not concerned with time's flow, only with what happens and why. Physical cosmology treats the past not as a series of moments that can be dated as future, present, and past at different times, but as a fixed actual structure that can be measured by any extensive grid that can be applied. Thus a Big Bang cosmology might apply a Zenonian analysis to the first moment—remember Zeno said that any motion could be analyzed into an infinity of steps because before you could complete the first unit you would have to go halfway, and to do that you would have to go halfway to the first half, and so on. Probably, however, because of quantum phenomena a Zenonian analysis would be unhelpful as there would be too many empty analytical units. In fact, the Big Bang can be analyzed physically only as the process of expansion, not as the first move out from a previously existing unexploded core. The analysis of a first moment of time, in contrast to the first units of extension in the extensive continuum of an explosion, is metaphysical, not a matter of astrophysics.

No matter whether time's flow has been a Steady State or started with a Big Bang, the character of time's flow involves the three modes of time connected so that there is always a present that actualizes future possibilities and puts that actuality into the past. The date of the present changes as soon as it has become actual. There is thus a smooth flow from date to date in the present. At no time is there a break between the finish of one emerging present and the beginning of the next; at the next time there is already a new emergent becoming. At no time is there a transitional bump from one present to the next. The flow of time is continuous from one present date to the next, continuously adding to the past without jolts, and continuously shifting the future. Time's flow is smooth. This is an eternal state of affairs, as shall be argued now.

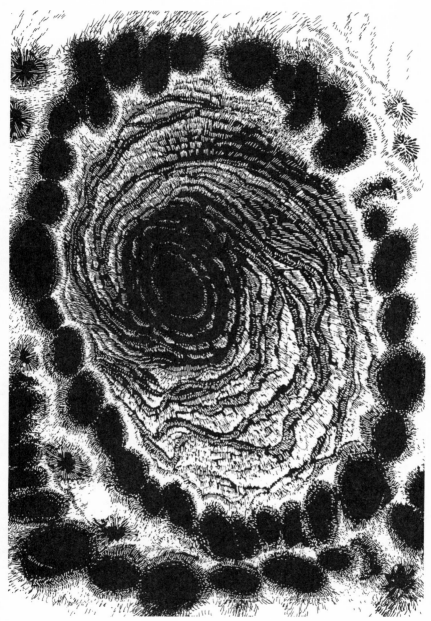

"A Black Hole, an image from Imagination" Neville 1993

Chapter Eight

ETERNAL TOGETHERNESS OF THE TEMPORAL MODES

The discussion has now completed its first pass at character-izing time, distinguishing and connecting the three temporal modes, past, present, and future. "Distinguishing and connecting" should not be understood in an old-fashioned substantialist way, as if they were three independent substances with some connections. Rather, they are three harmonies, each of which requires for its own being the conditional features derived from the others that, when harmonized with its essential timeliness, makes the modes temporal. Together they constitute time's flow.

The precise nature of the togetherness of the temporal modes is the topic of this chapter. The topic forces us to see time *sub specie eternitatis* and thus initiates a second pass over the topics previously investigated. The first section in this chapter draws out a distinc-tion between temporal togetherness and eternal togetherness. The second argues that the togetherness of the modes of time, in contrast to the togetherness of temporal things, requires an eternal context and analyzes why. The "ontological context of mutual relevance," which is required for the togetherness of the temporal modes, is the real structure of eternity and provides the stepping stone to the understanding of divinity to be developed in Part Three.

The third section makes the point that time and temporality are characteristics of determinate things, not containers within which temporal things are to be found. Thus time is in things, and things collectively are in eternity. The fourth section makes the obverse point, that temporal things are bounded by time, beginning and ending. No temporal thing takes up the whole of time but is eternal in its temporal finitude. These two sections presage the theological points to be made in Chapters 15 and 16, respectively; namely, that in one sense the infinite is in the finite and in another sense the finite is in the infinite.

Togetherness

Eternity was defined earlier as the togetherness of the temporal modes. Now that claim can be given some content. A distinction needs to be drawn between temporal togetherness and eternal togetherness. Temporal togetherness applies only to temporal things; indeed it is what makes them temporal. Eternal togetherness applies, among other things perhaps, to the temporal modes. They are not before or after one another, nor are they together in the same time, but in eternity.

There are many kinds of temporal togetherness that are not eternal. Temporal things may be together in the past, together in the present, and together in the future, in ways discussed earlier. Things may be together in the sense that one thing is in the actual past of a present happening and another thing in the present's proximate future. An actual thing can be together with a possibility in its future as mediated by a needed decisive present to actualize the future. And so on. Temporal relations of all the sorts are made possible by the conditional features each mode of time gives to and receives from the others. Temporal relations are what constitute things as temporal, making them by nature earlier, later, and contemporary with other things. Temporal things might also be eternal, or have an eternal dimension, as was suggested with regard to morally responsible persons in Chapter 4 and shall be argued in more detail in Chapters 13 and 14. But if things are temporally together with other things as earlier, later, and contemporary, they are at least temporal.

Eternal togetherness is another matter. At its most abstract it means mere nontemporal togetherness. In this sense, mathematical entities are related to one another. Slightly less abstract is the togetherness of formal elements that are lifted out of temporal things conceptually and make no intrinsic reference to temporal relations. "Knowledge is good," "might does not make right," "interdependent social systems tend to compensate for one another" are examples of this; of course, these could never be actualized except in temporal things, but then neither could mathematical relations.

A far richer dimension of eternal togetherness is constituted by the togetherness of the temporal modes. Furthermore, if the analyses of the modes previously given are somewhere near the mark, the senses of eternal togetherness in mathematics and systematic abstractions are to be accounted for as functions of the togetherness of the temporal modes, with the future being the locus of form that might be actualized. It is clear that the temporal modes themselves are not together temporally. Rather, it is their togetherness that allows for the temporal togetherness of things that are earlier, later, and contemporary with other things.

The richness of the eternal togetherness of the temporal modes comes from time's flow. The outstanding character of the temporal modes is that the date of the present is always changing. The present's mode is becoming, creativity, actualization. As soon as a present has completed the work of becoming, as soon as it is actually actualized — helpful redundancy — that moment, that date, has become past and something new is presently becoming actual. Not only is something new always becoming — the present is steadily moving on to new dates — but the past is always growing and the structure of future possibilities is constantly shifting in response to the decisions made in each moment of present actualization. Each particular date marks specific and historically particular changes in the growth of the past, the actualizations of the present, and the kaleidoscope of forms in the future. Relative to any particular date, these changes are temporally related as past, present, and future. Yet the changes in the temporal modes are always happening because that is the eternal togetherness of the modes. Without the eternal togetherness, there would be no temporal changes. Therefore, the eternal togetherness includes the extraordinary dynamism of the constant changes of things within each of the temporal modes. Rather than eternity being static, it is inclusive of all the changes that, with respect to any temporal date, are in mere temporal relation to one another. Eternal togetherness does not gather temporally diverse changes into one time; to believe so is to take one mode of time, the present, to be the paradigm for all time. Eternal togetherness is a different kind of togetherness entirely. Although always conceived in relation to time, and thus part of the same topic as time, eternity's togetherness is not temporal togetherness. It is rather the condition for and inclusive of all the changes involved in temporal togetherness. Eternity is the condition for and inclusive of time's flow.

The argument for eternal togetherness here is tortured and backstepping. Because our language all comes from temporal sensibilities, there is no univocally eternal language in which to explain eternity. The argument analyzes time and shows what time needs in order to flow that is not itself temporal. Eternity thus has been characterized as simply a condition for time. Indulgent readers might follow the argument so far, but surely more must be said about eternal togetherness and its intrinsic characters to be convincing.

The Ontological Context of Mutual Relevance

The eternal togetherness of the temporal modes is the context in which they are relevant to one another so as mutually to constitute time's flow and each individually to be a temporal mode rather than sheer creativity, sheer fixedness, and sheer form. Thus eternal togetherness can be called a context of mutual relevance. Indeed, because the context is what allows for the possibility, occurrence, and actuality of temporal things, it can be called an *ontological* context for mutual relevance. This notion can be analyzed further by recurring to the metaphysical theory that allows temporal modes to be understood in terms of their essential and conditional features, thereby coming at the idea of eternal togetherness from a new angle, not from an analysis of the conditions of time alone.

The argument was made in Chapter 6 that each temporal mode, although connected to the others, is unique and stands in a relation of otherness to the others. This is possible because each temporal mode is a harmony of interconnecting conditional features and unique essential ones. The modes are related to each other by the conditional features. But with respect to the conditional features, their essential features are mutually external.

As harmonies, the modes each require both its conditional and essential features. In fact, the essential features are determinate because of their harmonization with the conditional ones, and vice versa. The essential objective everlastingness of the past requires both its future-derived structure and its present-derived actuality to have something objectively everlasting. The essential creative changingness of the present requires the potentials from the past to have something to change and the possibilities from the future to have something to which to change them. The essential normative formality of the future requires actual potentials from the past to give determinate shape to possibility and the dynamic creativity of the present to make those constantly and everflowingly relevant. The temporal modes would not be temporal at all without the harmonies of their essential and conditional features.

This means, however, that there must be some kind of togetherness more basic than temporal conditioning that allows the modes as whole harmonies to be together. For, unless the harmonies including the diverse essential features were together, the modes themselves could not be together sufficiently to condition one another. The context in which the modes can condition one another, and thus be what they are, mutually related temporal modes of past, present, and future, is a context that includes the essential features as well as the conditional ones, the ontological context of mutual relevance; and it is eternal, not temporal.[1]

This "proof" of an ontological context of mutual relevance is not innocent, because it constitutes a crucial step in the "proof" of divine creation and the characterization of God as eternal in Part Three. It will be argued there that the only thing that could constitute an ontological context of mutual relevance is an eternal divine creative act and that the eternal dynamism of time's flow constitutes what we should mean by the life of God. Because so much hangs on this argument, it is well to take another look at it.

The background premise of the argument is that one accept the metaphysical hypothesis that determinate things are to be understood as harmonies of essential and conditional features. If one does not buy into that hypothesis, or something very like it, then the argument for the ontological context of mutual relevance does not hold. It will be recalled that three general dialectical arguments support the hypothesis. If one denies essential features, then one cannot account for the integrity of things over against one another, and they must be allowed to have mere relational reality; and ultimately there is only one relation, a relation without distinct terms, a Bradleyan absolute. If one denies conditional features one is left with an atomism according to which things can be related only by having relations forced from without, and the "forcing from without" is itself a relation that refers back to prior grounds ad infinitum. If one denies that the conditional and essential features are directly harmonized and says instead that they are related by some higher term, then the relation between the features and higher term wants an account, again ad infinitum. Once one accepts the metaphysical hypothesis, the argument for the ontological context of mutual relevance follows schematically.

Let A and B be determinate harmonies. A's features include essential ones, eas, and conditional ones derived from B, cbs. A might also contain conditional features from C, D, and so on. Similarly, B contains essential features, ebs, and conditional features from A (and perhaps elsewhere), cas. Now A and B are *conditionally together* by virtue of their conditional features: A contains cbs and B contains cas. But the conditional features do not exist in the larger harmonies by themselves. The cbs in A would not be determinate without being harmonized with the eas; similarly the cas in B need to be harmonized with the ebs. Therefore, for the conditional togetherness of the cas and cbs to be possible, there must be an ontological togetherness in which the essential features of each thing, the eas and ebs, are together so that A and B can be together. Because the essential features are what give A and B integrity over against one another, the ontological context cannot include the essential features of A among the conditions of B or vice versa. Therefore, the ontological context of mutual relevance must make A and B mutually relevant without reducing their togetherness to some higher thing. Rather, their togetherness constitutes a new harmony.

In the case of time, we have seen how the temporal modes both are conditioned by one another and have essential features over against each other. Time's flow is the result of their ontological togetherness. The togetherness, however, is not temporal but eternal. Eternity is the ontological context for the mutual relevance of the temporal modes such that time flows.

To show that an ontological context of mutual relevance is required for the temporal modes to be together and thus be themselves as temporal is not to show what that context is. The nature of the ontological context is the topic of the next part. The remainder of the discussion here shall flesh out what the eternal context does for temporality.

Time in Things, Things in Eternity

The modes of time are not things in themselves but harmonies characteristic of the enduring world of things. This is not an innocent position because many of the thinkers of modernity have construed time (and space) as a gigantic container for temporal things. Newton believed that, for instance, as did Einstein over against Whitehead, who believed that temporality and spatiality are "immanent" within things, as he said. The position here agrees generally with Whitehead.

Suppose for a moment that time is a thing itself, a large container. What would it mean for a temporal thing to be "within" time? It would have to have dates that are earlier and later than other dates; if the thing endures through time, the dates internal to itself would be related as earlier and later. If the thing acquires these temporal properties from its location in the containing time, what could it be in itself without the temporal properties? Are its parts not temporally related? Must it not be the case that the thing intrinsically and necessarily must already be temporal for it to be able to be "in time"? A similar argument holds for space. How could a thing be said to be "in" space if it were not already spatial to begin with? To be "in space" or "in time" is already to be dimensional and extensive in those ways. Thus space and time are what result from the spatial and temporal togetherness of spatial and temporal things. "Where" and "when" there are no spatial and temporal things, there is no space and time. This result accords with the suppositions of contemporary physics according to which both space and time are functions of the propagation of light and other moving elements.

If time is a function of temporal things with futures, presents, and pasts, then time needs to be defined by the dates of temporal things. The duration and temporal context of a given temporally extended thing can be marked off by dates. Dates are interdefined by some measure or metric. But there is no one natural metric for dating things. If the metric for dates is taken from past time, as it is in science, they mark unit structures such as revolutions of the earth or the period of decay of atomic particles that can be matched to the structures of the enduring thing; such is chronological time. If the metric for dates is taken from present time, as it is in moral thinking, it marks off decision points. This discussion has frequently taken a present moment of creative actualization as the unit to be measured in a metric of time. A "proper date" will be defined in Chapter 11 on this metric as the moment of present becoming. If these metrics are combined, as they are in historical thinking, they mark off significant decision points of many things relative to one another—the chronology serving as a metric frame for relating different chains of decisions. If the metric is derived from future time, as it is in therapeutic thinking oriented to wholeness, it marks off ideal stages of development and change. Most of our thinking moves easily and without confusion among all these metrics, although often supposing chronological time as the coordinator of metrics because it alone is relatively uniform.

Understanding an enduring thing on an historical metric, each of its dates is susceptible to all three modes of time. The date of the proper location of an incident is future before that date is actualized, past after having been actualized, and present when occurring. After all of the thing's proper dates have been actualized, after it has ceased to be present or to have any more future, its identity then consists in all its dates in all three modes. That is, it clearly is all past. But part of the character of each of those past dates is to have been a present once, and a future for perhaps quite a while before that. That is an eternal identity, as was suggested in Chapter 4.

The enduring thing's eternal identity is to be temporal. This means that the thing's career was always changing, with a constant move of creative decisive actualization from one moment to the next, with a constantly shifting future from the standpoint of any date within the thing's existence, and with a constantly accreting actual past. The kinds of relations among the dates include all those possible among the modes. So, for instance, at one time, June 15, two dates, July 15 and August 15, are both future, one more distant from and dependent on the possible decisions in the other; at another time, July 15, one date is present and the other future, and June 15 is past; at another time, August 15, two are past and the other present; at another time, September 15, all are past. The full identity of the enduring thing that lasts at least from June 15 to September 15 eternally includes all these.

If the enduring thing is a person, its eternal identity consists in all the conditions we noted in the concluding section of Chapter 4 That is, every moment of the person's life save the last is one for which there is a future; the future of a child is ordinarily wide open, that of an adult thickly bound by obligations, that of an elderly person severely circumscribed by physical limitations. Because of this future character, every morally freighted decision has consequences affecting moral identity. Every moment of the person's life save the first also has a past, with some commitments stemming therefrom; the commitments from the past during childhood are minimal but they are denser for the person at a more responsible age. Every moment of the person's life has a proper location of presence, relating to past and future. To the extent the person's identity is self-determined, it is through the cumulative character of these present moments, and they vary at different stages in life regarding how much and what sorts of things are at stake in decisions. Without all these features, it is impossible for a person to be morally responsible for a past act, morally capable of undertaking an obligation, or morally culpable in the present for the future or past. Only because personal identity is eternal, like the identity of any enduring thing, can the most salient features of human nature be understood.

Human nature apart, it is now apparent in what sense time is in things, because temporality is a character of things rather than things being temporal because they are in time. It is also apparent in what sense things are in eternity, because their real identity includes the identity of all their proper dates as each is in all the modes of time. The togetherness of the thing's proper dates is not only linear; in fact, it can be linear only with respect to one given date being specified as the orientation or present date. The togetherness of the same date, say July 15, 1992, as future, as present, and as past is not linear like the togetherness of June 15, July 15, and August 15, but eternal, containing within it the movement of the changing present.

Things in Time, Time in Eternity

The eternal togetherness of the modes of time in a thing's identity should not be confused with any temporal identity. Things come to an end and people die. The fact they eternally have a future for any of their dates does not at all entail that they have a future at some date after their death. To be sure, whether there is more life for persons on a different plane after life on earth is an empirical question, one most of us are not desirous of investigating prematurely. Many of the religions of India take reincarnation, life after life, to be a part of common sense. Some unusual memories certain people have might be evidence for multiple lives or for life on a different plane. Reincarnation has great power in explaining how people can be born with such different life chances in a universe that is supposed to be moral. Yet most of us who have been educated through modernity do not find the evidence for reincarnation convincing nor its assumption a good part of common sense; most of us also do not believe that the universe is intrinsically moral, although we might believe God is moral. Furthermore, from Socrates onward the European tradition has suspected that life is understood only insofar as one faces death; a finite end is somehow important for taking each moment of life with proper seriousness.

So it is commonly assumed that people's lives are bounded by birth and death. Part of their eternal identity is not to have any proper locations in the dates after their existential end. Not to acknowledge this is to believe in a doctrine of immortality that disguises the existential import of death; it will be argued in Part Four that immortality is a valid belief only as symbolic of eternal identity.

Similarly, because things eternally have all their dates past and also all their dates present does not mean that they exist before the proper date of their creation or birth. To believe they do is to have a false doctrine of predestination. Predestination is a valid belief only as a symbol for the relation of God to one's eternal identity.

Within time, things have only the dates of their proper locations, no dates before or after. To be "within time" is always to be relative to a present proper temporal location. Within a proper present, the future is still indeterminate in part, as marked by the chains of decision with which future possibilities are structured. Within that present, certain things are past and not others. Within that present as embodied in a particular becoming, many other things are happening contemporaneously as coordinated by a common past and common future. From the standpoint of any present time, only fully past things have a whole eternal identity. Fully future things have no identity as past or present, and contemporaries are cut by the same standpoint of the present. The relation between one's temporal identity within time, at a time, and one's eternal identity is one of the main themes of religion, to which the discussion shall return in the concluding part.

To be *merely* "within time" is not necessarily to be temporal. To be only within a present moment of becoming is to be at a now that, by itself, does not flow. The now only comes to be. Time's flow requires actualizing something that is thus transformed from future possibility to past actuality. Time's flow changes the structure of the future and the content of the past. Time does not flow at a time but through time, through dates that successively are future, present, and past. Time's flow requires the death of the now and the birth of new possibilities. Time does not flow within time but within eternity.

Therefore a proper philosophic acknowledgment and understanding of time's flow requires an acknowledgment and understanding of eternity. Eternity is not something static, as we have seen, like a Whiteheadian eternal object, but something inclusive of the changing dates of the present. Only in eternity is the dynamism of change significant.

Precisely because we experience the flow of time our experience is not wholly within time but at least partly within eternity. To be sure, mere experience of time's flow is not a full grasp of the eternal identity of everything or even of the things whose flow we note. But time's flow provides a glimpse of the eternal character of temporality.

Part Three

Divine Eternity

"Microwave Radiation Fluctuations, left over from the
Universe's Explosive Birth"   Neville 1993

Chapter Nine

ETERNITY AND GOD'S BEING

God as a Question

Eternity on the one hand makes one topic with time. On the other hand it is part of the question of God. In the Western theistic religions eternity has sometimes been identified with God. Or God is said to be the eternal one. Or eternity is to God as space-time is to finite creatures, the context and form of life. In the religions of Greece, India, and China, the gods may be immortal but they certainly are not eternal, nor do they have the position of ultimacy ascribed to divinity in the monotheistic religions. What is eternal and unconditioned in those religions, where such is identified, is itself the mother of time, change, endurance, and immortality.

The nature of God is the central question of theology in monotheistic religions. Whether there are interesting parallels in the religions that are not monotheistic, and how those parallels are to be assessed is the central question in comparative religions.[1] Those questions must be answered by detailed and painstaking examinations of the issues. No conception of God can be taken for granted today as the "traditional" one. Nor do any of the various a priori theories of religious parallels make much sense. It might be that there are several ultimates, such as God and creativity, and that religions differ by focusing on one or the other.[2] It might be that all religions are getting at the same thing with only historically divergent vocabularies.[3] It might be that religion is a strictly anthropological category referring to rites or social structures with no commitment about ultimate things at all.[4] It might be that there are simply differences between religions with no similarities. Each of these possibilities needs to be investigated case by case.[5]

The purpose of this chapter, however, is not to compare historical conceptions of divinity with parallels in other religions and relate them to eternity. Rather the purpose is to develop a conception of the substance of eternity, to ask what in fact can serve as the ontological context of mutual relevance for the modes of temporality. The symbols for this shall be taken in the first instance from the monotheistic West, particularly from Christianity. But the explication of the symbols is driven by the logic of the idea of eternity, not by historical associations, at least in the main. It then will be possible here and in subsequent studies to see how far the same logic finds expression in nontheistic symbols. Ninian Smart and Steven Konstantine (1991) have gone far to show that the divine has two families of expression: in one, associated with Western theism and some Hindu theism, the divine is conceived to be something like an individual agent with a personal moral character; in the other, the divine (though that word is misplaced) is conceived to be like a principle, as in Mahayana Buddhism's Emptiness, the Tao, or Neo-Confucian Principle. The word *divine* is misplaced somewhat in describing the "principle" families of conceptions of the ultimate, because many of those religions have hosts of gods that are not ultimate for whom divinity language might be used. But because in the West at least the language of divinity as been appropriated to the ultimate, we shall continue to use it to describe both the personal agent and the principle families of conceptions of the ultimate. Theravada Buddhism, which denies any metaphysical ultimates, is a major religion that makes no use of the notion of the divine under any interpretation. With due deference to those traditions that employ "principle" conceptions of the ultimate and deny "personal agent" conceptions, we shall nevertheless call the ultimate *God* in this discussion. It will soon be obvious that the philosophical conception of God developed through the discussion of eternity transcends both the personal agent and the principle models, although it can be instantiated or specified in both of those conceptions.

False Images of Eternity

The inquiry into the nature of eternity must begin negatively, with a criticism of popular but false and misleading images of eternity. There are at least five: eternity as static form, as the *totum simul*, as total determinate fact, as normative goodness, and as the unmoved mover.

Eternity Not Form

As frequently recognized, eternity is often ascribed to form as such because form is not inherently temporal and does not change. Mathematical relations, for instance, are what they are whether or not any temporal things exhibit them. Universals are what characterized things in time but are not themselves temporal. Plato argued that forms are necessary to mark temporal changes and characters, but cannot do so if they themselves are temporal. Philosophers in the East as well as the West have defended various and conflicting theories about the reality of form. And, in a way, form can be called eternal in the bare sense of not being obviously temporal.

Yet form is clearly not eternal in the sense of eternity required to be a context for the togetherness of the temporal modes of past, present, and future. Eternity in the full sense must include within it the dynamic changing of the dates of the present, and this is precisely what pure form cannot represent. In fact, part of eternity is the constant shifting of the formal structure of the future as decisions are made in time's flow. Eternity in some sense must be the measure of form, not the other way around.

If the arguments made earlier about the character of the temporal modes are valid, then the attempt to characterize eternity as form arises from the privileging of the future. Form cannot be the ontological context for the essential elements of the past and future, that is, for objective and everlasting actuality or for dynamic actualization, nor can it be a proper context for the shifting forms of the future's own possibilities. Those elements are precisely what need to be related to form for real temporality to be possible.

Eternity Not Totum Simul

The image of eternity as *totum simul,* popularized by Augustine and carried down into the idealist tradition, is an extrapolation from the present. In Augustine's account (*Confessions,* Book 11, Chapters 26–31), mind measures time's flow by expectation of the future, attention to the present, and memory of the past—all of which are in the mind's present. Although our finite comprehension is partial in all three respects, the divine mind completely grasps all at once (*totum simul*) without loss or distortion. Because God creates time, according to Augustine, the divine mind is not literally within time nor limited to a finite present. Yet by knowing things that are in time, God encompasses all times into the *totum simul* present of expectation, attention, and memory in which divine eternity consists. The fundamental model of eternity here is presence to mind or consciousness. In the modern era, during which consciousness has seemed to be such an important Cartesian category, Augustine's fundamental model has seemed plausible even to those who would reject his Christian elaboration of the nature of God.

The difficulty with the *totum simul* image for eternity is that it cannot acknowledge the real passage of time in which things come to be, flourish, and die. The present of expectation-attention-and-memory is static. If the divine mind were to attend to what things change so that now one thing would be present to attention and then it would be past while another thing is present, there would not be one *totum simul.* Rather, there would be two mental states, neither of which is in the same present as the other except as remembered or anticipated. Augustine would not say that divine eternity is a temporal sequence of eternal presents of expectation, attention, and memory.

Charles Hartshorne (1948) and his followers, however, would say something like that. Hartshorne would claim that at any moment God does have a comprehensive vision of all that has gone before, all that can be anticipated within the limits of what is then determined, and all that has just happened. That divine vision itself adds a complexity to the cosmos, to which the rest of the world responds, so that in the next divine moment there is a new comprehensive vision of the new whole. In no sense, nevertheless, would Hartshorne say that God's vision is eternal. Within itself, each divine moment is an activity of integration, and the passage from one divine moment to the next is a plain temporal passage. So Hartshorne's view, whatever its strengths and limitations, is not a candidate for a *totum simul* theory of eternity.[6]

Harold Oliver (1981; 1984) follows Hartshorne to a great degree in the analysis of the present moment of experience, and he follows Augustine in the strict denial of reality to the past and future. From this he concludes to a kind of eternal immediacy to present experience that is concretely an absolute relation; the subject and objects of the experience are abstractions from or mere perspectives on the concrete relation. So, too, terms are merely aspects or perspectives on relations, which alone are really real. Because the apparent plurality of relations is in fact a relation of relations, there is in the end only one real relation with nothing external that could distinguish aspects or have perspectives on the ultimate relation. *Reality* is not temporal, for Oliver, because there is no past or future. But *experience* is temporal in the sense that we experience time as passing; we experience the past as remembered and the future as anticipated. Although it might seem that we go from one moment of experiencing the whole immediately to another such moment with a different content, in fact we only seem to remember that we do that in any one moment. Oliver thus asserts what only can be called a grand theory of eternity while saving the *appearances* of the passage of time from future to past. But the theory entails denying the reality of time while distinguishing the question of reality from the phenomenon of the appearances of temporal passage. To say that time really is the opposite of the way it appears is a high price to pay for this theory. Furthermore, the argument works only by sustaining a solipsism of the experiential whole relation. In ontology, Oliver finally claims that there is only one real relation, the most inclusive one or God. Divine solipsism is not as pricey a theory as personal solipsism in Western traditions that have legitimated panentheism. Nevertheless, as the highest or absolute relation God either experiences or causes a lie consisting in the internal illusory appearance of the passage of time. At any rate, *totum simul* is not a good image for eternity if it must be the context for real passage.

Eternity Not Total Fact

The representation of the eternal as the whole of determinate fact takes its root from past time. The image of all of time laid out before the divine mind has had great appeal, particularly in periods where physical determinism was an attractive supposition. The relation between God and the world in the deist theory can quite properly be called *eternalistic,* even though it was sometimes expressed as God creating a predetermined whole on the "first day" and letting things unroll from there. The eternity in this model is not so much a character of God, who has little character whatsoever, but of the world: the world eternally has the character of fully actualized fact even if its "actual existence" unrolls day by day. Part of what Kant meant by claiming that "existence" is not a predicate is that it makes no difference whatsoever to the character of things whether they are future, present, or past.

That precisely is its weakness as an image of eternity for the ontological context of the mutual relevance of the temporal modes. For the factuality denies the dynamism of the present and the shifting openness of future possibility. Eternity at the price of all temporal flow is a price that ought not be paid, because time does flow.

Eternity Not Pure Goodness

The images of eternity as pure normative goodness and as the unmoved mover have a classic place in Greek thought and its inheritance to the present day in the West. The two images are associated with Plato and Aristotle, respectively.

Plato identified the Form of the Good as eternal and gave different accounts of it at different points in his career, as noted earlier. In the Republic (Book VI, 509b) he described the Form of the Good as creator of the world and the condition for the possibility of relating knowable entities to knowing faculties as light relates visible objects to vision. The Form of the Good is not itself an object that can be known, but is known only in its expressions in structuring ways of harmonizing things to achieve value. Unlike Whitehead, Plato did not believe that there are eternal and everlasting finite forms of things, but that, any time certain things must be mixed together to achieve a certain value, dialectic could bring out the form that would harmonize them. The Form of the Good is what makes harmonious things harmonious. In the early dialogues Plato investigated the candidate components and patterns of integration for such values as courage, virtue, love, immortality, beauty, piety, and in the Republic, justice. In no case could there be a successful formula for the value-form, which there surely should be if forms are eternally determinate. But in each case the outcome of the dialectic was an understanding of just what things go into the mixture to be formed and just what kinds of patterns are appropriate and what kinds deleterious.

In this early (or middle) Platonic theory much is explained about why things happen in time the way they do — to gain or lose value of this or that sort. But the theory does not attempt to explain how the modes of time are different and together. The reference in the Republic to the creation of the world is not developed there and the world of time's flow is discussed at length only regarding two topics. In the allegory of the cave, that world of flux is identified as the true world for human life and the world of contemplatable truths is represented as a seductive escape. In the discussion of the ideal curriculum, the world of flux is identified as the true arena for learning what goodness really is, by the experiential acquisition of a sense of good timing through administration of the provincial governments. The eternity of the Form of the Good is exhibited in the context of time, but does not provide a context for time's modes itself.

Subsequent to the Republic Plato dealt in greater detail with the cosmological questions of time. Most commentators take seriously the "likely story" told in the Timaeas by the Eleatic character, Timaeas, for whom the cosmos consists of a set of static forms copied from a blueprint and a chaotic "sphere" of unformed matter. The lessons Plato wanted to draw from that dialogue all had to do with how the various versions of creation and formation of the world are organized around achieving value. But he adopted temporarily the assumption, rejected elsewhere, that the forms are to be thought of as a preexistent static realm. In the dialogue, it is clear that, on the one hand, temporal flow is being explained as created and, on the other hand, is presupposed as the context within which the demiurgos does its work. Like the Republic, the Timaeas says much about the relation of form to change in reference to goodness, but not much about the ontological status of time itself except in mythic terms.

In the Philebus, however, a dialogue roughly contemporary with the Timaeas and one of Plato's last, a clear distinction is made between form or limit and what makes something valuable, as noted previously. What had been united in the Republic's account of the Form of the Good—both value making and structural form—are separated in the Philebus. The four causes in the Philebus—Limit, the Unlimited, Mixture, and the Cause of Mixture—are probably Plato's answer to Aristotle's theory of four causes (Neville 1989, Chapters 5 and 6). They are the ultimate things to which appeal is made in understanding or explanation. The Cause of Mixture is the late version of the Form of the Good, that which gives measure and due proportion. But it is in a position of equality here with form (Limit), that diversity which is to be formed (the Unlimited), and the Mixture or actual changing world. Normative goodness in this late theory does not count as an image of eternity that provides the context for the temporal modes, although Plato's theory recognizes them.

Eternity Not an Unmoved Mover

Aristotle's theory of the unmoved mover whose self-sufficient fullness of being is the motive for all other motions is a more likely but still misleading candidate. The likeliness in the candidacy of the unmoved mover is in the very richness of reality in that conception of God. Being complete act, the unmoved mover contains absolutely everything; hence, if there is a reality to past or future as well as present time, the "act" in that reality must be present within the God that is thus the context. The misleading part comes from the very richness of the notion of being ascribed to the unmoved mover; namely, such complete actuality that no change is possible. In Aristotle's account, change takes place only when something actual lacks something else it might have. Because the unmoved mover lacks nothing, it cannot change. Nothing in the unmoved mover could then correspond to or recognize the diversity in the modes of time and the dynamics of time's flow. The unmoved mover must be oblivious to temporality, as to everything else that is only partially "in act." Therefore, although there may be some plausibility to the claim that motion is for the sake of imitating the self-sufficiency of the sort enjoyed by the wholly actual unmoved mover, there is none for the possible claim that the unmoved mover provides the context for time's flow. To the contrary, time's flow is the chief thing that the unmoved mover cannot explain, only the shape and motive for the flow. Like Plato, Aristotle is clear that the final causation exercised by the unmoved mover itself must be in a larger context along with form, matter (which provides the potentiality for change), and making (which provides the actuality).

The negative lessons gleaned from this brief critical review of images of eternity are these:

1. Eternity is not static.
2. Eternity is not to be modeled by vision, mind, or consciousness, as "presence."
3. Eternity is not to be modeled by determinate fact.
4. Eternity is not to be modeled by goodness or that which makes things good.
5. Eternity is not to be modeled by fullness of being.

These negative warnings about eternity derive from the strictures about temporality developed in earlier chapters. The opposite question must be asked now about eternity from the standpoint of God. If God is to be eternal and somehow provide the context for time's flow, what is it God cannot be?

God Not an Individual

To put the matter crudely, the one thing God cannot be, to provide an eternal context for the temporal modes, is an individual separate as eternal or cosmically everlasting from the world as temporal. Yet this is the most popular image of God in Western theism: God is an individual who is internally perfect, who creates the world, and who relates to individuals person to person. Construed in anything like a literal way, God cannot be an individual in this sense because God would have to be in a larger context that includes both the divine being and also all the beings in the world. If this context itself is temporal, then yet something else beyond God and the world is required to provide the eternal context of mutual relevance. If the context is eternal, then God cannot enter into personal relations with people, because personal relations are temporal involving give and take. If the context is eternal, the divine individual cannot be said to endure, for endurance means lasting through a stretch of time. If the context is eternal, then God cannot be said to be individuated as a singular being over against the world, determinate with respect to the world, while the world is changing; God as individual cannot be determinate with respect to the world without changing while the world itself changes. Process theologians have made excellent and telling criticisms against this view of divine individuality as eternal, perfect, and personal. Their own view is that God is temporal, individual, finite with respect to the world, and personal in a literal sense; this will be examined in Chapter 10.

After the process philosophers, Paul Tillich (1951) made an even more profound criticism of the idea of God as an individual. He argued that everything in the world is conditioned by standing in contrast with polar opposites; this is something like the position defended previously that each thing has essential features and also conditional features connecting and distinguishing it from other things. The conditions for things conditioning one another, however, include an unconditioned ground of the being of the conditioned things, an ontological context of mutual relevance. If the ground is itself conditioned, some deeper ground is needed to relate it to what it conditions and so forth. Recognizing the common assumptions about God as an individual, Tillich (1952) described his conception as the God beyond God, the unconditioned ground beyond any determinate God. He appealed to the mystics for the logic of his experiential path to God, and he employed the arguments about idolatry to show that any determinate God cannot be unconditioned enough to be the real God. Because time's modes are among the fundamental polarities, the unconditioned ground of being might very well be or provide the eternal context for their mutual self-definition.

If God is not to be conceived as an individual, a wide door for communication is immediately opened to all those nontheistic religions that treat eternity with categories other than a supreme individual, categories akin to principles. At the same time, however, it is important not to lose contact with the religious sensibilities of the theistic traditions that have been so attentive to history's actual movements and time's flow. Therefore it is important to call attention to some aspects of the development of the idea of God in theistic religions. The positive characterizations to come of divine eternity depend on maintaining crucial contact with theistic as well as nontheistic traditions.

Theistic Themes

In recent years it has become customary to set Jerusalem and Athens at odds with one another, to say that the Hebrews understood God properly to be an individual and that the early theologians made a deep mistake by employing Greek philosophic categories to explain this. Few misreadings could be more serious than this.

The ancient semitic idea of Yahweh began as part of a polytheistic pantheon. Yahweh was the God who, out of many other gods associated with cities, adopted and was adopted by the wandering tribe of Hebrews. Yahweh's distinctive feature at first was his willingness to move with his nomadic people. The character of their relationship was not that of Yahweh defending a home, as the Mesopotamian and Egyptians gods did for their urban clientele, but was that of protecting them during their travels.

The experience of drought and famine made it clear that the nomadic life could not be adequately protected, resulting as it did in the Egyptian captivity; so Yahweh was the God who extricated the Hebrews from minority status in Egypt and led them to what was to be a home of their own. As a traveling protector, Yahweh was depicted as a warrior; as a lord of the homeland, he was depicted as a king.

These and most of the other images are all of Yahweh as an individual, frequently as an individual god among others or as an individual God heading a heavenly court of lesser deities or angels. The problems of religious leadership in ancient Israel, up through the time of the early kings, for example, through the ninth century B.C.E., was to keep the people at the worship of Yahweh alone rather than allowing them to include the worship of the other gods, mainly fertility goddesses and their consorts, along with Yahweh. By the time of the early prophets, however, the idea grew that there is only one God, and that the others are not gods at all but empty objects of idol worship. After having had a minor empire of its own, Israel began to suffer reverses at the hands of other nations. The prophets noted that Yahweh was the God of all those other nations as well, guiding their destiny as Israel had always hoped for itself.

By the time of the Babylonian Exile, and perhaps because of contact with the cosmological speculations of other nations in the ancient Near East, the prophets concluded that Yahweh was not only super-king over all the nations but also the creator of all nature. The Psalms contain many early references to God's creating the world, and it became clear that the conception of God as creator was in part defined by its relations to conceptions of the world. Whatever the world is, God is the creator of it. As the prophets and other writers such as the author of Job became more sophisticated in their conception of the cosmos, their idea of God became larger and larger, far less a literal person and more one about whom the question of human personal analogies had to be raised issue for issue. In the book of Job, for instance, the depictions of God holding heavenly court and wagering with Satan (Job 1–2) are clearly postmythopoeic uses of images as metaphors. The author was being literary, explicitly not literal. In the same book, the main topic is whether the moral categories for administering fortune as a reward for good or evil can be applied to God, and the straight answer is that they cannot. Those who apply such analogies have no standing with God who creates the pillars of the earth and flies on the wings of the morning (Job 38).

The strategy of the author of Job was to use images and metaphors as ways of relating human questions to a context to which the human scale of cultural measure was known not to apply. For religious purposes, it is satisfactory to think of God wagering with Satan. But when those religious purposes blend over into questions of morals and theodicy, the images and metaphors are stretched beyond their appropriate limit.

The driving dialectic behind this development was always to seek out the most ultimate category for understanding God that preserves divine lordship. That is, whatever the people of Israel are, God is their lord; whatever the world's nations are, God is their judge and destiny; whatever the world is, God is its creator. Given the evolution of the idea of God in Israel, the earlier stages were not dropped to leave but the latest priestly and rabbinic sophistication. Rather, all the layers of development were kept and employed for religious purposes, with questions of literalness arising only when the context made a symbol seem inappropriate. No one was confused by the claim that God is a rock (of salvation). Perhaps some were confused by Jesus' claim that the kingdom of heaven is ruled by someone more like a loving parent than like a warrior, especially when Jesus went on to deny human personal characteristics such as sexual identity to life in heaven. When the early Christians claimed that Jesus was right about the Hebrew God as creator and that Jesus was also divine in some sense and so was the Holy Spirit, theology was born as the discipline for understanding the contexts in which symbols do and do not apply.

Though of Jewish origins, Christianity arose in the Hellenistic world. Indeed, Judaism had been in that world for over three centuries by the time of the first generation of Christian disciples. The idea of sophia, translated easily by Christians into the logos cited by John, made sense in the Hellenistic context in which the highest divinity needs mediation to the rough stuff of the world. The earliest Christian theologians such as Justin Martyr employed Hellenistic categories as much Jewish in their origin as classical Greek.

The Greeks of the time were polytheists like the Hebrews of a millenium earlier. Their dialectic, logic, and secular irony were far advanced of the Hebrews. But they did not entertain, except perhaps in Plato and his school, the dialectical drive to formulate an ultimate principle under which the entire cosmos could be represented as created and over which the principle was lord. Plato's naive claim that the Form of the Good is creator of all had not been developed with a religious passion. Aristotle's theology was similarly disconnected from religious passion. The Greek religious passions were devoted to the mystery cults that were relatively primitive in their polytheism, though perhaps entranced by astronomy.

The patristic Christian theologians, and after them the early
Muslim theologians, used middle Platonic, neo-Platonic, Stoic,
Epicurean, Cynical, and Aristotelian concepts to interpret their
conceptions of God and to structure their attempts to show how
God is related salvifically to history in Jesus, the Spirit, and in the
influences of prophecy. Although derivative from the classical
speculations of Plato, Aristotle, and the other founders of those
schools, the uses to which the "philosophical" categories were put
were controlled by the semitic drive toward articulating ultimacy.
Athens served Jerusalem from the first century on.

The contribution of the Greek concepts was not insignificant,
however, but it was to show that categories other than personal
ones allowed of greater ultimacy. Thinkers from Origin to Augustine to Aquinas were careful to be able to say that God *in some sense*
is personal and is correctly addressed in the forms of the Psalms,
the prophecies, and the Gospels; but none of those people conceived God as a personal individual in any sense literally like a
warrior or king. Each of them, and surely all their contemporaries,
was concerned to sustain contact with the biblical language and
traditional formulations for the sake of the imagination-shaping
guidance of piety. But equally each was concerned to avoid the
idolatry of making God so small as to be part of the world. Each
knew that once God was conceived to be a being *with* the world, a
larger conception of something *beyond* God and the world is
operative.

Therefore it is quite in line with the Western theistic tradition
to undertake a reformulation of the eternal that at once relates to
what is necessary to ground the diversity among the modes of
temporality and also expresses from appropriate metaphoric perspectives the rich achievements of cultivated piety. If these concepts also translate into symbols that express the rich achievements
of the cultivated piety of traditions that do not conceive of an
individual God who is perfect and personal at a nearly literal level,
so much the better.

One more negative point needs to be registered. Much of
Western piety has gone beyond the spiritually real metaphors of
personal address to and from God to a kind of cheap fellowship.
Understood in a metaphoric sense, one can indeed encounter God

in the morning in the garden with the dew fresh on the roses. Taken in a chummy sense, however, that piety involves a commitment to a temporal companion-God who could never be eternal and who is just as much at a loss about the passage of time as ourselves. That kind of piety undermines true religion and must be resisted. The God in the back garden is also the rock of salvation to which geology is irrelevant and the principle of harmony to which the attribution of jealousy and pique is abhorrent. The prophets were right to see that the crucial controls over the conception of God, mediating and judging all pious expressious, are the way in which God is conceived as creator of the world and the way the world created is conceived. Creation of the world is the place to look in finding a positive conception of eternity as the ontological context of mutual relevance.

Chapter Ten

ETERNAL CREATION

Theological Ideas of God

For the reasons expressed in the preceding chapter, the hypothesis concerning creation *ex nihilo* to be presented here has not only the independent merit of its philosophic case but also considerable weight of tradition. The theory of creation *ex nihilo* here is not the same as that of any earlier thinker down to exact details, admittedly. It does, however, express the general point made by thinkers such as Augustine and, before him, Origen, that everything you can think of is created, even time itself. The question of what God is apart from creation is extremely complicated in the history of theology. But in the instance of every theory, the interesting characteristics of God are those that are functions of God's relation to the world, as creator, judge, redeemer. Even mystics who long for the aseity of divine transcendence do so precisely because it is a human fulfillment and thus related to the world at least so far. For Christians the important characteristics are often those God has by virtue of divine incarnate presence within the world, as Christ and Spirit.

Many of the early Christian theologians down through the European medieval period accepted the Aristotelian account of perfection mentioned in the previous chapter; namely, that it consists in being wholly actual. Wholly actual, God has no potency to change and therefore must be immutable. If God is creator, judge, redeemer, and so forth relative to the world, and God cannot change, then God must be those things apart from the world, the argument goes. For an unchangeable God could not become redemptive in response to a world in which people freely sin. This position was pushed to its logical extreme by the Calvinist supra-lapsarians who said that people were created determined to sin and that God was determined to be the redeemer even before any fall (supralapse) that would make redemption relevant.

More to the point of the early Christian theological controversies about the Trinity, if Jesus in the world is the divine Christ or logos and the Holy Spirit is the active character of that logos, then God apart from the world must include not only creator-father but also logos-Son and Holy Spirit. This led most of the early theologians at least to adopt the symbols if not the nearly literal intent of saying that God is an individual comprising three persons, all without regard for the world as such, a position described as *immanent Trinitarianism*. (The view that God has multiple identities, say three persons, only in relation to the created world is called *economic Trinitarianism*.)

Recently Ninian Smart and Steven Konstantine (1991, Chapter 6) have explicitly defended an immanent Trinitarianism of the following sort. Beginning with the worship of the Christian community, reinforced by many close parallels and interesting assessible divergences in other traditions, they argue that the persons of the Trinity are three different centers of consciousness making up one divine life. The unity consists not in an underlying substance (*homoousia*) but in a common divine life. Each of the persons can legitimately be the subject of devotion and an orientation point for spiritual growth, with the understanding, implicit at least, that the three are all part of one divine life. Among the best features of Smart and Konstantine's discussion of the Trinity is its careful situating of their position relative to both ancient and contemporary alternatives and their treatment of how the Christian symbols for the Trinity relate or fail to relate to important symbols in other religions.

Their argument is surely correct to situate itself in the worship, liturgical, and spiritual practices of religions, Christian and otherwise. Theological conceptions that do not find reinforcement as formulations of deeply corrected habits of the heart are not likely to have any referential base in which they might be true. But this point, that God's diverse manifestations are addressed diversely in religious life, is compatible with economic Trinitarianism and its parallels in other religions (such as Brahman as *sat, cit,* and *ananda* or as Shiva, Vishnu, and Brahma; or the Mahayana doctrine of the Three Bodies of the Buddha; see Smart and Konstantine, pp. 170, 174–178). The difficulty with the Smart and Konstantine position as an immanent Trinitarianism is that it introduces very determinant differences between the centers of consciousness that are the divine persons, and this requires a further ontological ground for the three to be related enough to have a common divine life. This critical dialectic shall be traced in the remainder of this chapter.

The logic of the traditional immanent Trinitarian argument holds only if one adheres to the Aristotelian conception of perfection as requiring no change and insists that the conception applies to God irrespective of creation. (Smart and Konstantine, not traditional in this regard, hold that, though immanently and apart from the world God is a social Trinity, God still changes in response to the world.) If one has a different metaphysical conception or affirms that God creates the metaphysical conditions and is not conformed to them, then the argument for an independent triune (or otherwise personal) God apart from the world fails its logic. For instance, if God creates the principles for sameness and diversity, such as essential and conditional features, then God cannot be three in one apart from that creation.

The conception to be presented here of God as creator *ex nihilo* provides a different metaphysical conception of God and does affirm that God creates the metaphysical conditions. Therefore the present hypothesis does not speak about God as an individual apart from creation. Nevertheless, it will be incumbent on our argument to maintain contact with the motives of the classical theological conceptions in both theistic religions and non-theistic ones, especially as regards the theological assumptions of religious life.

The central divine reality, according to the theory to be presented here, is the creative act of which the world is the immediate terminus and that itself constitutes God as having the characteristics of being creator. These characteristics turn out to express, in very general form, a kind of economic Trinitarianism. The plot of the argument thus needs to swing between a consideration of the world and a consideration of its creation or a consideration of God as creator and a consideration of the world as God's eternal deed. The previous chapter and the first section here have concentrated on ideas, good and bad, of God. The next section turns to the definition of the limits of the world. The section after that considers process theology's attempt to relate God and world. And the concluding section makes the argument for creation *ex nihilo*, the conception of eternity to be defended here. Then Chapter 11 will examine how creation is expressed in the world, especially as regards the creation of time; and Chapter 12 will swing round to discuss God, whose internal dynamic life is constituted by time's flow.

Conceptions of the World: Closure

The dialectic driving the historical development of the conception of God as creator is not the metaphysics of divinity but the advancing conceptions of the world that God is supposed to create. In the Western traditions these have included roughly the world of tribal success, of national prominence, of international justice, and of nature itself. This dialectic must now be thematized and brought up to date with regard to contemporary physics's conception of nature.

People's conceptions of the sum total or boundaries of the world can be expressed by the mathematical notion of "closure." Closure is the characteristic of a set of things defined by a particular operation or trait; it might be internally infinite but is definite with respect to what falls outside it as not sharing the trait. For instance, the set of even numbers has closure, infinite though it is and distinct from the odd numbers.

What God is understood to create has a kind of closure that identifies it as created. In Genesis 1, Yahweh creates the order of the world but not the chaos ordered. In Hellenistic speculation God creates the plain of Earth, but what about the vaults of heaven? The Gnostics answered that the Earth and lower spheres were created by a God of limited virtue whereas the higher heavens are immaterial and perhaps not even created at all; the Christians argued to the contrary that all the heavens are created, material or immaterial.

The conception of the world's closure significant for theology in the modern world was stated by the physicists of the European renaissance who said that whatever is in the world can be measured, in principle, and the measure expressed in mathematical terms. The identification of what there is to measure has developed in fantastic ways since the renaissance focus on stars and vortices. The elaboration of more complex kinds of mathematics has aided this expansion of our understanding of the vast variety of things. Galileo, however, could take a quick Ph.D. in physics at a contemporary university and see that his original notion of what "understanding the world" means has only been augmented, not fundamentally changed. For contemporary astrophysics, closure is defined by the terms employed in mathematical models of the Big Bang and its alternatives.

Early in modern European history thinkers such as Descartes recognized that mental phenomena are not easily brought under the aegis of the mathematically measurable. Psychology had developed as an ape of physics to such a degree by the end of the eighteenth century that Kant could entertain the hope of mathematizing mind, a hope sustained down to this day. But Descartes's strategy was to call attention to the determinate phenomenological characteristics of mind's operations and content, so that subsequent thinkers could develop sciences of consciousness, language, and signs. In all these, what is studied are determinate differences and similarities.

What unites the cognitive ideals of mathematizing physical science and the human sciences (or the human arts of understanding, enjoying, and making) is the conception of determinateness. To be in the world is to have a determinate (or at least partially determinate) identity, to be determinate in these respects but not those, to be determinate with respect to these things but not those. Although there may be no "standard" mathematizable measure for all aspects of the human condition, at least there is the measure of determinateness, and the determinate characters of things can be the objects of inquiry. Precisely for this reason the metaphysics introduced in Chapter 5 and developed since for the understanding of time and eternity has focused on characterizing identity as determinate through its essential and conditional features.

Suddenly in the early modern period the closure of the world was seen to be much vaster than hitherto imagined. The world consists of all things that are determinate. All of these things, in principle, are subject to investigation, perhaps even scientific understanding. The result of this realization in the early centuries of the modern period was that theological explanations were pushed back in favor of scientific ones. In principle, science ought to be able to explain why things have the determinations they do and why they occur in their locations rather than somewhere else or not at all. If the world has the closure of all determinateness, then any question "What?" ought to be subject to human scientific or humanistic inquiry, not theology.

That there exists a world at all with closure remained a theological question, but one without much scientific interest; recall the passage from Hawking quoted in Chapter 1. Where is God the creator relative to the system of determinations: outside, inside, or nowhere? The deists quickly answered that God is outside the system of closure; God creates the system and then has nothing else to do with it, because science provides internal explanations of everything else. The deists respected the "that" question for the world in addition to the scientific "what" question. But once answered—God made it—all the remaining questions had to do with what God made; there was nothing interesting to ask about God because all interesting questions were about determinate issues. The early deists supposed a fairly traditional conception of God as an individual, perhaps even a triune individual; but the supposition was pointless and had no real content. After some generations of recognition that the deist theology was religiously irrelevant—religions want very determinate things such as salvation or sanctification—God dropped out of the popular Enlightenment world-view. If God makes no difference to the "what" of the world and only "what" questions are interesting, God is an hypothesis Laplace and other scientists could do without.

The next step was to say that the question of God as creator, the "that" question, is "meaningless." The arguments to show that the "that" question is meaningless all presuppose that only determinate issues, the explanations of things by determinate principles, are meaningful. Meaning itself is assumed to be limited to what lies within the closure limits of the determinate world. The logical positivists of the twentieth century brought this logic to its conclusion. Yet, as the deists saw, that "that" question is of a different order from the "what" questions.

If God is not outside the world, whose closure is determinateness, then perhaps God is the totality of the world itself. Pantheism, the name of this position, has an ancient lineage going back to nature mysticisms East and West. In the tradition of modern European philosophy or theology there have been two major representatives of pantheism, Spinoza and Hegel. Although no simple summary can do justice to either thinker's theory, they can be sketched with regard to their answers to the question of "where" God is relative to the closure of the world.

Spinoza argued that only one substance, God, exists. As a whole, of course, it is not determinate with respect to anything else, and so is infinite or not determinate. But internally God can be regarded in two ways, as the determinate world (deterministically related part to part) or as the creating or manifesting of the determinate world. The first he called *natura naturata,* "nature natured," and the second *natura naturans,* "nature naturing." Conceived as one substance, God is nature naturing; but looking at the world, the determinate totality of the world, nature natured is all there is. For Spinoza, science handles nature natured and ethics (or theology or philosophy) nature naturing. God is no individual outside the realm of nature natured, no additional determination, nor is God within nature in a determinate way.

Hegel largely approved Spinoza's scheme but added subjectivity and developmental or dialectical unfolding to it. For Hegel God is Spirit dynamically seeking determinateness. The beginning of the dialectic consists of four figures: being, nothing, becoming, and determinate being. Being is positive reality but has no features that distinguish it from nothing. Therefore Spirit is becoming, which is the bringing of determinate being out of nothing so that there is something. "Something," however, is the most abstract idea of determinateness possible, so Spirit must go on to produce sameness, difference, something else, and so forth. The dialectic produces real nature as analyzable by science and also the course of history. Spirit is always the whole in process, each most inclusive positive "stage" seeking its other and then requiring their integration, which in turn is determinate and needs its determinate "other" and so on.

The difficulty with even these sophisticated forms of pantheism has to do with whether the wholeness that totalizes the world is a determination over and above the world, or whether it is just the fit of the world together. If it is an extra determination, then in fact God stands outside the world, and all the arguments against the deist position apply. An infinite regress of relations is required to connect the unifying determination with the plurality of determinate things it is supposed to unify. If it is not an extra determination, then the wholeness of the world is trivial; there is no meaningful totality to the world, just the bunch of things, finite or infinite in number, that fit or do not fit as they do. In this alternative, pantheism is no theism at all. Spinoza's fate was to have fallen to the latter criticism and to be judged an atheist. Nature naturing adds nothing to nature natured, and nature natured is just the secular world. Hegel's fate was the opposite. Because God as the dialectic of Spirit is always required to move on beyond any determinate state, Hegel was viewed as never being able to account for a sufficiently determinate world to satisfy science. Even Hegel's account of history could not acknowledge the simple determinateness of people and events who are not caught up in the great historical dialectical schemes — people have true reality for Hegel only insofar as they play roles in the larger dialectic. So Hegel's pantheism fails by virtue of not attaining to a world for God to be "all of." Spinoza's position is metaphysically the more interesting because, if the account of nature naturing can be strengthened into a theory of creation *ex nihilo,* his position is not a pantheism at all but one rather like that defended in this book to account for eternity and time's flow. Spinoza, however, was not friendly to the radical contingency implied in creation *ex nihilo.*

A further alternative answer to the question of where God is relative to the closure of determinateness is to say that God is on the inside. God cannot be conceived as the creator of all determinate

things because divinity itself is among those things, interacting in
various ways, including those ways having to do with religion and
perhaps morality. God among the determinations might be infinite
in ways appropriate to divine closure, but still can be conceived to
be within the larger world of determinations set over against and
determinate with respect to other kinds of things such as physical
realities and finite spirits.

Early in the modern period, those who thought God to be
determinate and within the realm of determinations were the
advocates of miracles. They believed that the world was set up to
behave a certain way naturally, and that God sometimes intervenes
to make things happen differently. This of course was objectiona-
ble to the truly modern scientific thinkers who attempted to explain
away the traditional miracles as either false reports or as having
some underlying natural explanation. David Hume (1779) argued
that nothing could ever be shown to be a miracle rather than just an
as-yet-unexplained happening. Believers in God as the being with
the world who interferes to exercise gracious providence often had
deist conceptions of the creation and differed from the deists in
believing that God stays around to interact with the determinate
world created. Strict deists would rightly object to this, however,
because if God makes specific empirical differences within the
world then God as cause is among the determinate things within
the world and needs to be understood scientifically, as one of the
"whats," not as creator of the "that."

In the twentieth century various schools have defended a view
of God whose being is finitely within the closure of determinate
things albeit perhaps infinite in other ways. William James argued
this position. But the most important and fully developed school is
process theology, which needs now to be examined on its own
account. Process theology would accept the general characterization given here of the world's closure as consisting in determinateness. For the actual world in contrast to God, process thinkers
believe that determinateness consists in positions in an extensive
continuum. But not only this. Determinateness both for finite
actual things and for God too consists in having definite acts of
existence that have singular position and relation to other definite

acts of existence; determinateness consists in making a different place and nature for oneself relative to the rest of the world.

Process Theology

Responding to the additional motive of wanting to ascribe pure moral goodness to God as a determinate agent, process theologians from Alfred North Whitehead (1926; 1929) and Charles Hartshorne (1948; 1962; 1970) to John B. Cobb, Jr. (1965; 1967), Schubert Ogden (1966; 1986), David Griffin (1973; 1976), Lewis Ford (1978), Marjorie Suchocki (1986; 1988), and others have been quite clear to reject conceptions of divine creation of the entire world, especially of time. Their extremely subtle theories account for divine causation and interaction with the world, but not for God's being the creator of the determinate realm as such.

Any happening, in the process theological account, is a vector of the interactions of divine projections of worthy possibilities and the creative responses of the things in the finite world. Some authors have pointed out that this gives theology no empirical content; God can never be cited as the reason why things turn out this way rather than another because God only suggests the best possibilities, and what happens is always instead the result of finite things responding in their present moments of creativity to that divine lure among many other influences. In a larger sense, however, the process hypothesis is empirical in that it does provide categories for interpreting a rich history of religious experience. It also treats metaphysics as a kind of high-level science that articulates very general interactions among determinate things. God and the physical world are both represented and explained by the process system as functioning within the principles of determinateness.

There are five general difficulties with process theology, specific objections to its systematic categories aside.[1] First, it fails to recognize, resonate with, and advance the dialectic of God as creator and sole lord of the world, thus abandoning a great tradition of experience and reflection. The reasons process theology gives for abandoning that tradition are mainly two. The tradition of God as creator has been associated with the view that

God is a coercive cause of the world, metaphysically denying freedom and encouraging the political model of despotism. True, in some kinds of Calvinism and perhaps in other traditions within Christianity and other religions, freedom has sometimes been denied; nevertheless, far and away the main groups of theologians and religious traditions affirming divine creation have also affirmed human freedom and responsibility. Only if God is conceived as "another individual" over against us could God's action seem to limit us like a despot's would; if God rather is felt as "closer to us than we are to ourselves," in Augustine's phrase, then divine influence is not externally coercive and is compatible with freedom. This is not to minimize the problems of accounting for human freedom within a created world (see Neville 1974 and 1978).

The other reason for abandoning a strong creation doctrine is to exempt God from blame for evil. Process theology believes that God's best intentions are limited by always having to work with a world of antecedent conditions, making the best of what is perhaps not so good, and by having to respect human freedom to do the worse in the face of the better. But this argument depicts God as moral in exactly the same sense that a truly goodwilled person is moral, except that God is supposed by process theology to be unable not to take everything into account and required to present wise lures to the world based on this superior knowledge. To cut theology off from the great tradition of divine creation in order to conceive divinity as of limited ability to interfere, like a human, and morally well-intentioned, like a good person, is questionable. It is a special twist on the movement within European theology since Calvin to shift theology to anthropology.

Second, by making God a moral agent within the world, one interacting among other determinate things, process theology gives a rather literal reading of the metaphors of morality in religion, subordinating the religious feelings of awe and terror to those of righteousness and supplication defined in fairly narrow selfish senses. This point is continuous with the preceding one, but points to problems with the worshipfulness of God. However much God is conceived to be moral, or moral-plus, God is also in nearly every religious tradition conceived to be aweful and terrifying, the *mysterium tremendum,* as Otto showed (1917). In some sense, if God is Lord then God is responsible for the earthquakes and Satan. Therefore process theology commits itself to too domestic a God. Yet this liability and that in the first point are prices that process theology and its neighbors are generally willing to pay to fit God into the world defined by determinateness.

Third, process theology is liable to refutation by any alternative metaphysics of determinateness that does not need the hypothesis of God to explain things in the world. One of the things the God of process theology is supposed to do, for instance, is to provide subjective aim to the exercise of creativity in finite things; perhaps other sources of that subjective aim can be hypothesized of a wholly secular nature. Donald Sherburne, a distinguished process philosopher, has made important contributions to aesthetics and ethics but has carefully excised the idea of God from his philosophy (1961). Thinkers such as Justus Buchler (1966) and David Weissman (1989) are close to process philosophy in many ways but do not accept any theological notions into their systems. None of this is to say a priori that a metaphysics is better without God than with God if one can get away with it; to be sure, the metaphysics defended in this book adopts much of the process theory of nature and completely rejects its theology in favor of a different idea of God.[2] But in making God a part of nature, or a being right alongside nature and subject to the same metaphysical and moral norms, process theology readies itself for dismissal by other naturalisms. Process theology is not persuasive to secular people who are willing to accept reductionist accounts of religious experience and have alternative approaches to subjectivity.

Fourth, process theologies deny intelligibility to the idea of creation *ex nihilo*, yet that idea is presupposed, albeit hidden, in the process conception of creativity. The denial, of course, comes from the old proverb, *ex nihilo nihil fit*, out of nothing nothing is made. But the validity of that proverb is the very point at issue in intelligibility. Do we understand ultimately by seeing how things fall under higher principles and categories? Or do we understand by locating the points where they are composed in all their parts? If principles and categories themselves need to be understood in their existence and normative status, then the latter, the locating of points of creation, must be possible in at least some cases. The sequel shall defend the idea of creation. The process case is in self-referential difficulty, however, because even the process idea of creativity, a temporal principle, exhibits and depends on creation *ex nihilo.* The Category of the Ultimate, as Whitehead called it (1929, Part I, Chapter 2), is affirmed by all process theologians and has three components: many, one, and creativity. The Category of the Ultimate is that wherever there is a many, a new one is created out of that many, thereby increasing the many by one. What distinguishes the new one from the old many? Its components, at least in their origins, come from the old many. But anything that makes the new one new and constitutes an addition to the old many can not have been in the old many and therefore must have come *ex nihilo.* Any new immediacy, any novelty of pattern and objective addition to the old, any new and distinct space-time position — all these are not in previous actuality but are created in the moment of the new one *ex nihilo.* The creativity in the process Category of the Ultimate is of course not the same as the ontological creation of the entire world *ex nihilo* because the past many provides raw material for creativity to work up into the new one. But the difference between the Category of the Ultimate and divine creation *ex nihilo* has nothing to do with the *ex nihilo:* in both cases everything that is novel arises from nothing and not from antecedents. The difference consists only in the point of whether what is new works on antecedent materials or produces a product that is novel in its entirety. For process theology, each actual occasion is a combination of the old many plus the spontaneity of creativity, which is *ex nihilo.* If creation *ex nihilo* is unintelligible in the case of ontological divine creation, it is also unintelligible in ordinary temporal creativity in the Category of the Ultimate. And if it is intelligible in creativity, it is intelligible in the case of divinity.

In fact, the process scheme can easily be adapted to a larger theory of divine creation *ex nihilo.* Whereas the divine creation theory says that the whole of time's flow is created eternally, where that creation shows up within time is in the spontaneous creativity of emergence or becoming or actualization of the present moment. The fact that the present requires actualized facts from the past as potentials and forms from the future as possibilities illustrates only the fact that eternal creation *ex nihilo* cannot be limited to the present moment but involves the creating of temporal things in all their modes. This is to jump ahead of the argument, however.

Fifth, process theology is rendered highly suspect as theology if it can be demonstrated that the entire determinate world is in fact created *ex nihilo*. If process theology should be able to show that cosmology requires a being who acts like the process God in addition, still that intraworld being is not God at all, however necessary it might be to finite things. The real God is the creator, and the process God would have to be a creature. The next section shall attempt to make out the argument for divine creation *ex nihilo*.

The context of the argument might usefully be recalled here. The conception of "world" since the beginning of the modern period has been defined by determinateness as its closure. For physicists, the mathematical models for cosmology and particle physics characterize the closure of determinateness. For others, particularly students of consciousness and social realities, other forms of determinateness are normative. The relevant theological question is whether God is to be conceived as outside the closure of determinateness or inside or, if neither, where? The whole? The deists placed God outside the world's closure, and process theology places God inside, neither successfully. Pantheism cannot be sustained, as we have seen. Creation *ex nihilo* as interpreted here is another alternative.

Creation *ex Nihilo*

If God is not outside the world of determinate things nor the boundary nor inside, is there a "place" at all for God? There is no place in a univocal sense, but then, in the hypothesis of God as the creator of all determinate things *ex nihilo*, God is not an individual needing a place. As creator of the whole of determinateness, God takes on the features of being creator. Thus, the determinate features of divinity, such as being creator (and hence perhaps judge, redeemer, etc.), would themselves be the product of creation. God's character in the determinate sense is among the created things. Apart from the creation, God is indeterminate, indistinguishable from nothing, and unproblematically nowhere. Apart from creation, there is no "where." God's character arises from the act of creation itself, as a finite agent's moral character is in part the consequence of the moral actions, not the deterministic cause. Creation *ex nihilo* is not a doctrine about God as a thing or an individual, but about God as the creating of the world itself. Thus the location of God is not somewhere, in or out, but in the ontological contingency of the determinate things.

This conception does not suffer the deist's fate of making God irrelevant to the determinate world, because the determinate world is the very terminus of God's creative act. God is in every determinate thing, suffering with the suffering and enjoying with the joyous, not as an external observer or prehender but as immanent cause, responding to individual things eternally by creating other things. Nor does this hypothesis of creation suffer the pantheist's fate because God is not identified with the world except insofar as the world is considered the product of the creative act. Nor does this theological conception suffer the process God's fate of being too much a part of the world, too domestic, too much governed by the principles and norms governing everything else, for God the creator creates all these, including the divine character as creator. How can this conception be made plausible?[3] The character of creation *ex nihilo* is to be understood in three features: the creative source, the creative act, and the created product.

The created product is whatever is determinate; science and other human cognitive endeavors address what this is. God's character as creator is included among the determinate things and is studied by theology. The specific characters of God as loving, responsive, suffering, and the like are also elements of the created product. For theological purposes, God as creator is especially expressed in the transcendental properties that characterize all determinate things. These transcendental properties constitute the material for a revised doctrine of the logos in Christian theology, of Saguna Brahman in Hinduism, of sophia in Judaism, and so forth.[4]

The creative act has the form of the product and the unity of creating all the determinate things together. If the world of determinations is highly unified, then the creative act has a tight unity, perhaps like the act of a finite person. In certain respects the world does have a tight unity with a subordination of parts and wholes, and relative to those respects, teleological arguments for a creative personal agent make some sense. If the world is loosely unified, the creative act has that character. In many respects the world seems impersonal, a bizarre combination of brute mathematical law and chaos among the items of human significance. In relation to these the creative act seems more like a principle or sheer energy. The act is at least as unified as the togetherness of all the determinate harmonies with their different essential features.

The source would be nothing at all, not even source, if there were no creation. Apart from creation it would be wholly indeterminate, indistinguishable from nothing. This is what saves the doctrine of creation *ex nihilo* as developed here from postulating an individual God hanging around outside the created order, avoiding the line of sight of astronauts. But there is the creation and God is not apart from it. Given the creation, the source is that on which the determinate world absolutely depends. If the source did not create, there would be no world; hence the absolute dependence of the world.

The relation between God as ontological source and God as determinate product is wholly asymmetrical in a causal sense. The source cannot itself be determinate, except consequentially in the role of being source, without itself having to be created. Therefore, the source apart from creation would be indeterminate, and it has no determinate character that would require relation to the created world except those characters arising from the creation itself. The threefold character of creation *ex nihilo*—source, act, and product—is among the determinate things created, as a kind of transcendental metaphysical condition. Because the threefold character is among the determinate things, it is amenable to articulation by our theological understanding.

Can creation *ex nihilo* provide an interpretive model for theism's God? This needs to be treated as an empirical question and analyzed according to the various elements asserted of theism's God. Surely it does provide an important addition to the dialectic of creation in the theistic traditions, responding to the modern definition of the world's closure as determinateness. It also responds to other theological motives such as ascribing supremacy and lordship to God. The extent to which creation *ex nihilo* can be represented with the metaphors of a causal agent with personal intentions, judging and acting to save the world, depends on what is found in the world. If the world is ordered as the product of a personal intentional agent, those metaphors apply quite directly. If there is a history of salvation, then God the creator is a savior. For Christians, the character of the Christian God depends on the worldly character of the Christ and the work of the Holy Spirit, not the other way around. And so with regard to the more diverse and general forms of holiness: the ways by which holiness is possible display the graces of the creator.

By virtue of the same empirical status of characterizations of creation *ex nihilo*, that concept lends itself to investigation as an interpretive tool for those religions whose metaphors are oriented less to individual divine agency. This is not to say that creation *ex nihilo* is an adequate frame within which to interpret Buddhist emptiness or Confucian principle. But it is not ruled out as a more literally individualistic hypothesis would be. The validity or usefulness of the creation *ex nihilo* hypothesis for comparative religions is an empirical issue (Neville 1991a).

The theory of creation *ex nihilo* can be shown to fulfill the need discovered in the previous chapter for an ontological context for mutual dependence of finite determinations. The problem there, it will be recalled, was this. Determinate things are harmonies of conditional and essential features; if this were not so they could not be determinately related and determinately different. Now the conditional features display all sorts of interactions and mutual conditioning of things, but only presupposing their harmony with the essential features. In what sense are the essential features of different determinate things together? Not in any of the senses supplied by conditional features; indeed those senses are dependent on a deeper ontological togetherness.

The ontological togetherness required for mutual relevance is that the different things be created together. They are simply made to be together as the product of the creative act. Their "being created together" is the ontological context, whose reality lies in the act of creation *ex nihilo*. If the context were itself determinate, such as a super-space-time, then some deeper context would be required to relate the determinate context to the determinate things it itself relates. The context therefore must be indeterminate except in that it has the structure of what it contains or contextualizes; God as creator *ex nihilo* is precisely that, indeterminate except with regard to the determinations created. If the ontological context were only nothing, then there would be no real determinate things, no world; God the creator is not nothing, nor only indeterminate, but the actual creator. The context only can be the making of the determinate things out of an indeterminate nothing, creation *ex nihilo*. If the ontological context were anything else it would be either determinate, and thus require a prior ontological grounding context, or it would be only indeterminate, and hence contextualizing nothing.

The actual determinate world exists; it needs an ontological context of mutual relevance; only creation *ex nihilo* can serve as that ontological context; therefore the world is created *ex nihilo* in its comprehensive determinate characters and God is this creating conceived as source, act, and product. Here is the promised "proof" arising from our metaphysical hypothesis.

The explanatory power of the creation *ex nihilo* hypothesis lies in its pointing to the making or the action of making. This is a kind of ontological empiricism, a noting of the creative power in the determinations. Some thinkers will insist that this is no explanation at all, that explanations necessarily have to explain determinate things by more determinate things. But this objection consists in insisting only that all explanations must be within the realm of determinate things. Why is that so? Are not explanations designed to show why determinate complex things are what they are? At one level, this is done by citing higher determinate principles. But when the subject to be explained includes the principles of determinateness as such and all determinate things including the explanation, nothing determinate could supply the explanation even though what is to be explained is a determinate complex.

Sometimes it is objected that an explanation by appeal to a making is not intelligible, that it has no analogies in common experience; process theology's version of this objection was discussed earlier. To the contrary, every time we assign moral responsibility to someone, including ourselves, we do so on the basis of what the person adds to the entire situation that obtained before the alleged moral action. To the extent the action can be reduced to determinate antecedents, those antecedents and not the agent are responsible; similarly with acts of artistic creativity and, upon reflection, with most acts by which we compose our lives. Finite agents are never without limiting conditions and antecedents, and so the analysis of responsible action often seems to reduce to these. But precisely those elements that make for responsibility are the ones that are spontaneous and *ex nihilo*. The whole issue of responsibility is an analogy for understanding through identifying the acts of composition. In the case of divine creation *ex nihilo*, there is no novel rearrangement of antecedent parts, but absolutely everything is created.

The argument of this section has not been merely to pose an alternative hypothesis to various theistic responses to the modern understanding of the world's closure, although it has done that. The argument also has claimed that any recognition of determinateness, at least as articulated in previous chapters, must acknowledge an ontological context of mutual relevance and that creation *ex nihilo* is precisely that context. A determinate thing cannot be that context, nor can the context be a thing that is absolutely nothing. The former would require a further creator, and the latter would account for no determinate world. The creation itself is what provides the ontological context. The next question to ask is whether the hypothesis makes good sense of eternity.

Chapter Eleven

CREATION OF ALL TIMES

The state of the argument is that we have defended the plausibility of the hypothesis that the modes of temporality are together eternally, and that an account of what eternity means might be helped by recurring to the metaphysics of essential and conditional features with which the temporal modes were originally explicated. An examination of the togetherness of harmonies of essential and conditional features in general gives rise to the consideration of the theological hypothesis of creation *ex nihilo*. The togetherness of essential and conditional features requires an ontological context of mutual relevance, and God conceived in one way as creator *ex nihilo* serves as that ontological context. The argument has been very complex, never staying long with one chain of links but pulling in one strand after another as if making a rope. Perhaps the best metaphor for the argument is that the metaphysics of essential and conditional features is the warp upon which the woof of time and eternity has been woven along with the woof of God and creation. The temporal problematic needs to own up to the phenomenology of time's flow, whereas the theological problematic needs to own up to the living realities of religious life. Now we need to develop the pattern of both themes of the woof and show how the theological idea of creation *ex nihilo* provides the eternity required for time's flow. That is the topic of the present chapter. Its reverse, in Chapter 12, is to show how the temporal contents of eternity constitute the inner life of God.

The Analysis of "Proper Dates"

The first step in relating creation *ex nihilo* to time's flow is to ask how the hypothesis displays the creation of the temporal modes. The first answer to that question is, "all together eternally." That is, the past is not made "before" the present or the future or any such temporal arrangement. This point has been discussed several times previously. The second answer is that what is created are temporal things, and these have a temporal order relative to their proper dates.

A thing's proper date, according to the definitions stipulated earlier, is the date of its actualization, however that is identified and measured and regardless of whether the actualization is present, past, or (possibly) future. Before that date is in present time, the thing is properly future; and after it has occurred, it is properly past. The temporal ontological constitution of a thing therefore can be understood in terms of its proper date. The proper date of a thing can be analyzed most completely as its present time, although the date must also be analyzed as future and past.

Noting that things have a proper date was the basis for what Whitehead (1925) criticized as *simple location*. He pointed out that things can enter into other things, really and truly enter into them, at subsequent dates. Those subsequent dates are proper to the other things, but not to the entering thing. The temporal location of things is to be understood in terms of their proper dates and the contrast with "multiple location" or participation in the proper dates of other things.

The discussion of proper dates enriches the theory of temporality and createdness. As such it is a matter of heavy metaphysics, reviewing categories vaguely introduced before and explaining them in more detail. These categories will reemerge in Chapters 14–16 as the basis for the covenant interpretation of the human condition.

Four elements enter into a thing's present existence at its proper date: form as possibilities for actualization, components as potentialities, the actual mixture of these in the singular happening, and the cause of mixture in the spontaneous creativity of the moment. An analysis of the existential createdness of the thing at that date requires elaborating on each of these. The categories, as mentioned earlier, derive from Plato's Philebus (see Neville 1989, Chapters 5–6).

Form

Possibilities are forms by which the components might be harmonized. Forms for integrating a given set of components differ by three factors: complexity, simplicity, and density.[1]

Complexity is the number and diversity of components that can be integrated by the form. Any form except the sheer repetition of the entire past involves some elimination of components so that they are not actualized in the present happening coming to be. Any form also may require transformations and reductions, substitutions and homogenizations of the components. The less this is done, and the more the form allows the components to be reactualized in the emerging happening, the more complex the form. Complexity aims to allow you to have your cake and eat it too.

Simplicity is the way by which a form arranges components to achieve identity of focus, with each element having parts like itself. Simplicity makes possible massiveness of actuality. Complexity in certain ways is the opposite of simplicity. Maximum complexity can be achieved by bare forms of conjunction: this and this and this and this. But no item is reinforced by being with other items, no component is made more massive or intense by harmony with the others. Maximum simplicity is a kind of internal homogeneity.

Density is the degree of maximization of both complexity and simplicity. The greater is the complexity, the greater the density deriving from the various separate actualities of the diverse components. The greater is the simplicity, the greater the density deriving from mutual reinforcement. The density of a form is of course its value, as pointed out in the earlier discussion of form in Chapter 6, enjoying both the separate values of the components and the reinforcing values from having them together this way rather than some other. Degree of value in density is not easily measured on scales of comparison because an increase in complexity can be made easy by a decrease in simplicity and vice versa.

Different forms achieve different kinds of values for the same set of components depending on whether they favor complexity or simplicity and how. The complexity of a Jack-of-all-trades, master-of-none is at the opposite extreme from the simplicity of the idiot-savant. There are circumstances when each would be preferable to any other sort of person; but in most circumstances we rightly prefer to be and associate with people less extreme, people who have found life forms for maximizing higher degrees of both complexity and simplicity.

The forms for the potential components of a particular happening or present moment of a thing differ in their value, and the actualization that results from the present creativity will have the value of the form actualized. Forms are not relative merely to the components in a particular happening, however, but are part of the unified field of the future for all present happenings. Thus a thing has not only the value actualized in itself but also the values of the various roles it plays in the larger field. To analyze a thing is to analyze not only its own embodied form but also its structural connections with other things and the values achieved elsewhere because of its identity.

A structural analysis of forms treats them as overlapping hierarchies. That is, a form internally is the integration of a set of components, each of which has a form, and so forth. Internally, the form is of greater density or value if its component structure is both more complex and massively simple. The density can be described as a contrast; that is, the more the complexity can be preserved downward in the hierarchy and integrated in reinforcing ways upward, the more the top of the hierarchy will contain very few but massive and complex elements juxtaposed in sharp contrast. A harmony is not itself a determinate "third term" integrating lower level components, but a sheer juxtaposition of things that hang together because of their mutually integral natures. The harmony of a thing's own components can enter into contrasts with other harmonies according to the structure of broader possibilities. Form is whatever patterns articulate possible integrations. Part of understanding a thing at its proper date is understanding the forms it exhibits and in which it participates on a larger scale.

Components

The components of the existential createdness of a thing at its proper date are the potentials for its coming to be. These are all the past things, previously actualized, with their integrated structures and achieved values. The great metaphysical lesson of Whitehead was that the potentials for actualization are themselves the real actualities of the past. Those actualities have their own proper dates, which are past, and they are potentials for actualization at the proper date of the newly emerging happening or present moment of a thing. Thus actuality is multiply located, both at its proper location and also in whatever subsequent states of an enduring thing or subsequent happenings that can include them. To understand a thing at its proper date is in part to understand its components and their own proper dates. Only in this way is it possible to understand both how the components are real things in their own right, functioning actually in the emerging proper date, and how the proper dates (and proper places) of those components are perhaps external to the emerging thing and constitute a field for it.

Actuality

The actualities of the past are varied and structurally connected with one another. The connections are themselves varied, ranging from deep mutual implications that require rigid repetition to converging and diverging vectors of forces. Sometimes the potentials that come to a moment are so determined in their interrelations that only one outcome of the coming-to-be is possible; this is causal determinism. But most often, especially concerning affairs on a human scale, there are many ways by which the components can be mixed. The ongoing hang-togetherness of the universe, exhibiting both continuing determination and also freedom of variation and chance encounter, is structured by rhythms and pulses. Subatomic particles have a vibratory character and so do human bodies, generations, and historical events.[2] When a present happening has happened, its actuality consists of the combined actualities of its potentials, however modified, with possibly new forms actualized that were not in the previously actualized components.

The mixture in the existential createdness of a thing at its proper date is precisely what is actualized then and there. This includes a selection and modification of the actual components from the past and a selection from among the possible forms for integration. This mixture is what is existentially important about the moment. In the course of an enduring thing, it is the change or continuity that is this moment's significance for its identity. For human beings, some moments affect their whole being and much of the world around them, and these are weighted with moral considerations. The mixture achieved in the moment might be a significant act of will or commitment. Important or trivial, the mixture achieved in the present coming-to-be is how the thing engages its own time, structured by the past facts and future possibilities. The mixture achieved is what is the moment's contribution to the actual past, a contribution that might be a potential also for the future.

The mixture is that moment's singular identity. It contains the value of the forms actualized, and contains also the value of excluding those forms that were possible but were not actualized. Part of the guilt of the bank robber consists in not actualizing the possibility of walking past the bank. The value achieved in singular identity is not always to be understood in good versus bad terms, however. By reading this book, the reader is at the moment excluding the values that would be achieved by attending to friends and family or by having a sensual good time (assuming that there are things more sensual than reading this!). The values in the mixture are those of different *kinds* included and excluded, not just or even those of different degrees. Part of understanding a thing in its proper date is understanding its existential mix; whereas the sciences are most often interested in form and components, historians, existentialists, novelists, poets, artists, and other analysts of meaning and consciousness focus on the mixture as such.

Cause of Mixture

The cause of mixture, or causes of mixture, are those elements in the creative process of coming-to-be that select among the possibilities and transform the potentials so that they can be actualized together. These "causes of mixture" are whatever determine the process of integrating all the conditions from past and future into the value achieved in the mixture. In other language, the causes of mixture are the essential features of the thing in the proper moment of coming-to-be. There seem to be at least three sorts of essential features as causes of mixture.

One is the essential features among the actual potentials. All the potentials are at least conditional features of the moment; but some might also be essential ones in the sense that they determine the process of harmonization. Inherited DNA that determines bodily structure and growth would be one example. Moral commitments made in the past or morally freighted actions affecting moral identity in the present are other examples.

A second kind of essential feature for coming-to-be is future possibilities defining the ongoing identity of an enduring thing. Again, these might be bodily possibilities having to do with continuity and programmed change, historical ones such as always being the child of particular individuals, or moral ones such as obligations. The essential features from the past and future determine how a present happening relates to the other elements in the ongoing identity of enduring objects or long-lasting institutions or situations.

A third kind of essential feature for the present is the spontaneous creativity itself that selects and actualizes. The privileged position the "present" has had for defining existence and divine "presence" stems from this spontaneous creativity. On the one hand this decisive actualizing creativity is the inmost essence of the moment. In human beings, it is the instant of decision. Unlike some existentialists, who exaggerate the importance of the instant of decision, it is important to recognize that a person's prior identity and future obligations also play large roles in making that decision point meaningful. By itself, without essential connections to past and future, the instant decision is absurd and humanly meaningless. But the instant of decision is not by itself; it is indeed part of an ongoing life and larger community of people and nature. For that reason, the decisive actualizations made there are at the heart of personal responsibility.

On the other hand, that spontaneous creativity is the presence of the creator making something actual in the moment. The person is never complete in the moment alone, requiring also past and future elements. The instant of decision is an abstraction from the ongoing life of the person in nature and community. But it is where God enters into time to make a temporal difference. After the moment is actual fact, things are different from what they were before.

"Two Authors" Theory

In a sense, there are two authors of every decisive moment, God and the creature in the moment itself. The spontaneous creativity in the moment is part of the larger singular creative act by which God creates the whole world; it is part of the act of creation *ex nihilo*. At the same time (no pun intended) that spontaneity is the event's own self-definition. Where the event is part of a person's life, it is part of the person's own self-definition.

Some thinkers in contemporary theology like to speak of cocreation, where people are said to have responsibility along with God for the creation. The point is easily misunderstood. It makes no sense to say that God and humans divide the work, God handling some part of creativity and people other parts. This is the strategy of process theology in its attempt to say that we alone, without God, are responsible for some things, including evil, whereas God is responsible for other things, never including evil. But this is to deny God any part in the creation of human beings (in process theology, God helps set up only their possibilities). Far better it is to recognize that the creativity by which we define ourselves and by means of which we take responsibility for what we do and are is the same creativity that is part of the larger divine creative act of which the whole world is the product.

The senses in which human beings are responsible for their actions and self-constitution need to be spelled out in terms of their freedom from constraints, the openness of their possibilities, their abilities to act, to understand what is at stake, and so on. Surely people are responsible sometimes and not other times, and the circumstances make the difference.[3] Whether the divine act of creation is to be understood as responsible in that very same sense depends on how closely the analogy of the moral agent is to be applied to God: not too closely, according to Job. Part of the meaning of human responsibility is that there is a continuity of personality such that in various ways we can objectify a moment of decision, stand back, and decide in and about it. By contrast, divine creativity has no form whatsoever save for its decided products in themselves, as connected within the eternal creative act. Only creation within time is to be understood as a process of decisions; the divine act is immediate, with no intervening steps that could be like a process of deliberation. The complexity in the divine act is the togetherness of its products.

There is no conflict between divine creation and human freedom unless the creator is seen as an external agent who might force certain options upon a person. All temporal realities, those having nothing to do with freedom as well as those that do, are created so that, in their present moment of arising, what is added spontaneously to the previously actualized components arises *ex nihilo*. But this is another way of saying that, for the emerging entity, that creativity is its self-causation. Its previous character determines it just to the extent that its past sets limitations; its present character is in process of arising through the selections and decisions that make up present becoming. Whether the person, or the person's society, is free depends on the empirical case. Is the person in chains? Has the person developed capabilities of acting on the basis of intent? Does the person in fact have real options? Or does the situation preclude them? Or has the person failed to keep options open? Has the person a carefully developed set of values according to which to choose? Are these engrained in the habits? All these are empirical issues, and the real state of affairs has two authors: God as the general and therefore in most instances trivial creator, and specific temporal causes, some of which are beyond human control and others of which are matters of moral responsibility.

For most matters of human concern, the relevant causes are finite and temporal ones, those for instance that expand or limit freedom, increase or diminish prosperity or security, those that make for pleasure and happiness or that cause suffering and grief. Because the creator is the source of absolutely everything determinate, God is the ground of all things. This in itself is trivial from the standpoint of advancing human interests, because the important distinctions have to do with identifying those causal processes to embrace, to avoid, and to attempt to control. Nevertheless, at every moment of time, God's creativity is taking place, and it is necessary to enrich our hypothesis by showing in more detail how this is true.

The Temporality of the Creative Act

What is the temporality of the divine creative act? At the proper date of a happening, there is form, which is future possibility; that form as future must be together with the emerging present so that something is possible to happen. At the proper date are also the components that are the past actualities functioning as potentials. There must be a togetherness of the past with the present creativity that actualizes them in the emerging happening. Those past actualities also had their own present at the proper date of happening, and creativity was present then both in their own past components and in the creativity that took place. Creativity is present in the moment transforming some of the possibilities to actualities by means of the past actual components. As in process of coming-to-be, divine creativity is attaining to a date. As completing the actualization, the divine present activity has a date. For the divine creativity to be at work at a particulate date as a proper present, that creativity must be of a piece with the creativity making the formal future and sustaining the past as actual. To understand this it is necessary to look at proper dates as future and past. This extends the discussion of proper dates.

The future whose proper date is a year from now can be schematized in terms of a vague hierarchy. That is, a year from now the reader will be "dead or alive" (but not both); decisive events over the year will determine which. Under the "alive" disjunct in the future, the reader will be "in the same place as now or in x, y, or z places" (but not both here and there and also not in some other places that cannot be reached by any means in a year). The reader's own future is part of a much larger interacting field of possibilities that will be made more specific by decisions as the year progresses. By the time the future date comes so that it is the immediate possibility of a happening, its vague forms will have been made sufficiently specific that the decision process within the creative moment of its proper happening is sufficient to decide all alternatives left vaguely open. As the year wanes and the proper date of what had been a year off approaches its moment of existential presence, its formal structure changes. The divine creativity in making the forms is united with that in each existential decisive present to constitute that shift.[4]

When the proper date of an actualized past happening or thing recedes into the past, its own meaning is elaborated as its sequellae are actualized. Whether the past happening can continue to be a potential in subsequent events, the farther it recedes into the past depends in part on the structures and continuities of its increasingly long connections with the living present. Its capacity to be a potential depends also in part on the spontaneous creativity in the current present happening. Not only does that creativity actualize the potentials that are given, it also identifies what counts as the set of potentials. That a thing has become past means it is ready to be a potential in any subsequent happening. But whether it will be in the actual past of the present happening depends on the creativity initiating the present moment. Each happening develops into its own droplet of existential spatial and temporal location. The structural limits to these happenings are set by the common actual past elements and the common possible future. But that something happens, which defines the resulting space-time locations, comes from the initial selective process of potentials in the coming to be.[5] The divine creative act thus both relates the present arising to past facts to get them as potentials and relates contemporary happenings to one another.

The argument has now run through in static fashion the ways by which the temporal moments of a thing's proper date are together with one another so that their essential features are mutually relevant. The creator is present at each date as providing its future possibilities and its past potentials, as well as its present creativity for actualization. A moment properly dated in the future has God creating its formal character, God having created the actualities to be integrated, and God in the present decisions that give the future its shifting structure. A moment properly dated in the past had God as the previous creator of its own potentials, God as the source of its creativity, and God providing the possibilities it actualized; subsequent moments add to its meaning, and God is present in those in relevant ways. The relations that define the temporal differences between the different dates are all eternal relations, not temporal ones. This is what has been exhibited here.

The Nontemporality of the Creative Act

Time's flow, however, is not like this static description of differences among dates. It involves the constant shift of the date of the decisive present. As soon as one date has come to be, it is past and a new arising has begun. How is God "at a given time"? Popular religion asks whether God knows now what the world will be in a year. The answer depends on whether God completely exists now, and the answer is no. God is "now" only partly, in the part that is presently dated creativity; but God equally is creative of the past and future. God is eternal. Therefore it makes no sense to say, except by abstraction, that God is now. To the extent that God is only now, God "knows" nothing more than is determined now about the future. But God is not "only now."

Much of theistic piety is modeled on a conversation with God, where God is truly and fully now, waiting for us to speak and respond, and responding differentially to us from the divine point of view. Given the eternity of creation, this can at best be a symbolic representation of how we relate to the creator. By all means it must be admitted that in many circumstances this kind of personalistic representation is appropriate. It is said that there are no atheists in foxholes and, if a sudden believer assumed to have predestined calamity addresses a God, the believer argues might and main to evoke a divine decision to alter providence. But most people also understand that this personal conversation is in another context only metaphorical. Providence is deeper than our druthers and our goods are difficult to map onto divine priorities. The very idea of God "knowing the future," as if the divine were a mind projecting about a distant happening, is a metaphor with extremely limited application. Chapters 12, 15, and 16 will give a more precise account of the senses in which God responds to temporal human needs and prayers.

The analysis of the divine presence in the temporal modes has employed the categories of form, components, mixture, and cause of mixture. These are transcendental properties of what it is to be a temporal thing and function much like the Christian theological notion of the logos. They are that in and by which things that are made are made. By analyzing the forms, components, mixtures, and causes of mixture in nature, people, society, and institutions, we attend to the "that" question regarding their existence.

The "what" questions of scientific and other modes of thought fall into these four kinds and their various combinations. The sciences can ask just what forms are possible and actual, and what their structure is relative to one another. We can understand things by analyzing their component and antecedents, determining regularities and marking unusual actualizations. We attend to concrete matters by determining just what is actualized relative to the potentials and possibilities. And we specify the values of things, inquiring how things might have been different and what difference that would make in value. The subtleties of analysis of human intentions, responsibilities, and cultural achievements and failures all are variations on the "what" question relative to form, components, mixtures, and causes of mixtures.

Those categories themselves, however, place the divine creation in things. The mutual conditioning of the determinations and their various essential features constitute what things are. But that those things are at all is a function of the creation in concert of their forms, components, mixtures, and causes of mixtures. What is this like from the standpoint of eternity itself? How should we conceive the internal dynamics of creation? Is it fair to speak of a divine life?

Chapter Twelve

GOD'S ETERNAL LIFE

Time's Flow *sub Specie Eternitatis*

Time's flow is badly represented by the analytical placement of creation in the temporal modes, as depicted in the previous chapter. Not that this depiction is mistaken or even that it can be neglected in understanding the passage of time. But all that the analytical depiction can show is the systematic interconnections and changes that take place as present moments become past, changing the future possibilities and giving way to new moments of decisive creativity. Chunk, chunk, chunk go the droplets of becoming.

Time's flow can be appreciated only *sub specie eternitatis,* for it is in fact a proper trait of the eternal creation *ex nihilo,* only partially grasped by finite beings in present consciousness, behind the veil of memory and anticipation. The eternal act of creation does not take time, for it encompasses all the dates of things as each is future, present, and past together in order for present time to move on. Yet the eternal act of creation, as regards the creation of temporal things, is characterized by an infinite internal dynamism. Although not taking time itself, the eternal creative act includes the singular pulse of present decisive creativity from moment to moment in infinite serial order. The mathematical complexity of seriality is only now being explored by contemporary physics.

Time's flow is fully real only as the internal character of the eternal act in which all times are together in an infinite singular series of continuous transformations. There are no times between present bursts of creativity; the finish of one is the beginning of others in a smooth flow. The smoothness cannot be understood from the standpoint of considering the sequence of present moments itself, for each of these stops and another comes to be. From the standpoint of the eternal act, however, there is not only the series of fits and starts of the present shifting from date to date. Rather there is also, and essentially coordinated with the present, the successive growth of actuality in the past, each new actual moment added continuously, without temporal break, to what came before. Together with this is the continuous reconfiguration of the formal structure of the future, modified by each decision everywhere; the shifts in the future should not be imagined as a sequence of stills but as a continual movement of boundaries.

Thus the internal constitution of the creative act is a dynamic eternal transformation in which things past, present, and future are together, in which there is a continual transformation of each mode as the actual past grows, the present shifts dates, and the future is in constant formal movement. This transformation is ordered by the singular sequence of time, and for things within the time, their location is temporal with some things past and others yet to come, depending in part on what is happening. Yet within the eternal act itself, the location at a particular temporal moment is an abstraction from the whole that contains all moments in continual transformation. The eternal act is not a stasis within time, but a creative act that includes temporal flow within the larger context of the togetherness of all the modes. The eternal act does not change, because it does not endure from one moment to the next. The temporal things within it change, however, actualizing efforts that add to the past and shift the future's possibilities.

This section completes the metaphysical description of time's flow relative to the eternity of the act of creation. The threads of temporality and the threads of theology are now both woven into the metaphysical warp. But the tapestry is still too abstract.

Images of Time

The dialectical reasonings that allow us to grasp how the temporal is contained within the eternal — and only that standpoint involves time's most conspicuous trait, that it flows — calls for metaphoric envisionment. Of course the eternal act cannot be literally envisioned, for it is not a temporal or spatial thing, not a conceivable object of vision. Time's flow itself is a rather good metaphor for eternity, but it casts attention back to the location within time of that which passes and comes to be. Every great reflective culture has attempted to image eternal dynamism, appreciative of the literal impossibility.

India

From India have come images of consciousness and the dance. Brahman is like a great self, unitary behind the flow of objects across consciousness. Without the dazzling passage of objects, consciousness is empty, not transcendent-of-change-Empty but dull-empty-empty. Thus consciousness is never without its river of changes, but still comprehends them all together so that, when pressed as to what Brahman is in itself, the answer is given that Brahman is utterly without qualities, Nirguna Brahman.

Balancing this "mentalistic" metaphoric motif is Siva's dance. The dance, which is our temporal world, has no existence save as Siva dances. Siva is the true reality on whom the dance depends utterly, and yet is as nothing unless dancing: Siva is only a dancer. There is no necessity in either Siva or our dance that Siva dance our world: that is just the play he has chosen. There may in fact be many other dances as well, although that is not our concern. Both Brahman as pure transcendent consciousness and Siva the dancer represent the dynamics of time within a time-transcendent "doing," an intending or a dancing.

China

China also has two major metaphoric motifs for the temporal within the eternal, integrated and reinforcing one another even more strongly than the Indian. The Tao that cannot be named is the mother of the Tao that can be named, and the latter is the temporal flow of events exhibiting structural transformations of yin and yang (*Tao Teh Ching*, Chapter 1). Underlying the flow there is a deeper sense of genesis that is not temporal. This is expressed explicitly in "orders" of creation such as expressed by Chou Tun-i: Nonbeing, then the Great Ultimate (or perhaps Nonbeing *and* the Great Ultimate), then the extension of yang, then contraction to yin, then the structuring of movement into elements and finally the 10,000 things of the changing world.[1] Only the interactions of yang and yin to form structures involve temporal passage, which is contained within or supported by Nonbeing and Being from whose eternal dynamic relation it takes its genesis.

The other Chinese motif starts from the wholly temporal flow, which is articulated as the changing interaction of Heaven and Earth. Heaven and Earth are eternal, each in its own way, and the dynamic world is the result of their interaction. In Sung and Ming Confucianism Heaven was reinterpreted as Principle and Earth as Material Force. The Tao is the processive development and changing of actual things by reconfiguring material force. Principle directs the reconfigurations, not so much by supplying Platonic-like forms but by defining what harmoniousness would be. Principle is normative and always addresses every swirl of changes uniquely. Principle is always the same, however, always what would make a plurality of conflicting changes harmonize. The Schools debated many theories of the unity or separateness of Principle and Material Force. But they all acknowledged the constancy of change and the transcendent unity of Principle or Heaven. Principle is that in any temporal thing which is its incipience for growth or change.

The West

The symbol in the West for time within eternity is life. Ordinarily, life is conceived as a trait of some temporal processes that come to integral focus, grow, and die—all to be understood from within the temporal order of dates of present existence. But life's metaphoric scope is quite extraordinary. To be truly alive, spiritually alive, is to be far more than biologically alive. It is to be both responsive and creative to a heightened degree. The responsiveness of true life involves adjustment of everything in one's self in the response, no walled-off privileged core. The creativity is to make every response more than reactive, more than "an equal and opposite reaction," but a transformation of the whole by virtue of the quality of the response. Living things in the primary reference of the term are in a larger context, responding to external events and acting externally in response while also coordinating internal changes. Applied to the creation of the world *ex nihilo,* there is no larger context. Responses are internal responses of part to part, and actions also are the creative ones constituting the determinate world. The eternal creative act is Life in a heightened sense of that term, living by virtue of the infinite dynamism of its temporal product.

Of course, another image of time now is associated with the West; namely, scientific time. Two sources contribute to the specialized scientific image as mentioned earlier, the microscopic and the macroscopic. Microscopically, time is the metric defined by atomic decay, and macroscopically it is defined by the models of the projection of light used to speculate about the Big Bang and alternative theories. Both are compatible with the theory of time's flow presented here and with the hypothesis of creation *ex nihilo.* Yet clearly the scientific image of time bears no similarity to the image of time as Life within eternity. The scientific image of time is formed exclusively by metrics whose structure is to have even parts outside of even parts—every minute is exactly as long as the minutes before and after. The scientific image prescinds precisely from the eternal togetherness of different dates in each of the temporal modes and from the internal dynamic of eternal change. It recognizes exclusively the complex connections of seriality as defined by before and after in motion. The scientific image of course is not mistaken or misleading, only abstract relative to some of the most interesting features of time, especially from a moral and religious point of view. Science does not address the ontological constitution of time, only its shape when measured by particular metrics, perhaps the shape of its first moments.

The symbol of Life is the one to be developed here, although it is obvious that the symbols in the other traditions have their own potential for giving cultural content to the arguments made about eternity and time's flow.

The Singularity of Creation: God

At this point the argument returns to the issue raised earlier concerning whether creation *ex nihilo* legitimates representation of the creator in the symbols of theism. There may be other, nontheistic, symbols that legitimately represent the creation, but the issue here has to do with the God of the Western religious traditions. The earlier argument showed that God ought not be represented in any nearly literal way as an individual apart from or along with the determinate things of the world. That individualistic representation of God as *a being* is not adequate because, if there were a perfect being with infinite divine closure alongside the world, there would still have to be a deeper creator to make possible that alongsidedness in an ontological context of mutual relevance.

Nevertheless, the divine creative act has a singularity that requires that we speak of *the* creative act and this singularity underlies the legitimacy of monotheistic language. Because the creative act must create all harmonies eternally together, with their essential as well as conditional features in mutual relevance, it is one singular act. Creation could not be a succession of acts because then a prior creation would be required to make them mutually relevant so as to be successive, just as eternal creation is required to provide the context for temporal succession of future, present, and past. Only one singular creative act could be the ontological context of mutual relevance for the many changes constituting time's flow. The monotheistic impulse both West and East was directly on target. But it should not be applied to a single God who endures alongside the world. Its application is to the singularity of the creative act, which singularizes the source and also the product of creation, the cosmos. The singularity of the cosmos does not entail that the cosmos is a totality in any strict sense; indeed there are deep problems with the idea of totality (see Neville 1992b, Chapter 5). Singularity allows that the cosmos consists only in the determinations that exist or will exist in their determinate and indeterminate relations. Because the creative act is singular, we may speak of and address the singular, God, referring to the act itself, its source, or its product considered under the aegis of being contingent on the creative act. Better yet, God refers to all three together, because this is what is, lives, and contains the divine life.

The theological significance of the term *God* is now closely linked with the eternity that provides the ontological context of the mutual relevance of the temporal modes in time's flow. Without

saying that God is a determinate individual that must be located
relative to the boundaries of the world's closure, we can still speak
of God as the singular creator. What can be said about the life of
this creator?

Divine Responsiveness: God as Living Creator

According to the creation *ex nihilo* hypothesis, God the creator is
the singular and eternal creating of the world, including its
temporal elements. This eternal creative act is a living singularity in
the metaphoric sense stated earlier. The act contains an ordered
infinite dynamic of transformations in which the flow of time
consists. The divine life, albeit eternal in having all distinctions of
time together in the creative act, swirls internally with the dynamic
flow of temporal things, with each decision, each accreted actuality, and each possibility infinitely responsive to each other and the
whole infinitely creative. The living God is not immortal Wotan
thundering across heaven after his Valkyries but the eternal divine
life within which every temporal happening takes place and within
which every temporal thing also has an eternal identity, a togetherness of all the proper times in all the temporal modes. Finite
things are eternal only insofar as they are fragments of the divine
eternity.

    To be able to represent God as responsive to human needs and
suffering, and responsive in another sense to prayer, is deeply
important for religion. Although divine responsiveness is of course
symbolic — God is not *exactly* like mother — it is nevertheless very
real to people. The most obvious way to represent divine responsiveness is by analogy to human responsiveness, with a model of
God as a humanlike individual. This is the way pursued by process
theology in the face of traditions that say God must be much bigger
than that. We have rejected that way for many reasons and
therefore cannot appeal to it to represent divine responsiveness.
Divine responsiveness must instead be represented within the
eternal act of creation.

    The first step in understanding the possibility of divine
responsiveness is to recall that eternity does not mean static fixity,
as if the past supplies its image. Rather, eternity embraces the
changing natures of all dates together in all the modes of time.

Therefore, in general divine responsiveness is to create things in determinate relation to one another—with mutually harmonized and relevant essential and conditional features—so that one thing is responsive to another.

In particular, divine responsiveness must be understood from the standpoint within time of a person in need of a divine response, say to a petitionary prayer or rescue from danger or despair. For the person in need at the particular present time, the past is fixed and the future is partly open. The person hopes that the future contains the petitioned or needed things that constitute the divine response, and that those particular options are the ones that will be realized. If that needed future is in fact realized, then God has responded to the need.

Although in eternity all things are together from the standpoint of the person with the partly open and needy future, God's response is still open. Notice that even if the theologically relevant response does come about, it still needs temporal causes. If a child is about to be run down by a truck, and the divine response is to prevent that, the result might be accomplished by a pothole that causes the truck to careen away. Or it might be accomplished by a moral agent who dashes heroically into the street to snatch the child from danger. In the former case we might call the pothole providential, and in the latter case we would say that God works through people. In both cases, the eternal creation relates the problematic situation to a satisfactory outcome by the mutual relevance of future that will be actualized to the present need. From the standpoint of the present needy person, God's response is future and is part of the future's openness.

A disbelieving secularist would look at the future and observe that whatever happens does so because of natural causes, the pothole or the adventitious hero. That is true so far as it goes. If eternity is not the togetherness of the temporal modes and the sequence of temporal modes is understood without eternity, the secular disbeliever would be right that this is just as far as it goes, no farther. For the "providential" future to be indeed providential, one must see that the mutual connection of needy present with the actualization of the right possibilities in an open future is a matter of their direct togetherness in the eternal act of creation. Indeed, if we are to avoid a vicious determinism and predestinarianism, it is necessary to say that divine responsiveness requires the eternity of God rather than the everlasting temporality of a divine enduring individual. Chapter 15 will develop some of the consequences of this point.

Through many twists and turns, bringing threads into the metaphysical warp from many directions, we have now completed an argument for God as creator *ex nihilo* of the world of determinate things. God is not to be conceived as an individual alongside or in addition to the world, but as creator whose content is the world itself, including the divine character resulting from creating. Recall the alternatives.

Deism was an inadequate representation of God on two counts. First, it construed God as an individual apart from the world, and second, it construed the temporal world to be apart from God, each irrelevant to the other. Deism was right only in its insistence that the "what" of the world amenable to science and other cognitive endeavors depends on the "that" of divine creation.

Pantheism seems to be the opposite of deism in its claim that God is just the world as a whole. God is not an individual except in the sense the world as a whole is individual, and the world is not apart from God in any sense whatsoever. In addition to the difficulties detailed in Chapter 10, an error of pantheism is that it conceives God to be simply a large temporal individual; pantheism cannot represent the eternity of God.

Pan*en*theism is the view that God is the world plus more, a higher unity. In a sense, creation *ex nihilo* is panentheistic, because the world is the terminus of the divine creative act, and the act and source are not reducible to the world. The eternal life of the divine creation, of God, is more than the temporal lives of the creatures. But what is "more" is not something determinate apart from the world. The "more" is the character God takes on in creating the world and therefore is itself part of the world, "world" being defined as whatever is determinate.

It is far better to describe God as the great living eternal creator within which "we live and move and have our being" (Acts 17:28). God is one, because the act of creation must be unified: it is the ground of all the diversity among the determinate things, the ontological context within which even things' essential features are together in mutual relevance. God is eternal, because within the unity of the creative act all times are together; the eternality of those connections is what makes possible the temporal flow of time. God is living in a superlative sense because the eternal act has as its terminus the infinitely dynamic transformations of the singular time flow of the world.

As living, God is not a form, not a comprehensive Now, not an infinite actuality, not a principle of goodness nor an imitable self-sufficiency. God is the creator present in each thing, moment by moment and in our past and future. Those diverse temporal locations of divine creativity constitute the eternal divine life itself. In itself, the divine life contains our world on its foundations, our beginning and end, our joys and sufferings, regrets and anticipations, all together in the definitive being of the divine act.

O LORD, you have searched me and known me.
You know when I sit down and when I rise up;
    you discern my thoughts from far away.
You search out my path and my lying down,
    and are acquainted with all my ways.
Even before a word is on my tongue,
    O LORD, you know it completely.
You hem me in, behind and before,
    and lay your hand on me.
Such knowledge is too wonderful for me;
    it is so high that I cannot attain it.

Where can I go from your spirit?
    Or where can I flee from your presence?
If I ascend to heaven, you are there;
    if I make my bed in Sheol, you are there.
If I take the wings of the morning
    and settle in the farthest limits of the sea,
even there your hand shall lead me
    and your right hand shall hold me fast.

If I say, "Surely the darkness shall cover me,
    and the light around me become night,"
even the darkness is not dark to you;
    the night is as bright as the day,
    for darkness is as light to you.

For it was you who formed my inward parts;
    you knit me together in my mother's womb.
I praise you, for I am fearfully and wonderfully made.
    Wonderful are your works;
that I know very well.
My frame was not hidden from you,
when I was being made in secret,
    intricately woven in the depths of the earth.
Your eyes beheld my unformed substance.
In your book were written
    all the days that were formed for me,
    when none of them as yet existed.
How weighty to me are your thoughts, O God!
    How vast is the sum of them!
I try to count them — they are
    more than the sand;
    I come to the end — I am still with you.

(Psalm 139)

Part Four

Eternal Life

Chapter Thirteen

THE ETERNAL IDENTITY
OF PERSONS

Immortality and Eternal Life

Part of the time passion of the modern world is a preoccupation with the religious quest for eternal life or immortality. The
preoccupation is both negative and positive. There are people who
go to great lengths to deny the possibility of eternal life, immortality, or an afterlife of any sort. The denials often take the form of an
antisupernaturalism and are made in the name of Enlightenment
rationalism and secular humanism. The positive preoccupations
are fearsome affirmations of the afterlife, tales of dying and
resuscitation shaped to the Bardo Thodol, and New Age channel-
ing from and to "departed" spirits.

These passionate distortions of the time sense, these desperate
attempts to make time be less or more than it is, stem from a true if
misguided feeling for the problematic of eternity. Rather, because
time and eternity are one topic, the passion is a stretching for the
eternity obscured by the modern representation of time.

The great religious and theological traditions have developed
more balanced views through centuries of self-criticism: more
balanced on the one hand and more daring on the other. The
balance comes in putting metaphoric limits on the contexts in
which the great symbols are used. The daring comes in embracing
directly the eternal dimension of life that is *not* to be represented as
just more and better time.

185

Although the distorted time passion of the modern world has
led it to disguise the eternal as immortality, as merely more time,
our discussion has made clear that time and eternity are two
distinct parts of one topic. Time cannot be appreciated in its true
dynamic temporality without eternity, and vice versa. If eternal life
were merely more time, life without the temporal cutoff of death,
neither temporality nor eternity would be grasped in their true
nature. The truth of the matter is that human life is both temporal
and eternal, and not one without the other.

Martin Heidegger was entirely correct to say that the great
question of the twentieth century has been that of Being. He was
also correct to see that at least one way into the question of Being is
through the nature of human being and the human condition. But
he was part of the problem, not of the answer, to associate the
problems of Being and human being with time. He failed to see that
Being and human being are eternal as well as temporal. Hence he
developed a deficient view of temporality that led not to the
religious theme of eternal life but to preoccupation with death
(Wyschogrod 1985). In advocating an authenticity that consists in
"being toward death" while caring for the world, Heidegger
undergirded an excessive individualism that was the opposite of
what he intended but that has become the emblem of the declining
tradition he represented in the twentieth century.

Temporal and Eternal Identity

How is human life constituted by eternity as well as time? What is
human life's eternal dimension in relation to its temporal dimension? At the end of the fourth chapter it was argued that personal
identity requires a peculiar transcendence of the present moment.
A person's identity in the present moment, especially moral identity, is never merely that present moment but is also the eternal
togetherness of all the person's moments in all temporal modes. The
bank robber on trial today includes within today's identity the still
innocent potential bank robber before the robbery and also the
robber actually lifting the money. The home buyer today is also
today the person whose identity includes the possibility of paying
off the mortgage, the possibility of the moment of actually paying it

off, and the possibility of having paid it off. The analysis of the temporal modes in Chapters 5 and 6 and their eternal connections in Chapter 8 have now shown how this is possible. More, those analyses have shown how no mode is possible without being together with the other two; the eternal togetherness of the modes of time is *necessary* for real temporality, for time's flow.

The argument regarding personal identity can now be generalized in summary form. A person's identity consists of all the proper dates of the individual's life eternally together in all the temporal modes. At any one time, there is a serial ordering of dates such that some are then actualized and fixed and others are an ordered, somewhat open future. For *any* and *all* of the person's proper dates as present (except the first and last in obvious ways), this fixed-open cut obtains. And every date is together with all the others as past, as present, and as future. At no present date is it *then* determined what the future will be except as present conditions determine it. But any present date is eternally together with all future dates (and all past dates) in their present and also their past temporal modes. There is no present time at which all dates are future, except before birth, nor at which all dates are past, except after death. Yet within the set of proper dates of a person's life, each date is eternally together with all the other dates as each of them is future, present, and past.

The argument from Chapter 4 concerning the bank robber and the mortgagee shows how the present is together with past and future if it is to be present at all. That is, in addition to the ways by which the past is inherited into the present, say in memory or causal traces, and to the ways by which the future is anticipated in the present, the real past of the actual robbery (and the innocence of the previous day) and the real future of the possible payoff are eternally together with the present to give the present its meaning as morally connected with the past and future.

An analogous argument holds for the togetherness of the present and future with the past in order for the past to be past. A past moment could not be in the past of time's flow without subsequent present moments to add to its meaning and without shifting futures to extend its structure. Similarly, an analogous argument holds for the future's eternal need for the past to give it specific diversity to unify and for present moments to shift its possibilities toward actualities.

Within time, then, a person's identity is wholly temporal with meaning derivative from the eternal connections of temporality. Within time, a person is responsible for the actualities of the individual's accumulated identity in the past and is responsible also at the present moment for refining the humanly relevant open future. Precisely because the present fixes itself as past, the person is finite and lives cumulatively and asymmetrically from earlier to later times. Only at death, when there is no more relevant open future, is the person's responsibility for life over. The actual life lived, with all the points of personal responsibility, with all the conditions of identity and change, is definitive of the person. Within time, that life is set with the finiteness of the past-future cut for each present existential moment. Within time, each present moment is together with the future moments as *possibilities* for present action and past fact, not as existentially present or actually past. Every religious tradition has symbols for the finitude, inexorability, and singularity of temporal life.

Most of all, life is a problem of how to live toward death with accumulated actual identity. The past is now gone and cannot be changed, only taken responsibility for; the future is not yet and may hold no promise of a second chance. Karma is the Indian way of understanding this; judgment, guilt, and the possibility of redemption the Western.

Within eternity, however, a person's life as temporal is whole: whole as an infant laboring with innocence and a dreadful future, whole as a mature person coping with past and future obligations, whole as a person stepping into chilly Jordan. Eternally a person is *not* just who that person is now. Eternally the individual is what the person could be, what the person comes to be, and what the person is and has been relative to what the person could have been. Within eternity, the person is never only at a present moment, never only faced with a future, never only a finished story but eternally all three. Within eternity the person is responsible as an innocent, responsible as a chooser, and responsible as a finished life. Within eternity, each future date is together with each present as existentially present and actual fact, as well as possibly present and actual. Within eternity the past is never gone and the future is never not yet; within eternity personal identity is whole.

Do we live then in time or eternity, or both? Both, of course; but this is problematic. While we are living, with some future to be realized, we are not fully eternal at any present moment. There is a gap between our existential reality fixed by the proper date of the present and our eternal identity that will not be fixed in time until death, albeit fixed in eternity. Precisely because we are temporal, we cannot gainsay that temporal task and pretend to be living as if everything were over. Eternally it is not over until temporal life has been lived through. Without the fullness of our time, we are incomplete as temporal beings, and our eternal identity is only as temporal beings.

Death's Allure

Now the allure of death is apparent. Not only an escape from pain and failure, not only a return to the womb, not only the entrancing opiate of oblivion, death beckons as the completion of temporal identity and the full achievement of who we are eternally. Our eternal identity is worked out in time precisely because each moment of life must be lived through as present, made to be actual, deciding the possibilities.

The allure of death is ambiguous, however, because who we are in time is who we are actually. A life badly lived is eternally badly lived. A life unredeemed is eternally unredeemed. A life lived well is eternally well-lived, but who fails to think that things could have been done better? One of the great joys of getting older can be the sense of satisfaction and self-actualization that comes from having lived as one has and having made the choices (especially the hard ones) one has made. Even if the major decisions are satisfying, however, no one is satisfied with all the minor ones.[1] The significance of the actual historicity of time lies in the religious doctrine of judgment. The temporal identity we are given by circumstance and give ourselves by choice is also the eternal identity that is the whole truth about us.

Consciousness of personal identity thus must be bifocal. On the one hand, within time we are temporally situated with a fixed past and open future, surrounded by morally freighted elements.

On the other hand, within eternity this situatedness is but part of the story. As temporal beings we do not have any eternal vision. We can imagine our eternal identity only from the standpoint of an eternal God. At any finite time we cannot know much of our future and have forgotten much of our past. But by identifying with the divine eternal context we can approach our eternal identity as a mystery that bears on present conduct.

The chief instance of the relevance of our eternal identity for present conduct is in the approach toward death. On the one hand, we are *at least mortal.* We are responsible for our time, for facing up to the finite options of our future, for actually choosing over the finite course of life, and for coming to terms responsibly with what we have done. Every moment, every year, every lifetime is to be lived through only once, and what we do relative to the temporal dimensions of that time is what constitutes our finite and actual identity.

The sense of immortality to be denied in conjunction with this point is the popular view that there is always more time so that nothing counts irrevocably. In common piety we can always profess remorse at sins and a desire to wake up to the important religious demands, and then back-slide to the old bondage and spiritual unconsciousness with the confidence that "later" we will get serious. Against this the great religions teach mortality: "To-night might be your last so repent now!" "Be here now!" "Wake up!" "Live toward death, not away from it!"

The great religions all know that even when life after death is used to symbolize the eternity of human life, this does not mean merely more of the same, like a resuscitated corpse. Lazarus was significant not because of his new life but because of the surprising divine power exercised by Jesus in recalling him from the dead. Buddhist karma is not mere continuance of life, but another life in another body, with new chances and circumstances. For those religions that believe in reincarnation, the succession of lives is never taken to mean that we can do anything we want because there are an infinite number of extra chances. On the contrary, the doctrine of karma says that everything we do in a finite time is fixed and consequential, not only for this life but for all successive ones. Contrary to what Western critics sometimes think, reincarnation and karma *increase* the sense of responsibility in the finite, hence of the significance of mortality: each deed, each life, is dead, fixed, and influential once it happens. So we are at least mortal.

The eternal dimension of human life certifies, however, that mortality is not the last word. When thinking about the ending of our time, there is a greater meaning to life than its simple conclusion. Therefore, religious sensibilities have often expressed the eternal dimension in a denial of mortality even while recognizing that something nontemporal is at stake. Popular representations of the life of the faithful in heaven, or of the unfaithful in hell, in Hindu, Buddhist, Taoist, Christian, Jewish, and Muslim traditions, have many differences regarding entrance requirements, length of stay, emoluments, catch-22s, and circumstances. Yet they are agreed in being fantastic. Everyone down to the least sophisticated understands them to be fantastical representations of what cannot be really as the representations depict. This is so both for those who have some other idea about what might be more accurately descriptive and those who think exclusively in the terms of the fantastical representations. Temporal life of the sort we know on earth, be we rich or poor, is simply not enough to be the added meaning people feel when they stretch for eternity, even when we can imagine expressions of that added meaning only as qualifications or transformations of that temporal life.

The Western philosophical tradition itself has recognized this, the tradition that so often has been pitted in skepticism against religion. In Plato's Phaedo, Socrates, who is about to be executed, conducts an extended inquiry into the question of whether the soul, especially his, is immortal; the dramatic point is to give comfort to one of his disciples who has lost control in premature grief. One after the other, the traditional arguments for the immortality of the soul, as well as some original with Plato, are reviewed and refuted. In the end, Socrates says "Nevertheless!" and proceeds to tell a myth of passage through the underworld that makes life worth living and death worth bearing, to the relief of all. The message is that, even though immortality is not exactly failure to die, or even a continued life, the meaning of life is more than its apparent temporal structure would suggest. Life is eternal as well as temporal.

Some process theologians have argued for what is called *objective immortality;* namely, the doctrine that a religiously significant sense of immortality is that one's life continues to be influential in subsequent events. Not denying that one's subjectivity ceases with death, the doctrine of objective immortality asserts that part of one's reality consists in the effects one continues to have in what comes after death. Religiously this has been an important dimension of reverence of ancestors, who continue to be immortal so long as they are remembered. Some African tribal religions and Chinese Confucianism find much of the holy in the sustaining of immortality in memory. Some process theologians argue that the world is too fickle to keep objective immortality going very long, and that God's memory by contrast is infallible in this respect. Thus, individuals are objectively immortal because God remembers them and makes them a part of the divine life after they cease their subjective reality. Whatever truth there is in any of these senses of objective immortality—subsequent events, human remembrance, divine memory—objective immortality is not the continuation of consciousness or subjectivity. Objective immortality recognizes that a person's responsible life is bounded by birth and death, however far its moral and other consequences might reach. Objective immortality is not religiously significant as a denial of death or finitude.

Having admitted the importance of affirming death as the *eternal* actualization of responsibility, the point at which Heidegger was correct, the importance of the eternity of human life must also be affirmed to understand the being of humanity. Heidegger said that death constitutes the temporal horizon within which we find meaning. That is plainly false. We are part of natural processes billions of years old and that have an unimaginable future. We play roles in food chains and construct and deconstruct the biological niches in which we and other species live. We are parts of families that antedate and will succeed us, parts of societies and processes of civilization. Although our roles vary from the trivial to the important in all of these, the limitations of our birth and death may be hardly important at all for these processes. Regarding most of the affairs in which we participate, to "live toward death" would be outrageous narcissism.

Furthermore, for us to focus on our own death, however important that might be for bringing us to attention regarding responsibility, is to capitulate to individualism. For, other people, social structures, institutions, and nature would be interesting only insofar as they play roles within the horizon defined by death. The life of the community, and the larger community with nature, is not all that much defined by the mortal horizon of any one individual. There were doubtless many roots to Heidegger's Nazism beside his attempt to use notions of time to do the work of eternity. The preoccupation with death and the substitution of a mythic past for eternal identity were not inconsequential, however.

By some irony, opposite to Heidegger's preoccupation with time is the focus of the Kyoto School on the present as the locus of being and nonbeing. Nishida (1987, pp. 128–136) said that the present is the temporal locus of motion, which alone is actual; it is the locus of the act of will that transcends immediate consciousness. The past has no absolute and fixed reality, only the spatialized reality that consciousness gives it. Some process theologians join the Kyoto School in claiming that the past is gone and the future not yet, and that therefore the present is the only reality. By virtue of the creativity expressed in the present, according to the process conception, there is a simulacrum of eternity. But this is only to confuse time and eternity, however, not to acknowledge them both. Because of the denial of reality to the past and future, neither the Kyoto School nor the Hartshornean process theologians can acknowledge persuasively the dynamic character of time nor cumulative responsibility. And because eternity is represented only by creativity constituting change, not constituting a genuine new reality, the dimension of creation *ex nihilo* is lost from the Kyoto and process theories. Both temporal finitude finalized as death and the eternal life by which we are more than any or all of our times in the mode of the present are necessary to understand the being of the human or the world's Being.

Several references have been made to the individualism that results from the existentialist focus on death. The point needs to be stressed more positively. The eternity of human life is not merely the eternal togetherness of different dates of a person's life. Our eternity is also an eternal connection with absolutely everything else in the cosmos with respect to which we are determinate. Thus we are in necessary connection with one another, with nature, and with the social institutions and habits that mediate our conditional interactions. Our eternal individual identities are part of a larger eternal community of identities. We are together not only conditionally—although that surely is true—but also ontologically. The specific characters of our community are given by the various conditional features by virtue of which we are determinately related. But the being of the community itself is an ontological fact. For this reason, the metaphor of "covenant" has high plausibility for articulating the normative dimensions of the human condition that will have to be discussed shortly (Neville 1991b, Chapter 5). The covenant idea will be introduced at greater length in Chapter 14.

Judgment: Standing in Eternity

As alluded to earlier, the eternal identity of persons means that they live "under judgment," to use the biblical phrase. In this relativistic age, concentrated on living for the moment, that conclusion may be even more startling, surely more threatening, than the claim that people have eternal identities. The argument that the human condition is to live under judgment thus deserves to be laid out at greater length.

That there are normative dimensions, for instance matters of justice and morality, of beauty and piety, or truth and the representation of value, is not genuinely deniable. A scheme for classifying the normative dimensions shall be presented in the next chapter, although little store needs to be set by this or any other scheme. That there are normative dimensions to life means that we live up to the norms where they are relevant or we fail to do so; the most usual case is that we honor them in part and fail them in part. Taking "moral identity" in the broadest sense, the moral identity of most of us is a mixture of rectitude and guilt.

The eternity of human life has a special relevance for our temporal situation with regard to the normative dimensions; namely, that we are now and at all times under judgment. Being "under judgment" is complex. It does not mean that there is some external conscious judge thinking approving or disapproving thoughts. It means rather that our moral identity is exactly what it is, eternally and through time, for better or worse. Thus, at any given time, we not only have a fixed past and a future to be affected by our present choices; we also are the ones who once had an open future and chose to fix it; and we are the ones who will have to live responsibly in the future we are determining now. The issue eternity presents for our temporal situation is that any temporal worth to our present actions has larger consequences in establishing our eternal moral identity. What we do, relative to the normative dimension of what we ought to do, defines us as not only as eternally actual but as eternally under judgment for what we ideally ought to be. Our moral identity is eternally what it is.

The eternal character of our temporal life is often something like this. In childhood we are morally innocent, but in youth assert the rights of our desires and self-esteem over some of the standard normative dimensions shaping social life. Then we settle down, identify with the norms of social institutions important for work, friendship, and family life, and amend our youthful ways, making amends where possible. The responsible life of active people is hedged about by a near infinity of obligations because most of us have to take shortcuts and compromise; the more morally earnest attempt on balance to address the most important obligations, but we all fail at some things while succeeding nobly at others. Perhaps toward the end of life, like Cephalos in Plato's Republic, we focus special attention of paying up past moral debts. For each individual, there is an eternal moral identity that embraces something like this pattern. Eternally the person was an innocent child, eternally a heedless youth, eternally a morally committed but compromised adult, eternally a senior looking back to win justification. Eternally we are all these together. This means that as we stand in eternity we are under judgment day by day and, at death, cumulatively. No wonder the prospect of death, even of an eternal life in the sense specified here, is marvelously acute in focusing concentration on salvation.

Our dual identity as temporal and eternal means we cannot be only secular but also live within the religious dimension, even if only in denial. We are not only persons of moral identity, but also persons under eternal judgment.

Chapter Fourteen

THE DIVINE IDENTITY
OF PERSONS

Participation in the Divine Life

The eternal identity of persons is part of the eternity of the divine creative act, according to the arguments of the preceding chapter. Therefore, all that has been said previously about eternal life for persons needs to be reinterpreted with respect to the ways in which human eternal life is part of the divine life. Eternity itself is not the whole issue. The eternal divine creative act is productive of all of time's flow. Even the temporal parts of human identity thus are part of the eternal life of God, indeed, the dynamic part. Human *being,* temporal and eternal, needs interpretation as part of the life of God.

This way of thinking, equating the human with the divine by some kind of reference to participation, is associated more with Orthodox Christianity than with Roman Catholic or Protestant, more with many kinds of Hinduism rather than with Jainism, more with Mahayana Buddhism than with Theravada, more with Taoism than with Confucianism, more with Sufism and Cabbala than with mainline Muslim and Jewish groups. Counterbalancing the association of the human with the divine is a dissociation based on fear of idolatry. The human is *not* the divine in so many ways, and abuses of pretense and authority are tempting when that warning fails of being heeded. Nevertheless, in each of the religious traditions there are important senses in which the heart of human life is to become more nearly divine, closer to the divine, more nearly fulfilled in divine ways. The logic of the present position regarding time and eternity is that the eternal dimension of human life is explicitly part of the divine life. The question to be explored here is, just what part?

The answer to be offered is that human individuals are part of the divine life in three ways: as participants in cosmic process, as bearers of divine creativity, and as contingent pointers to divine infinity and freedom. These three ways correspond to the three elements that constitute divinity: God as given character by the created world that is the terminus of the divine creative act, God as the creative act itself, and God as the unconditioned source of the creative act, the source that is not determinate except as being the source of the determinate world. These three elements of divinity are distinguishable but not separable. The source is not source except in creating. The creative act has no character except from what it creates and its asymmetrical power of making mediates between the source for which nothing is necessary and the world whose very being is entirely contingent. The world has the integrity of its own specific character but the power of its existence comes from the creative act and its contingency depends for actuality on God as source. The discussion will deal with each of these aspects, beginning with persons playing roles in cosmic processes.

Cosmic Processes

Chapters 2 and 13 made much of the senses in which various times in an individual's life are eternally together, constituting the person's eternal identity. An analogous point needs to be stressed about a person's eternal togetherness, as well as temporal continuities, with all the other things with respect to which the person is determinate. The basic argument can be reviewed briefly for the purpose of guarding against an insidious individualism that easily associates itself with a concern for personal judgment and salvation.[1]

A person at some one, several, or all times in life is determinate with respect to a variety of other things. These other things might overlap the person's own time, come before or after it, be near or far, and involve various kinds of causal or contextual connections. The other things make a difference to the person, and these differences are rendered in the person's conditional features. The person might also condition the other things in various respects. All determinations of some things by others are functions of conditional features. All temporal and spatial relations are expressed in conditional features.

Persons, like any other determinate thing, are harmonies of essential and conditional features. The essential features are those that integrate the conditional ones and give positive uniqueness or ownbeing to the things. Without the essential ones, there would be no conditional features, and vice versa. Therefore, for things to be conditionally together with spatial, temporal, and other causal relations, they must be together as whole harmonies. Things must be together in such ways as their essential features are together, and these are explicitly not conditional ways; rather, their ontological togetherness is an ontological context of mutual relevance.

The hypothesis presented earlier is that they are together by virtue of being created *ex nihilo*. The ontologically creative act is the context of mutual relevance, and only by virtue of the eternal unity of this act can there be temporal relations among the creatures with changing moments of present existence. Time's flow is made possible by eternal togetherness.

The character of the creative act is constituted by the determinate things created, and its dynamism is constituted by their temporal pulse. Physical cosmology describes that character as the dynamic of the expansion of energy and matter since the Big Bang; human beings are but tiny evanescent knots of gravitic and kinetic forces. The universe has evolved into galaxies of suns and their planetary systems.

On at least one planet the molecular structures have coalesced to form proteins, living organisms, a variegated system of ecological niches, and the human species. In the natural history of evolution, human beings are late arrivals whose origin depended on very specialized niches but whose adaptability to various niches rivals the rat and roach. With the possibility of radical transformation of the earthly ecology and space travel, the future of the human species is highly unpredictable. On a cosmic scale, however, persons are members of a species that requires a peculiar balance of matter and energy that might not be characteristic of more than this epoch. Occupying this epochal place in cosmic and natural history is an important if universal and often unnoticed condition for all persons. So far, human beings have done very little to condition the basic processes of the cosmic epoch, compared to the evolution of hydrogen, say, and have done little more to affect the natural history of planet Earth, compared to chlorophyl, E. coli, or grazing animals. Current ecological crises consisting in rising temperatures caused by human industry and destruction of the ozone layer by the human production of otherwise scarce chemicals might make human beings more important determinative conditions within natural history. In all these natural dynamics, the human roles, however small and trivial, are eternally constitutive.

With social processes persons take part in the development of civilizations and the building of their own cultures. These too are parts of the internal dynamic life of God the creator. Within the life of God we are together with our forgotten ancestors and our unimagined progeny; perhaps even more important than biological connections, we are together with the antecedents and conse-quences of our culture. More specifically, we are parts of our own local communities, which are embedded in larger societies across the globe. What we do in our neighborhood often has determinable consequences, and the circumstances of our local environs are highly determinative of our own lives. The career of each person cuts through economic and political conditions, through ethnic, religious, and artistic customs, through legal, educational, and class structures, and a host of other systematically structured institutions. Persons are conditioned by and condition each of these, in greater and lesser degrees.

This review of the obvious is intended to call attention to the fact that individuals are not defined individually but by their connections with the other things and organized systems with respect to which they are determinate. Until this point in the discussion it has been possible to ignore the larger setting for individual life as if it were an unimportant abstraction. Yet these connections and their further connections to distant things are what constitute the solidarity of people with the rest of the things making up the divine life. The creation of the vast dynamic of the universe, temporally unfolding and eternally together, is the content of the life of God, of which each person is a small part as determined by participation in all the processes, natural, interpersonal, and institutional. The determinate identity of each of us is constituted conditionally by relations with other persons, nature, and institutions, each changing as we ourselves change.

Some religious thinkers have seen a purposive plan to the cosmic project. Some have taken the integration of diverse species and otherwise separate natural processes into organic ecologies to be indicative of purpose. Yet it is hard to imagine what divine purpose might consist of when projected to a truly cosmic scale: perfect entropic dissipation of energy? Ecologies and other examples of organic harmony seem to be particularly fragile and dependent on the parts being so attuned they just fit together. One need not take the step of affirming an anthropomorphic purpose to the cosmic project of divine creation.

Within the cosmos, particularly the human sphere, there clearly are better and worse ways of behaving; and human life is defined in part by the differing values in the possibilities open to it, by the obligations these values lay on action, and by the moral identity actualized by how well we fulfill obligations. The meaningfulness of human life consists in the semiotic structures of language, institutions, and other symbolic representations and in how well we behave relative to these representations. Individuals and institutions have purposes, even if the larger cosmos does not, and these purposes are part of a person's life within the divine life. That we should understand the individual's participation in society and the larger networks of nature as part of the divine life rather than merely the secular way things are is an important thesis.

Shift the focus now from our own participation in the cosmic project to the constitution of the cosmic project in the divine creative act. From the divine perspective, we are seen as parts of the larger swarm of processes. Whether or not we are important, we are essential parts of the *haecceity,* the thisness, of the divine life. Without us, the divine life would be different. Therefore, we should think of ourselves not only as eternal but as divine, or at least as part of the divine. Whether this is a comfort depends on how well we fulfill our local purposes. Though we stand under judgment, the divine has an investment in the outcome.

Divine Creativity

The second sense in which persons are participants in the divine is that individuals are bearers of divine creativity. The most obvious sense in which this is so concerns persons in present time. Whatever is given to an emerging present moment, the reality of that moment is its spontaneous working up of that given stuff into the new reality of the moment. The present does not exist in space or time but rather *becomes* a space-time entity. When it has become it is past. The spontaneous creativity in the present is part of the divine creative act. Although spontaneous in the sense that the creativity is something over and above the past events that are given, the present creativity is not entirely random. Two kinds of limitations obtain. On the one hand, spontaneity is limited by the formal properties of the future. On the other hand, it is limited by the actual structures of the past. The formal properties of the future not only determine internal conditions of unity for the emerging present, but also the connective forms relating this space-time present with others in a field. The actual structures of the past are what they are and can be combined or reconfigured only in ways that respect their fixed actuality. Where the possibilities and actualities allow only one way of emerging, the spontaneous present is deterministic; only the existential reality of the moment is novel. But it appears that the past can be integrated in many ways and that possibilities are not always few.

Present spontaneity in human beings is not particularly interesting unless the alternate outcomes at stake have semiotic significance on the scale of human meaning. Those that do are outcomes that express or deviate from previously developed character, that make a causal difference beyond the immediacy of the moment to other things that are semiotically representable, that have different worths relative to the ideals of action, and so forth. Present spontaneity is surely a part of the larger eternal act of divine creativity, such that divine creativity is present in any present, and thus is trivial as such. What makes the present divine creativity interesting is its making a difference to the semiotically interesting alternatives. When the creativity is the person's making a choice that determines the individual's character or causes a significant consequent, then creativity is interesting.

Persons of course also bear divine creativity in the mode of the past. All of the past conditions that enter into a present moment were once themselves present moments with spontaneous divine creativity. And their past components were once present as well, so on back indefinitely. If God were temporal and were only present, it still would be the case, as Hartshorne has argued (1962), that God never confronts past conditions that God had not influenced creatively at some previous time.

Similarly, people bear divine creativity in the mode of the future. In the present, the future is constituted by formal properties for things. Form itself is a condition for actualization and hence is created. Furthermore, future possibilities are options for what will be present creativity when the possibility comes to its own present time.

Therefore, at any present time, a person bears divine creativity in the past and future as well as the present. Moreover, even at a present time a person has an eternal identity, and eternal connections with processes of great extension. In consequence, in a person's eternal identity the person bears divine creativity in all its modes, as present, past, and future for each of the dates of the person's life.

The religious significance of bearing divine creativity was expressed well by Tillich (1951; 1952) in his theory of the power of being. That power is felt within one's own being, not only in the present but in the past and future as well. It is also felt in other things that are seen sometimes as expressions of the uncanny. Sometimes persons, events, or places can become particularly significant for the power of divine creativity in them. In principle, any person, event, or place could be so significant; yet in practice the perception of the divine in things requires a jarring dislocation of the ordinary cosmological connections of things that focuses attention on the ontological character of contingency.

Divine Infinity and Freedom

The reference to contingency calls attention to the third sense in which persons are part of the divine life; namely, as pointing to

God as the unconditioned source of the created order. This sense is peculiar because here people are witnesses to what they are not. Persons', indeed the world's, very contingency is a witness to the independence of the source on which we are contingent. Mystics in all traditions articulate this as they traverse the path of conditions to grounds or heights of uncontingency. Of course, insofar as the created world consists of all things determinate, the creator is the abyss, the great nothingness whose only character is to be the source of other things.

That persons in their contingency witness to God as source is not a function of their experiencing God as such. Regardless of experience, people are signs of God's aseity simply by virtue of being ontologically contingent. If someone were to read the sign, that part of the ontology of human being would be recognized.

The eternity of human identity is to be construed as part of the divine life in three complex senses. Because the whole of creation in its dynamic temporal unfolding is the inner life of the eternal creator, persons participate in God through their participation in those cosmic and social processes. Because that eternal life has its being as the terminus of the divine creative act, persons bear that creativity in the temporal and eternal ways they combine present, past, and future. Because human life and its worldly context are contingent on the asymmetrical productive act of creation, persons' contingency testifies to the aseity of God as source of all determinateness.

Participation in, the bearing of, and the witness to God as creator are the ontological parts of human life. In all these senses persons, and their societies and world, have divine identity.

The Religious Significance of Natural Eternity

This consequence means that persons are both naturally eternal and naturally part of the divine. Important as the complexities of this natural eternity and divinity are for understanding human ontology, the point is surprisingly flat from a religious point of view. Surely, from a religious point of view, what we do, or what God does specifically in and about us, makes a difference. What is the difference? Here is the point at which the popular religious representation of eternal life as immortality or life after death is on target. If we live beyond death, then there must be some place or quality of life to which we come that reflects the quality of our spiritual character before death. However fantastical, the representations of heavens and hells make the religious point about eternal life: do we get what we deserve?

To understand this question it is necessary to recur to the problem of the normative dimension of life and judgment. There are ideals bearing on most of what we can control. Although there have been many classifications of ideals in the history of religions and philosophies, the following reflects the cosmological structure that has been developed here (see also Neville 1991b, Chapter 5).

Every determinate thing, as we saw in Chapter 11, has a form with which it harmonizes its components; it also fits into larger forms. Every thing also has components stemming from various natural and social processes, components that in some instances are partly independent of their conjunction in the thing. Besides form and components, every thing is an actual mixture of these two, not just a possible formation of components by the form but an actualization of a structure that, when past, is fixed and concrete; the mixture of things is an engagement with the particular existential world. Finally, every thing, in its actual mixture of form and components, achieves some value or worth, both intrinsically and as a function within the larger context.

For human beings who have some real control over what they do and how they make their world and their own moral identity these four transcendental components of determinate things give rise to four kinds of ideals. Relative to form, there are ideals of righteousness and justice, the bringing of the best possible order to human affairs. Relative to components, there are ideals of piety, of recognizing and paying deference to the intrinsic nature and worth of the components of things, regardless of how they fit into the larger forms structuring human life. Put religiously, piety approximates attending to the world from the creator's point of view, appreciating every individual thing and process for its own loveliness and as the center of its own environment, without reducing it to some instrumental role in the economy of human justice. Relative to the actual existential mixture of things, there are ideals of authenticity and engagement, what Tillich (1952) called *faith* or the courage to accept one's circumstances and deal with them. The dialectic of engagement, authenticity, or faith has been developed by twentieth century existentialists, and it is not reducible either to righteousness or piety. Relative to value, each person has the religious task of finding a destiny or centered path of development in the world; the path has elements of righteousness, piety, and faith, but it is not reducible to them. The virtue of pursuing the religious Tao is hope.

The Covenant Conception of the Human Context

So righteousness, piety, faith, and hope are cardinal religious ideals, ideals that obtain transcendentally because every thing in every situation, including every person, has form, components to be formed, the actual mixture of form and components, and value. Furthermore, these ideals obtain with regard to any individual's relations with other people, nature, and the institutions that give human meaning, structuring the relations among people and natural elements. The way the Western "Abrahamic" religions have understood this situation is to say that people are created to be in covenant.

The covenant includes relations among people, with nature, and concerning the care of institutions; these relations are governed by the ideals of righteousness, piety, faith, and hope. Summing up both the diversity of types of ideals and the covenant or nature-person-institution character of the subjects of action, the ideal in the West as in the East is to love. Love is the ideal harmonizing all the rest, not according to a special formula or algorithm but according to a special creative force: love *makes* things with good form, respectable value, engaged actuality, and with directions guided by hope for centered destiny. This love is the human counterpart to divine creation, which creates things *ex nihilo* with good form, components, actual mixture, and appropriate value. As God's creation can be designated a kind of ontological love, so can human ideals for behavior within the creation. Indeed, the ideals of loving the creation are like those of loving God as creator of the creation. According to Jesus in the Great Commandment: Love the Lord your God with all your heart, with all your soul, and with all your mind. Love your neighbor as yourself (Matthew 22:37–38).

Within the created context in which we actually live and within which we must act relative to the ideals of righteousness, piety, faith, hope, and summarily, love, we fail miserably, even the best of us. The character we have worked out for ourselves, that we have been taught as children and pass on, that is as true for East as for the West, for the South as for the North, is the habit of choosing often the unrighteous rather than the righteous order, of behaving impiously regarding the components of the world where we could have been respectful, of alienating ourselves in fear rather than engaging in faith, of succumbing to despair rather than pressing onward with hope, and of lapsing into tired hatred rather than rising to creative love.

Some thinkers have attempted to supply a motive for this failure, for instance selfishness, pride, or lust for power. But these are themselves failures of the ideals. Basic choices are not made because of motives but simply by the choosing, and the alleged "justification" is turned into the motive by the choice itself. The fall into sin, or ignorance, or selfish disharmony is one for which we are morally culpable. As many religions put it, we are "born good," but somehow inevitably go wrong. Even if the choice is not attributed to the responsibility of each and every individual, our social structures are at least partly unjust, our social habits lack piety, our culture is filled with faithless alienation, and religion in the sense defined here is taken by many to be a hopeless enterprise.

Therefore, despite the fact that each and every thing is part of the eternal life of God, people and their institutions, and maybe even some parts of nature, exist in a *broken* covenant.[2] Sinful, ignorant, or ontologically disharmonious, people ordinarily are not what they should be either in their persons or in their society. Their actual status, under judgment, is thus a betrayal of their ontological status as parts of the divine. Divine elements they are, but failed divine elements. The very character of their religious path is to correct this and fulfill the ideals defining their situation. The problem of salvation is precisely to go from the actual human condition to the ideal one and thus to be not only parts of God but normatively good parts.

The divine identity of persons is not only in their natural eternity and various ways of being part of the God as creator, but is also defined by the general ideal of divinization. Specifically, that ideal is to reconcile the actual affairs of human life with the ideals, at least insofar as we can affect things within our neighborhood. Sometimes this has been described as the process of sanctification, or the pursuit of sagehood, or the way of the Bodhisattva or Arhat, or the holy person or saint. These representations tend to individualistic connotations. Yet what is needed is a restoration of the covenant, a mending of the forms, a recalling to deference, a new courage, and a hope despite despair for all people, nature, and institutions. Reconciliation of the actual with the ideal is not just a matter of intention but of actual accomplishment. It is a real achievement within the life of God.

If God were conceived to be an agent separate from us with a separate consciousness and intentions, then the situation described would be impossible regarding human freedom. Either our broken condition would be the result of God's will, because it is created, or it would be the result of our wills frustrating the creator's intent. The first denies the freedom and responsibility we obviously have, and the second suggests that the creator is not lord of our hearts, indeed is not fully creator. Hence the importance of bearing constantly in mind that the creator is not an independent being but the tripartite creating of the world. We are made in a context with ideals and capacities somewhat to control behavior. Our decisions then are both functions of the larger eternal divine creative act and our own responsible determinations of our moral character. God is not to be ascribed a moral character that instead is a function of the personal choices we have made. God is to be ascribed the character of a creator of a world with partially self-determining people in it, obliged by ideals of righteousness, piety, faith, hope, and love. Part of the divine character is determined by how well we live up to those obligations. Our obligation to do so comes from the ideals, not from any coercion of our wills.

Salvation: Redeeming the Time

Salvation consequently is the problem of redeeming the time. Individually and collectively, we *are* our time, and we are that eternally. The metaphor of divine judgment need not suggest that in addition to who we are there is another subject who divinely casts a judgment on us. Rather, the divinity in the metaphor makes us conceive God's judgment as an eternal registration of exactly who we are, relative to what we could and should be. There is no room for alteration or cheating in the judgment: it is an exact registration of a part of eternity in eternity. The eternal quality of temporal life ensures divine judgment everywhere and always. Because every temporal moment has its place in eternity, every moment is under judgment, indeed three judgments—as future, present, and past.

The religious problem of salvation is therefore not solved by attaining to eternal life. We have eternal life willy nilly. Precisely because our temporal life with its achievements and failures is eternal, it is ultimately serious and eternally under judgment. Those religious symbols that represent eternal life as immortality, not dying, or returning to life after death are then correct to ask about heaven and hell to solve the problem of place in the afterlife. Eternal life is something we have naturally, as a result of being temporal. Because we are eternally under judgment there has to be an eternal "place" for us.

But of course the afterlife symbol of eternal life cannot be taken literally because what is eternal is precisely our finite life with its temporal boundaries. As an empirical fact, reincarnation might be true; indeed, there might be a series of lives on several planes of existence, as Gnostics and some Hindus believe. Those temporal extensions do not constitute the special quality of eternity, however; eternity is the togetherness of the temporal modes no matter how extended or through what permutations.

The true religious problem occasioned by natural eternity is how to cope with the particularity of divine judgment. That is, how can we live eternally as holy people, given the fact that any way we live constitutes our eternal identity?

The logic of salvation common to most of the world's great religions is something like this. The ordinary human condition is to be focused on the temporality of things alone: to be lost in ignorance of the eternal, to be in bondage to sin, to suffer from the vicissitudes of temporal attachments, to be selfish for gain, or competitive. Each of these leads to unrighteousness, impiety, faithlessness, and despair. Salvation starts with enlightenment, symbolic or otherwise, about the eternal dimension of things and especially about how the eternal is the truth and source of our being, the creator who loves the creatures, the compassion to liberate people from the sufferings of temporal attachment, the power of harmonization that makes one's self part of one body with all things, the generative Tao that lets us swim easily in the moving Tao of things. Salvation's effect is to return our attention to the temporal from the perspective of the eternal. The problems of daily affairs can then be given their true weight relative to the path of spirit and justice, things in the world are to be loved and our character and institutions developed to effect that love, the suchness of things is to be grasped as the eternity of the temporal, our destiny as vehicles of harmonization is to be discovered and pursued, and life is to be cultivated to be the simple, spontaneous temporal expression of the Tao beyond naming. There are many important differences between Hinduism, Christianity, Buddhism, Confucianism, and Taoism and differences within these traditions. Nevertheless, the rough contours of the logic of salvation as sketched in the analogues expressed here are common to these and other traditions. The metaphysical commitment in them all is that temporal human reality is part of a larger reality, the eternal life of God; and the eternal divine life contains within it norms for persons and perhaps others to satisfy.

The chief problem of conceiving salvation is to understand how God on the one hand can be so close as to be creator, in whose eternal dynamic life we are parts, and on the other hand can be "other" to the point of addressing the broken human condition. How can God be with "with us" and not merely "merely us" or "over against us"?

Chapter Fifteen

GOD WITH US

The Otherness of God

Paul Tillich, in a remarkable paper entitled "The Two Types of Philosophy of Religion" (1959, p. 10), wrote, "One can distinguish two ways of approaching God: the way of overcoming estrangement and the way of meeting a stranger." Like Tillich's, the theory presented here of the eternity of a person's life within the eternal life of God belongs to the former type, which he called *ontological.* God the creator is not a separate being whom we might or might not encounter within the cosmos, as depicted by what Tillich called the *cosmological type.* Nevertheless, we must ask how human beings can be estranged from God if God is not then in some important sense a stranger. The other side of the question, asked in the previous chapter, is, how can God be apart from us enough to save us?

This problem is by no means confined to Western theistic religions. If reality is the Tao, and we are all part of the Tao, how can we depart from the Tao? How is it possible to return to the Tao if there is nowhere else? If Brahman is all truth, and consciousness itself is atman and Brahman, how can we be ignorant? How can we need enlightenment? If the true nature of every person is to be the Buddha, to embody the Buddha mind, why is this not obvious? Why do we need to take the Bodhisattva's vow of lifetimes of devotion to the enlightenment of others if we and the others are already Buddha?

The point of raising this question is not to revisit the problem of accounting for human sin. Enough has been said in the previous chapter about our self-constitution as failures with respect to righteousness, piety, faithfulness, hope, and love to indicate that we both choose sin, ignorance, and disharmony and structure our society and its institutions to teach failure and perversity to others, especially to the next generation.

Rather, the point of raising the question is to ask how God can act toward us to address and help remedy the human need for salvation. How can God be separate enough from us to be salvific if God is the one in whom we participate as creatures in the divine life? Or, if God is basically and most nearly literally to be understood as creator in the senses explored earlier, with what right, and within what metaphoric limits, do we look to divine providence, intervention, and succor? If we were not fallen in any sense, not sinful, ignorant, nor disharmonious and if we were self-consciously at ease with our place in the divine life understood both eternally and temporally, then perhaps there would never be an occasion to symbolize God as "other." Theistic language would likely be useless, and we would rather enjoy simply the gift of temporal and eternal being in connection with the rest of what we could attend. But this is not our situation. The religious concern with eternal life is not merely about our natural eternity but eternity under judgment and in need of salvation. How can we participate more in the normative aspects of the divine life? How can we be more Godlike? Closer to God? These questions suppose that God antecedently is in some important religious sense "other."

The metaphysical groundwork for this problem was laid in earlier chapters, especially Chapter 12, in the discussions of how God can be responsive to the human condition. Although the creative act is eternal, encompassing together all dates in all the modes of time, we ourselves are temporally bound. From our limited standpoint, where the future is still open and at which point the eternal actual resolution of our future connection does not exist, the future of God's address to us is "other." The character God will take in response to our needs and to our deserts remains alien to us in the present, however real it is in eternity. From the standpoint of the present, God's creation in the future is really other; the issue is not one of our ignorance. Even God does not *now* know what the future holds because God is never only *now*. For ourselves, who truly are temporal, existing now with a future still future, the future and God's special presence as redemptive or condemnatory, helpful or negligent, merciful or punitive, remains other.

Within this general metaphysical statement of the boundaries of the temporally finite within eternity, it is possible to be more specific about the otherness of God. Two lines of answer to the problem of the otherness of God can be taken.

Privation of the Human

The first draws its inspiration from Tillich's approach to estrangement. Because we in fact live in a broken covenant, in a broken condition, sometimes we represent ourselves as contracted into a narrow perversity when in reality we are part of the glory of the divine life, perversity and all. This is to say, recognizing our disregard for or failures regarding the norms that define excellence in personal and communal affairs, we estrange ourselves from the larger divine context. So, Adam and Eve hid from God when they discovered God knew they had sinned. We construct representations that limit our world unduly, representations that perhaps deny the larger divine world or that justify a small, selfish attitude.

Almost inevitably, these representation take our temporal place alone to be real, deny the eternal dimensions, and ignore the true cosmic reach of temporality. The time passion of modernity is itself one of the representations that constitutes estrangement. If we can think of ourselves as temporal only and as temporal only in a linear way with no perichoresis of past, present, and future in an eternal identity, then we imagine ourselves as effectively cut off from the fullness of creation. This explains why, in reaching for eternity from within the temporal alone, it seems to be just more time, immortality: the desire for immortality is an internal fret at our self-imposed estrangement to time.

Precisely because of these representations of the selfish world by which we impose our estrangement from the sweep of eternal creation, we can be both sinful and parts of the divine, ignorant and yet Brahman, struggling under the Bodhisattva's vow and yet fully

Buddha, in competition with the Tao and yet wholly and only sustained by it. On the one hand we are not separate or estranged from divine creation at all. To ignore our eternal side is an illusion, sometimes a dangerous one. On the other hand, the world of our constructed estrangement is real. It consists in the representations of narrow estrangement and in our actual, morally freighted, behavior formed by those representations. Although we enjoy the fullness and freedom of the divine, if we think we are bound to sin, if we act in accordance with that bondage, and if we teach others that this is the way of the world, then we are in fact estranged. From this standpoint, the eternity and greater scope of the divine seems truly other.

Therefore one important sense of the otherness or estrangement of God is a human construction, or misconstruction. When that construction is ended, when the covenant is restored, God in these respects will not seem other but will both seem and be the larger divine context of creation within which we live, move, and have our being. But how will that construction or misconstruction be ended? For that we turn to the other sense of God's otherness, the sense in which God brings salvation.

Special Grace

The second approach to divine otherness is to appreciate what theists call the *grace* of God, the unexpected and extraordinary happenings that in some special way contribute to salvation, enlightenment, or ontological harmony. Nontheistic traditions have analogues to grace.

In one sense, all creation is grace. Every element in the divine creation of the world *ex nihilo* is both a free and unnecessitated part of God's act and also a gratuitously and undeservedly received contribution to the world's reality. Grace in the general sense is God's completely unconstrained and free action that benefits the world, especially people, without regard for merit. All creation counts as grace in this general sense. And in this general sense, grace is therefore trivial as a special theological notion. We should be ontologically grateful for all of creation, but this is precisely nothing special.

The special sense of grace has to do with elements of creation that take place within the overall general scheme that in unexpected and unusual ways contribute to salvific benefit. In one sense these are all but parts of the larger, single divine creative act. But relative to human need, they are particular responses and specially gracious, like the pothole or hero that saves the child from the truck. When creation is specialized in these gracious approaches, God is seen to be acting as an other to benefit specific persons or situations in salvific ways. These fall roughly into three classes as determined by the modes of time.

Past Grace: Prevenience and Destiny

Divine grace inhabits our past; in the Christian tradition this has been called *prevenient grace*. Stated most comprehensively, the grace of the past is what forms destiny for people and groups. Developed most by the Confucian tradition, *destiny* means that special path, career, or opportunity for which one, or a community, has been specially prepared. The preparation might be in genetic dispositions, in luck of birth in the right time at the right place with the right class and right parents, in having the right talents, the right education, the right personal connections, with the right opportunities for work and experience, with the right ambitions and the wit to recognize the occasion of destiny. None of these prevenient conditions is miraculous. After all, everyone has to be born to someone at some time in some situation, have some experience, and so forth. Often what we think to be our goals in life turn out not to be our destiny. We develop musical talent only to discover that our destiny is in medicine. We are born rich with an obvious career in the elite class and discover that our destiny must be worked out in poverty. We think our birthright is useless and poverty stricken, that our life is a waste, that we have no destiny whatsoever except to be addicted to the instruments of despair, only to discover our destiny to be the heroic witness to some needy soul. The elements in the past that make up destiny are all natural happenings as they come to be in their own present time. Only in retrospect, as they are past conditions for present life, do we see that they are organized to define a destiny.

The occasions or contents of destiny might take many forms. John Irving's *A Prayer for Owen Meany* is one of the most striking stories of sudden destiny in recent literature. Owen Meany's destiny was to save a group of school children by snatching and hurling away a bomb in an incident lasting only seconds but in which he lost his own life. Yet this destiny had been prepared by a peculiarly pathological upbringing, by particular and odd friendships, by his accidentally killing his best friend's mother with a baseball, by his studies, by his unusual religious experience, by visions of his grave, and most strangely by compulsive practice and perfection of a basketball trick. The novelistic telling of the story seems sometimes contrived because the reader is led to believe that all these antecedent incidents are supposed to harbinger something for the future. In real life destiny usually falls on us without warning, without treating antecedents as anticipations. But after the fact, there always has to have been a history that brings us to the right place at the right time: Owen Meaning had to have been doing *something* to get 3,000 miles from home to where the bomb was at the right time with the right partner with the special skills needed throw it away and save the children. *Sub specie eternitatis*, God the creator (and John Irving) contrive the whole so that the plot develops freely. Most of us hope for a destiny of longer duration, with a less literal application of the crucifixion theme, and prepared for by less bizarre and obscure preliminaries. Albert Schweitzer had three distinguished careers, as biblical scholar, as musician, and a missionary doctor; each would seem to be more than fulfilling for most of us. Yet perhaps none seemed to him to be his real destiny.

The discernment of one's destiny is perhaps the most important preparatory part of education. It cannot begin too soon; but for most of us the question is raised only relatively late in life. Most of life is spent pursuing what seems interesting and that for which our talents seem ready. Only when in middle age we stop to take stock of whether our career, perhaps outwardly successful, is truly meaningful do we raise the question of destiny. Destiny is not often the work that seems to fulfill our antecedent preparations. Destiny is turning over our antecedent preparations to some special need in the world, to a job, an occasion, or opportunity for which we need to be able to marshall our antecedents. Destiny is the occasion or path to which our life can be given and that gives that life its central meaning. Whereas pursuit of a happy life and career is a secular cosmological way of viewing our circumstances, finding our destiny and giving ourselves over to that is the religious way. Apart from the destiny, a career's antecedent conditions are all accidents, mere fractions of creation. As conditions of the destiny, however, they are grace in the past and are creation's special approach to each of us.

Future Grace: New Possibilities and Freedom

Grace in the future is the creation of special and novel possibilities. Most of the problematic situations for human life, in its secular as well as religious dimensions, are characterized by deadends. If only the car would start, if only we had more money, if only Barbara were here now, if only a war were not going on, if only they needed someone like him, et cetera. We try to think of all the possible solutions, and each of them seems blocked.

With regard to salvation, we are in bondage to our sins and cannot get free for all the trying. We are blinded by ignorance and cannot find enlightenment despite our desperate seeking. We are caught in competition and cannot find the way to ease into the harmony of things regardless of the most strenuous efforts and the most cultivated techniques of relaxation. And suddenly, where there was no possibility before, a way out appears. A new way of life is offered and we indeed can take it. The old is gone, the new is at hand. The possibility structure of the future has been changed, it seems, and we have new life.

In one sense, the gracious new possibility is just part of the generally created structure of the future. It must conform to the logical requirements of pure form, and it must be structured to relate to the real potentials in the person's life. In the sense of special grace, however, the new possibility breaks through the constellation of possibilities that had previously structured one's habitual life. Partly this is a matter of suddenly seeing possibilities that had been there all along. But often it is coming up to a possibility occasioned by a new situation that offers a way out if only we are ready to abandon our previous life structure, at least in certain ways. This last is what presents the eternal God as a salvific figure focused on salvation of the individual here and now.

Present Grace: Ecstasy, Discernment, and a New Heart

Divine grace in the present is extremely complicated. On the one hand, divine creativity makes the differences that become the destining prevenient grace of the past in some present; these differences structure the future in special, novel ways by framing actualities to which the future must be schematized. On the other hand, there are peculiarities of divine grace that are special to the gracious significance of the present. We may divide these, perhaps artificially, into three forms: ecstasy, discernment, and heartening. Within Christian theology, all three are known as marks of the presence of the Holy Spirit.

Ecstasy is the grace by which we are dislocated from the habits of the past. Of course the present must cope with the limitations of the past; what is real and fixed in the past constitutes the limits within which we must work. Nevertheless, we often inherit habits of behavior that are far narrower than the real potentialities of past reality. Ecstasy, literally "standing outside oneself," is when these habits of self-constitution (or group behavior) are dislodged and one can reexamine the potentialities and possibilities. Ecstasy is celebrated in pentecostal and charismatic Christian groups, in spirit-filled Hassidic Judaism and Sufi Islam, and in various other religions. Although the classical meaning of spirit-filled ecstasy is a setting aside of the usual and the alien possession of the self or group by the new spirit, ecstatic behavior itself can be routinized and made a ritual. In this case it comes to fail as an expression of the divine dislocation of creativity. But where ecstasy is genuine, in small personal ways as well as in manners of congregational behavior, the grace of God sets people free from the bondage of stereotyped responses. Sometimes ecstasy is necessary to take advantage of the grace of God in new possibilities.

Ecstasy by itself is blind spiritual novelty, as ready for the "evil" spirits as for the good. Therefore, spiritual traditions have always been concerned to develop tests for the spirit. Ecstasy alone is a necessary but not sufficient condition for the real presence of the divine spirit working to renew the covenant. Discernment is the second element of grace in the present.

Discernment is insight into the forces that work for the good in distinction from those that work for the wrong. In nearly every

instance, the religious dimension plays a role. The forces that work
for good are also those that work, according to the images employed
here, for the restoration of the covenant, that bring one closer to the
ontological ground of righteousness, piety, faith, hope, and love.
Those that work for the wrong are destructive of the covenant.

According to spiritual traditions East and West, discernment
is an art learned through long labor and apprenticeship to spiritual
directors. Most of the reason for this is that spiritual discernment
means penetrating through sham. Human beings are artful deceiv-
ers no more effectively than in their own religious life. Another part
of the reason for apprenticeship is that discernment needs to be
made into a habit. Unless one is automatically on the lookout for
the spiritually important (and for secular blinders), one's attention
will be elsewhere. Discernment comes down in the end to the focus
of attention on what is real.

Although perhaps based on habits of attention, discernment
always takes the form of sudden insight. Even when we know to
look for something to happen of spiritual importance, the discovery
is a novel reassessment of things. Discernment appears as a special
grace because, whatever its conceptual and habitual antecedents, it
causes a reevaluation and reorganization of one's vision of the
subject. When the discernment is about one's own life, it leads to a
classificatory distinction between realistic and unrealistic, self-
serving views. Part of "new life" consists in a new level of
discernment.

Discernment also has practical consequences. That is, it leads
to new directions. The sudden discernment of what is spiritually
important leads to discernment of how better to live and the
commitments to achieve that new way. Discernment itself is not
identical with deliberation and dedication, although it may involve
them. Discernment carries the sense of the veil of ignorance falling
away and the light of new life appearing. Still, the new life
discerned becomes a new obligation.

The third form of gracious spiritual presence, beyond ecstasy
and discernment, is a "new heart." A Christian term for the
graciously reformed character described in nearly every religious
tradition, the new heart is a resolve and focus on the content of
discernment that would not have seemed possible prior to the
significant moment. John Wesley is famous for taking his conver-

sion to consist in the experience of his heart "strangely warmed" by an understanding of God's grace. Although there are many godawful but deserved jokes about the Wesleyan warmed heart, it expresses a profound truth about present divine grace. Wesley both understood and believed in the "appropriate" theological propositions about salvation long before the heartwarming experience; he learned no new theology then. But what he learned was that God's love, distributed universally to all people, was also given to him in particular. Of course he knew this abstractly before. But it did not convince him. After the heartwarming experience, he had the confidence and power to proceed to live a life of service to his religious calling. The warmed heart not only convinced him that God was present in him, fulfilling his destiny and opening new possibilities for Christian new life in England, but that he himself bore the power of God to do some of those new things. God no longer seemed to be an alien whose love was universal and *not* particular but was identical to the free spirit within Wesley that led to his monumental ministry. In the crucial practical respects, God for Wesley was simply the creator in whom he had his finite being and to whose extensive glory he gave himself. Doubtless this sense was fleeting and evanescent; Wesleyan hagiography is not to be trusted in the details. But the structure of the hagiography makes the point: the present spirit of God gives substance and power to the new life that is better reconciled to the covenant demands of righteousness, piety, faith, hope, and love.

Ecstasy, discernment, and the new heart are not easily separable. The first relates to freedom from the past, the second to attention to the present, and the third to divinization in the future. These relate specifically to Augustine's internal trinity of remembrance (freedom from its bondage), attention (to the sharp springs of spontaneous creativity), and hope (internalized to the plunge of the muscles). In each of these modes of present grace, God can appear first as the other who comes and then as the creator who is always here, "in and by whom we have our being."

Providence: The Infinite in the Finite

Providence is no simple Christian doctrine that signifies divine temporal predetermination. In fact, it does not signify that at all. All divine determination is eternal, working in each of the modes of temporality in coordination. At any given present, the future is partly open. Providence rather in respect to the past is that part of the eternal creation, dynamically comprising each date of a person's life in all the modes of time, that provides the conditions for living out a spiritual destiny. Providence in respect to the future is the provision of possibilities that lead to the restoration of the covenant. Providence in respect to the present is the provision of present grace in ecstasy, discernment, and the new heart that moves God from the alien appearance back to the inner and circumambient creator. Given the presence of ontological norms that we fail to honor and the habituated ways of fallen social and personal living, the eternal creator functions and appears as the temporal agent of remedy. Creation *ex nihilo* is special divine grace when it works to overcome the circumstance of human fallenness.

There are thus several senses in which God is with us. In general God is in our being as our creator: nothing that we are fails to be part of the creative act. God is with us also in all our participations in social and cosmic processes, binding us with those processes as the ontological ground of our mutual relevance to all things: nothing we can touch fails to have God in it and in our touching. God is with us in responding to our needs and petitions, perhaps not as we would want but in sure eternal connection with the rest of creation: God is in our needs and sufferings, our pains and joys, and in their measure and fulfillment. God is with us finally in redeeming our standing in eternity. God comes to us as other, but does not force us to perfection. God's prevenience teases us toward responsibility. God's freedom pushes hope in our face when we attach to despair. And God's present spirit ecstatically dislocates us, holds up the mirror of discernment, and warms our heart with the love that creates the cosmos. God the creator is with us as other and charmer, who lures us to responsibility.

Chapter Sixteen

GOD BEYOND US

Let us review the argument as we enter the concluding chapter. This book began by registering a complaint about our age to the effect that it divorces time from eternity, rejecting the latter, and thus pathologically pursues eternal matters under the false guise of more time. In religious matters this amounts to a barren passion for immortality as more time or a too-much-protesting rejection of immortality as supernatural. Subsidiarily, the age's rejection of eternity and a proper representation of judgment has led to a preoccupation with guilt, sometimes countered by militant relativism. The earlier chapters of Part Four have dealt with judgment in the proper context of eternity, and this concluding chapter returns to the religious problematic of immortality. The thesis to be elaborated is that, given the natural eternity of persons, the true meaning of immortality is resurrection in the Christian sense and its cognates in other religions where they might be found.

In Chapter 3 the divorce of time from eternity in modern philosophy was discussed, and throughout this book an alternative philosophy has been presented, centering around the metaphysics of harmonies of essential and conditional features. This philosophy has been used to interpret both time and eternity and, in connection with both, God as eternal creator. In passing, the recent speculations of cosmological science have been interpreted as illustrative of the metaphysics that also interprets religion.

In Chapter 4 the problem of personal identity was discussed, especially in its dimensions of moral responsibility. The topic was used both to lay out the diversities in the structures of time and to suggest that temporal life must be presupposed to have an eternal aspect with respect to responsibility through time. Because it is difficult responsibly to deny that we have moral responsibility, if it can be demonstrated that time and eternity have the character ascribed to them in moral responsibility, then even the most confirmed of religious skeptics ought to be convinced of the plausibility of our direction. Subsequent chapters analyzed time and eternity in more detail, giving arguments for the theory that at least are exhausting if not convincing.

Chapter 5 presented a defense of metaphysics as the construction of a hypothetical worldview united by certain basic concepts and then introduced the metaphysical notions of essential and conditional features of harmonies. The dialectical point was made that this metaphysics accounts for genuine diversity without conceiving things to be either out of connection with one another as in atomism or subsumed into highest relations as in idealistic and epistemological absolutisms. Chapter 6 then discussed the modes of time, past, present, and future, in terms of the essential features that constitute their ineradicable diversity. Chapter 7 discussed them in terms of the conditional features that connect them so that time flows. Chapter 8 explained how the togetherness of time's essential and conditional features is eternal.

Whereas Part Two pursued eternity by an analysis of time, Part Three came at eternity from another angle and showed how it is related to time through divine creation. Chapter 9 introduced the idea of God as a theological topic and locus for eternity, and set many limits on the kinds of abstract theological conceptions that are useful for giving expression to the assumptions of divinity in the practice of religions. Chapter 10 noted that the eternity required for time is related to the eternity of divine creation. The creator must be conceived in terms of a viable conception of the closure constituting the limits of the world created. Several alternative conceptions of God were examined in this regard, including that of process theology, and an argument was given for a particular conception of God as creator *ex nihilo*. That argument can be construed as a proof if one accepts the metaphysics employed as premises. Chapter 11 showed how creation *ex nihilo* relates to all the temporal modes diversely and together to constitute and contain time's flow. Chapter 12 showed how the creation of time's flow constitutes a dynamic life within the eternity of God.

Now in Part Four we have returned to the religious topic of eternity in and for human life. Chapter 13 reformulated the claim from Chapter 4 that persons have an eternal dimension to their identity, this time in the rich vocabulary developed about eternity and time's flow; the moral dimension of personal life amounts to standing under judgment. Chapter 14 argued that, by virtue of the eternal dimension of temporal life, persons individually and collectively, as parts of nature, participate in the eternal divine life; thus judgment on humankind is a divine concern for salvation, which means redeeming the time. Chapter 15, noting that the concern for religious change cannot be for eternal life itself, if people are naturally eternal, but for a quality of eternal life, discussed how God in creating can also be "other" to us so as to come with the graces of salvation. Now we have arrived at the practical question underlying the discussion from the beginning: if our life is both temporal and eternal, what is the true shape of the passion for immorality? The answer is resurrection.

Resurrection: Salvation and Damnation

The Christian doctrine of resurrection was originally developed in explicit contradistinction to the earlier Gnostic and Greek (and later Christian) notions of the immortal soul separate from the body. Resurrection as proclaimed by Saint Paul (e.g., I Corinthians 15) and depicted in the Gospels is the triumphal victory of the whole person, body and soul in continuity, over death. For obvious reasons, the symbol of resurrection has a chronological order: death has to occur first for resurrection to be its triumphant rebuttal. Nevertheless, the religious significance of resurrection is not an afterlife matter but a matter of what life consists in and how to live. The author of Colossians, after telling the Colossian Christians that they had received Christ (Colossians 2:6) and "with

Christ died to the elemental spirits of the universe" (Colossians 2:20) asserted they not only had died with Christ but had already been raised:

> So if you have been raised with Christ, seek the things that are above, where Christ is, seated at the right hand of God. Set your minds on things that are above, not on things that are on earth, for you have died, and your life is hidden with Christ in God. When Christ who is your life is revealed, then you also will be revealed with him in glory. Put to death, therefore, whatever in you is earthly: fornication, impurity, passion, evil desire, and greed (which is idolatry). On account of these the wrath of God is coming on those who are disobedient. These are the ways you also once followed, when you were living that life. But now you must get rid of all such things—anger, wrath, malice, slander, and abusive language from your mouth. Do not lie to one another, seeing that you have stripped off the old self with its practices and have clothed yourselves with the new self, which is being renewed in knowledge according to the image of its creator. In that renewal there is no longer Greek and Jew, circumcised and uncircumcised, barbarian, Scythian, slave and free; but Christ is all and in all. As God's chosen ones, holy and beloved, clothe yourselves with compassion, kindness, humility, meek-ness, and patience. Bear with one another and, if anyone has a complaint against another, forgive each other; just as the Lord has forgiven you, so you also must forgive. Above all, clothe yourselves with love, which binds everything together in perfect harmony. And let the peace of Christ rule in your hearts, to which indeed you were called in the one body. And be thankful. (Colossians 3:1–15)

An exegesis of certain of the themes of this passage can lay out the problematic of resurrection, the payoff expression of the concern for eternal life. The exegesis can also summarize many of the themes of the discussion of eternity.

First, the unexpected logic of the situation should be noted. Although the Christians are already dead and raised with Christ and are at this very moment resident with Christ in the divine kingdom, indeed precisely because of this already realized es-chaton, the Christians need to shape up and start living like regenerated folk. The passage marks a sharp distinction between justification or salvation on the one hand, which includes resurrection and current membership in the heavenly kingdom, and sanctification, which is the long and slow process of living with a correct orientation to the "higher things." In other words, the religiously significant sense of resurrection is a state in which people can exist while in the midst of temporal life and at a point where behavior appropriate to the covenant is still only a hope.

Second, the author makes a distinction between two orientations to temporal life, one toward "things below" and the other toward "things above." The things above are characteristic of the heavenly kingdom ruled by Christ. Heaven is not a separate place, because the Colossians are in it while remaining in town. It is rather God's order for the creation in which the commandments of virtue, summed up in love, are obligatory. The orientation of the Christians is to acknowledge the divine order and strive for it. The orientation of the others, those seeking the "things below," is for a selfish life out of touch with the divine order. In fact, the epitome of the lower life is greed, and the author calls that idolatry; this is to say, the lower life is not only to neglect the ontologically normative elements of creation but to make attachment to self into an object of worship and religious devotion. The author's list of vices in the lower life and virtues in the higher are a version of the more general scheme described previously in which the ontological norms are righteousness (right form), piety (proper deference to all the components of creation), faith (authentic engagement of life), and hope (commitment to a religious path).

Third, the norms of the kingdom apply to everyone, whether the people acknowledge them or not. Therefore, those oriented to the lower way are subject to judgment, to "the wrath of God." Just because people are selfish, and thus are unjust to one another, disrespectful and undeferential, cowardly when it comes to the truth of their situation, given to despair, and generally unloving, none of this means that the norms of the covenant do not apply. The ontological judgment about most people is that they are found wanting because of an orientation away from the covenant and thus are subject to the judgment, symbolized as the wrath of God.

Fourth, those Christians who are indeed oriented to living according to the covenant still are not necessarily very good at it.

The author of the passage exhorts them systematically to give up each of the old ways and struggle to attain to true holiness. Death with Christ to the old ways and resurrection to the divine kingdom does not depend on successful sanctity. On the contrary, spiritual death and resurrection are themselves conditions for taking on the new orientation and setting out on the road of sanctification. Nothing is said about how holy Christians have to be for salvation. In fact, the pursuit of holiness is a consequence of salvation in the sense of death and resurrection, not a condition. For people who are oriented to the eternal kingdom, temporal life is merely a struggle to give up the old ways and practise the ways of the covenant.

Fifth, the new orientation that constitutes moving explicitly into the kingdom, instead of being in it unconsciously and judged by its norms, comes from affiliation with Christ. Affiliation with Christ means at least three things referred to in this passage and explicated in diverse ways elsewhere in Christian scriptures and theology.

1. Jesus Christ as a salvific figure appeared in history, did and said the crucial things, and was made known to the Colossians. Thus he was available for affiliation. In one sense, the epiphany of Christ was just one more element within the eternal act of divine creation, historical in the way that every other person is an historical part of the creation. In another sense, the peculiar identity of Christ was such as to offer salvation through affiliation, so his historical appearance can be viewed as a special act of God for salvific purposes. Moses and the other lawgivers (Muhammed, the Upanisadic teachers, Buddha, Confucius, the Taoist masters, and so forth) are all historical figures that in one sense are simply parts of the larger creation and in another sense sources of special affiliation with salvific effects, or at least alleged such effects.

2. The religiously important elements of Jesus' life are epitomized with figures of abandoning the old life and taking on the new. The most direct of such figures is Jesus' crucifixion and resurrection, which is symbolized for Christians in

the frequent ritual of the Eucharist. Slightly more indirect
is the figure of Jesus' baptism, his immersion in the waters
of death, or the womb waters of prebirth, and reemergence
with a new divinely appointed identity. This is symbolized
for Christians in baptism as the initiation rite to the
religion. Then there are many stories in the Gospels of how
Jesus unties the bonds of sickness and perversity characteristic of the lower life by means of his own faith or by
calling forth the faith of others, thus releasing the powers
of God's kingdom. Other religions have similar figures
characteristic of their founder or founding law or condition
that mark the shifting from one orientation to life to another.

3. Affiliation with Christ means both accepting the power of
    the affiliation to make the difference regarding new life and
    then actually making the affiliation. The affiliation with
    Christ means taking on the figure of death and resurrec-
    tion as the way to understand one's own life, to accept the
    reorientation to living according to the norms of the
    kingdom or covenant, and then undertaking to be part of
    the body of Christ. The metaphor of the body of Christ (for
    instance, in Colossians 1:24 and 3:15) means that one joins
    with other Christians to continue the ministry of bringing
    new life begun by the historical Jesus in Galilee and
    carried out by the Church as the body of extension
    ministry.

For Christians, then, salvation as a whole means affiliating
with Christ in death and resurrection to be part of his body, that is,
the Church, continuing the ministry of bringing new life to people.
It consists in attempting to live more nearly in accord with the
norms of righteousness, piety, faith, hope, and love, recognizing
that we start off with deep habits formed by the orientation to lower
things. Although the language of "new life" and "resurrection" is
peculiarly Christian, there are parallels in most other great religions; for example, the "chosen people" or those newly faithful to
Allah.

Within the eternal life of God, wherein each person dwells
both temporally and eternally, there are thus (at least) two ways of

living. One is to be oriented away from the ontological norms that define what is essential in human life and society, toward selfish definitions of the human world. This way is not only chosen and reinforced by choice, it is institutionalized in customs and taught to infants. Perhaps no one grows up without first learning to live in this way.

The other is to be oriented toward those ontological norms, toward the covenant, and to be struggling to break the habits and social structures characteristic of the other orientation. In a quite direct sense, this second orientation involves both recognizing and striving to fulfill the normative aspects of the eternal creation within the limits of our control. Therefore, whereas it is true that each life is eternal in the senses defined, only some lives are "resurrected" in the sense of attempting to fulfill the divine destiny involved in our creation. The resurrected life is lived with the direct project of identification with God and the normative creation. Religions differ in their accounts of what accomplishes the resurrection or the switch to the new, ontologically realistic, orientation. For Christians the historical part of creation that consists in the life of Christ with which we can become affiliated plus the present expressions of God's creative love raise us above guilt and enable us to embrace the affiliation.

The question of resurrection needs to be sharpened here by asking about the "death" over which it triumphs. Is death simply the general finitude of actual life in which we have a finite number of years, after which nothing? Is death rather the fragmentariness of our lives, their failure to add up to a human-shaped biography, a specialized kind of finitude? Is death the spiritual death of bondage to sin, ignorance, and disharmony for which we, not the natural condition, are largely responsible? Death is all three of these, and eternal life and resurrection have special dimensions relative to each.

Conquering Natural Death of Finitude and Fragmentation

Human life is naturally and generally finite in several senses. One is always born into an actual finite situation. One lives only a finite number of years. One has some opportunities and not others. And one makes choices that exclude possibilities. In fact, even if one's life seems to enjoy a nearly infinite array of possibilities, as it sometimes seems to adolescents, none of those is a real possibility unless it actually can be chosen. Actually to choose one is to make at least some of the others impossible. Even if one chooses so as to expand the richness of one's possibilities, choosing always makes one more finite. The very possibility of responsibility comes from the finiteness of life in this natural and general sense.

Despite natural finitude there is a natural eternity to human life. Despite the fact there will be a time after which one's life is over, the eternal fullness of one's life is part of the eternal life of God. This is to say, in God we are eternally identified in our youth, in our responsible years, and in our time of accomplishment. This is not a static biography or a time of infinite possibility or even a sum of moments of choice, but all together in the eternal togetherness of ontological creation. Thus to the death of life's dated ending, we can say, "So what! My life is eternally dynamic in God."

Nevertheless, one can respond to the temporal finiteness of life by attempting to overcome it. If we cannot live forever, then at least we can try to possess as much as possible within the finite limits we have. This is the elemental source of greed and selfishness. Greed is the idolatry of thinking that, like God, we can "have it all" within a life that can have only its portion. Therefore, one can defy the limits to one's portion that are set by righteousness, piety, faith, hope, and love. In doing so one implicitly if not explicitly rejects the ontological context within which even that finite portion exists.

Resurrection over the death of finiteness means two things. First, it means recalling us to the fact that our true identity is our eternal life that is part of the eternal life of God. Our true identity is not our temporal life alone into which we can greedily grab as much as possible. Second, resurrection over the death of finiteness means returning to respect those specific limitations on our finite portion that come from the ontological norms of creation. And because life lived with a positive orientation to those norms identifies with the whole of creation, not just with what can selfishly be possessed by the individual, this dimension of resurrection is richer by far than anything the selfish person could imagine.

In addition to being generally finite, human life is naturally fragmented. More often than not a person's life does not add up in ways that are very meaningful. The reasons for this come from the fact that, like everything else, human life is a harmony of many different factors. The cosmic conditions of the solar system seem fairly stable right now, but our life plans can easily be upset in the next decades by ecological disasters. The economy might go sour just when we finish professional training. Or our discipline can be ruined by sudden inherited wealth. A bizarre accident can cripple or kill us unexpectedly. Sudden family obligations can ruin plans for ever. War, pestilence, and famine are controlled by forces that are not scaled to the needs of our individual lives. Even those people who seem able to bring coherence to their lives, whom fortune favors with stability or sudden benign opportunity, find their projects only half finished before they are forced to move on, and then ruined by those who come after. With respect to this pervasive and almost inevitable fragmentation, death is ruined meaning.

Despite the fragmentation of individual life, our lives both temporally and eternally are part of the much larger temporal world and eternal life of God. Whereas *our* projects might be fragmented, we usually cannot tell what roles our fragments play in larger patterns. What unwitting part have we in someone else's destiny? What causal part do we play in processes that have nothing about them of the human scale? We usually have no clue as to larger patterns. Yet the divine reality of which we are parts is not constrained by our meaning patterns. If we serve some larger purpose, hurrah. If not, then still we are part of the divine glory. So long as we identify with the larger life of God, our own life takes meaning from that. As C. S. Lewis so often put it, we have a right to our own story but not to anyone else's. We cannot demand that our lives be fulfilled in any larger meaning than the one we find within our own neighborhood. And within that neighborhood, our story is only to live with righteousness, piety, faith, hope, and love insofar as we are able. If that does not add up, we still are committed to life fulfilled in the greater glory of God. We relinquish the demand that our own lives be specially meaningful and rest in the infinity of divine creation.

Nevertheless, this relinquishment of meaning for our lives seems to many like death, a death to be embraced in cynicism. If life is not meaningful then it must be absurd, and if it is absurd, then anything is permissible, especially that which titillates with the similacra of divine right and power. Like Raskolnikov, people believe that, if life is wholly absurd, then the only meaning we can find is that in which we try to act like a God over someone else. Couple ontological cynicism with greed, and selfishness becomes blind and ruthless.

Resurrection over the death of fragmentation and absurdity is to recover the sense of the divine mother who embraces all our parts and sets us on the path to make what true meaning we can. True human meaning is to be righteous in our neighborhood, pious regarding our world and its environment, faithful in embracing our small corner of things accepting all the fragmentation that destroys big-deal meaning, hopeful for our destiny to be in the right place at the right time, and loving within our ken so as, like God infinitely, to balance finitely our concerns for the forms of things, their components, their mixture, and their worth. Resurrection over fragmentation means being united with God's creation, including its normative elements, in ways appropriately limited to our finite and fragmented position.

Conquering Spiritual Death of Sin, Ignorance, and Disharmony

In addition to the natural finitude and fragmentation of life, there is the spiritual death caused by sin, ontological ignorance, and willful disharmony. Although perhaps driven by the forces of greed and cynicism that lead to the abandonment or perversion of the ontological norms of the covenant, spiritual death is something more. Spiritual death results from our own responsibility, not from natural conditions. It consists of two parts. The first is the gradual withering away of connections with the creative powers of God, a loss of touch with the life-giving directives of righteousness, piety, faith, hope, and love. Sometimes without deliberately willing this, a life of greed and cynicism simply estranges one from God so that no way back can be found. The second part of spiritual death is a kind of positive bondage to that estranged life. Even when we want to pursue the ontological norms we cannot: as Saint Paul said, "For I do not do what I want, but I do the very thing I hate" (Romans

7:15). Though the truth of our residence in the divine life is before
us, we cannot accept it. Though we understand our ignorance and
know in what enlightenment consists, we cannot wake up to it.
Though we are moved by the forces of harmony and hate the
disharmony of competition, we cannot stop. Spiritual death is the
result of our own responsibility, continually reinforced, that ruins
the possibility of responsibility in spiritual matters.

Despite spiritual death, our real and true identity is within the
infinite life of the eternal dynamic creation. Spiritual death is an
unnatural construction of our own greed and cynicism. Spiritual
life is the truth of the matter in the sense of the eternal identity of
each person within the divine creation act. Spiritual life is simply
there for the taking. Spiritual death is an illusion to be conquered
by abandoning it and reconnecting with the human heartstrings of
righteousness, piety, faith, hope, and love.

Nevertheless, the powers of that illusion, the bonds of spiritual death, are stronger than the powers left to the spiritually dead.
Not only do our attempts to do good result in the opposite (Saint
Paul's complaint), what good we do seems more God's work than
anything for which we can take responsibility.

So resurrection from spiritual death, perhaps unlike resurrection from the death of finitude and fragmentation, requires outside
intervention. At this point the eternal elements of divine creation,
always and universally present, must be focused as special acts of
grace. God must act historically with persons or life-giving law or
some other actual thing, affiliation with which overcomes spiritual
death and provides the power of new life. Of course this is just part
of the eternal act of divine creation, itself an element in the divine
life. It can be viewed as a fulfulling or completing of the creation.
Yet for individuals and for spiritually dead communities, those
special gracious epiphanies are direct instruments of resurrection.
Acceptance of the new way, the new Tao, provides the orientation
to life lived in the covenant. The resurrected life is lived finitely, in
expectation of ordinary death some day, and fragmentarily, assuming that our works will not add up or last long. Resurrection is life
lived with attention on the obligations of righteousness, piety, faith,
hope, and love in our neighborhood. These obligations commit us
to amending both our world and our personal habits lingering from

the old common life. The resurrected life is lived not individualistically but as a citizen of the heavenly kingdom, in covenant with others, with nature, and with institutions; ultimately, with God.

Glory: The Finite in the Infinite

Given the unity of the topic, the resurrected life is both temporal and eternal. As temporal, the resurrected life is the acceptance of the divine creation as the context for life and the commitment to pursuing, within the finite and fragmented neighborhood of our situation, the norms that define humanity. As eternal, the resurrected life is both defined by its place in the eternity of creation and characterized by an emptying of its attachments to greed and cynicism. In place of those false fascinations with self, the resurrected life takes its satisfaction in the whole of God's glory. Any person's perception of that glory is limited and conditioned by the cultural perspective of the created context. The reality of the glory perceived, however, is the immensity of eternity within which time's flow is both possible and actual.

The final twist of the argument is to point out what has been implicit throughout the entire discussion of creation *ex nihilo*, that everything is, or is in, God the creator. According to the metaphysics of creation, the world is to be counted as the terminus of the divine creative act. There is no medium apart from God in which the world floats. It exists simply as God's act completed, or having arrived at determinacy. The world is *the created* to *God's creating* as *natura naturata* is to *natura naturans*. Time's flow is not the medium of the creative act from source to product but itself the dynamic product within which the divine act is source. The true reality of the world, and every determinate thing within its bounds, is to be part of God, the climax of the divine act.

The religious term for the fullness of God is *glory*. To experience divine glory is the *mysterium tremendum* (Otto 1917), *numinus* and profoundly fascinating. But the divine glory we know infinitely transcends anything we can experience. That transcendence itself is the source of the *mysterium tremendum*. From our analysis we know that the glory includes at least the vastness of creation dwarfing the human sphere, the ubiquity and power of the act of creation *ex nihilo,* and the infinite distance and fecundity of God as source.

Divine glory incarnates itself in the created world, but far transcends the specific values and ideals of the world. In our finite and temporal position we are obligated to the norms of the covenant, but divine glory includes the covenant and more. The passion of our finite existence is limited with regard to its own boundaries, but infinite with regard to its setting in divine glory. The satisfactions of our cobbled fragmentary lives are taken neat, but our satisfactions in God's infinite life comprise everything without measure. At our best we are earnest for goodness but are fulfilled in the glory sourcing good and evil. At our worst we betray the obligations of our neighborhood, we contradict our status as obligated, and we find our pride in ruin, destruction, and negation—but despite ourselves we are swept up in the infinite mercy that is God's glory. We strive for the culture of our society, for the welfare of our people, for the happiness of our loved ones, and for the blessed fulfillment of our own lives—yet the true worth of all that is that we live for God's glory.

The secret behind the point that time and eternity make one topic is that all the concerns of temporal life find their authentic object set in eternal glory. In the end there is only one topic, divine glory. If our argument concerning eternity and time's flow flies toward the mark, this temporal field is fully real, defines our norms and being, and is graced by the contracted presence of the creator. But by the same argument, the infinite glory of the creator in the end alone is real. Our eternal life eternally has a finite place in that glory. Beyond that, our resurrected life pours out to identify with the divine life in all its glory. Not only is God with us in finite life, the truth of our finite life is raised into the infinite life of God's glory.

Notes

Preface

1. To be sure, some extreme relativists do deny all validity to ideas of moral responsibility. I have dealt with some of the arguments about this in *The Puritan Smile* (1987a) and have developed some of the metaphysical underpinnings for objective values in *Reconstruction of Thinking* (1981) and *Recovery of the Measure* (1989).
2. I have recently addressed these three theological genres with *A Theology Primer* (1991b) developing a brief system of Christian doctrine, *Behind the Masks of God* (1991a) treating comparative issues, and a reprint of *God the Creator* (1992a).

Chapter 1. A Time to Rethink Eternity

1. See the articles by Powell, Lemonick, Wilford, and Browne.
2. Descartes articulated this theory first in his *Rules for the Direction of the Mind* and then more succinctly in the *Discourse on Method*. His *Meditations on First Philosophy* provided his metaphysical justification for the belief in simples (all these writings are in the *Philosophical Works of Descartes*). That belief, including the theory of analysis following from it, has limited applicability, however. Likely it can be applied to very little within the scale of human life without extreme distortions, although it might well be applied helpfully to the microscopically small and the cosmically large, which was Descartes' first intent. For a contemporary defense of Cartesianism, see Jerry A. Fodor's *The Modularity of Mind* (1983). For a biologist's use of contemporary Cartesianism, see C. R. Gallistel's *The Organization of Action* (1980). For a criticism of the Cartesian approach to analysis, see my *Recovery of the Measure* (1989), Chapter 2.
3. Peirce's remark is made in "A Neglected Argument for the Reality of

God," which is found in several anthologies and in *The Collected Papers of Charles Sanders Peirce, CP,* vol. 6: 452–493.

4. "Vagueness" as a logical notion was invented and explained by Peirce, again in his "Neglected Argument for the Reality of God." The theory of metaphysics to be explained here in the text derives from Peirce's discussion by relating metaphysics to science, religion, politics, etc., as the more vague to the less vague. For an extensive treatment of this, answering objections that philosophers and others have raised against the practice of metaphysics, see my *The Highroad around Modernism* (1992b), Chapter 6.

5. Much of the theory of hypotheses is sketched in his "Neglected Argument for the Reality of God." I have given a more thorough analysis of his theory, with texts from other writings, in *The Highroad around Modernism* (1992b), Chapter 1.

6. With the confirmation in 1974 that cosmic background radiation conforms to the blackbody shape predicted by the Big Bang theory, most scientists abandoned the Steady State theory. As late as 1988, however, Fred Hoyle, who first proposed the Steady State theory, argued that the Big Bang theory is *not proven* but is asserted by its advocates with a religious fervor (Hoyle and Wickramasinghe, 1988, pp. 116–118). New discoveries are alleged to offer greater support to the Big Bang theory; see Powell 1992, Browne 1992, or Wilford 1992.

7. Of course, Peirce anticipated Hoyle and Wickramasinghe by about a century; his statement is in the "Neglected Argument" paper. See also his 1898 essay, "Detached Ideas on Vitally Important Topics" in the *Collected Papers,* especially in *CP,* vol. 1: 553–569. I have analyzed Peirce's approach to the correction of habits in religious matters in *The Highroad around Modernism,* 1992, Chapter 1.

Chapter 2. The Fall from Eternity to Immortality

1. The thesis of my *The Highroad around Modernism* is that modernism and its alternatives in late nineteenth and twentieth century cultures, including postmodernism as a dialectical rejection of specifically modernist culture, are all merely late modern. They all are outgrowths, albeit different from each other, of the original genius of modernity.

2. Insofar as the formation of passions is a profound pedagogical task of culture, this "better assumption" is the educational moral of this book. The most sophisticated treatment of eternity and time in our century so far has been W. T. Stace's *Time and Eternity* (1952). But whereas his book takes

the problem to be a contest between religion and naturalism, as represented by science, the situation rather is that science itself raises the issues for which theology and religious practice need to supply responses. The phrase *time consciousness* of course is intended to call to mind Husserl's *The Phenomenology of Internal Time-Consciousness*.

3. Radhakrishnan believes that the early Indian theory of time arose as the result of attempts to reconcile the myriad accounts of creation in the Vedas with the equally strong beliefs that the cycle of birth and rebirth is endless. See Radhakrishnan, 1929, Vol. 1, pp. 513 ff. Perhaps the most influential expression of the theory of eons is in the Bhagavad Gita, 9:4–10:

By Me all this universe is pervaded through My unmanifested form. All beings abide in Me but I do not abide in them.

And (yet) the beings do not dwell in Me; behold My divine mystery. My spirit which is the source of all beings sustains the beings but does not abide in them.

As the mighty air moving everywhere ever, abides in the etheric space, know thou that in the same manner all existences abide in Me.

All beings, O Son of Kunti (Arjuna), pass into nature which is My own at the end of the cycle; and at the beginning of the next cycle I send them forth.

Taking hold of nature which is My own, I send forth again and again all this multitude of beings which are helpless, being under the control of Nature.

Nor do these works bind Me, O winner of wealth (Arjuna), for I am seated as if indifferent, unattached in those actions.

Under My guidance, Nature gives birth to all things, moving and unmoving, and by this means, O Son of Kunti (Arjuna), the world revolves.

(Translation from Radhakrishnan and Moore, 1957, p. 132)
4. Hua-yen Buddhism is the most sophisticated speculation about time and eternity, drawing on the whole of the Indian tradition, with considerable learning from China. For expositions, see Garma C. C. Chang's *The Buddhist Teaching of Totality: The Philosophy of Hwa Yen Buddhism* or Francis H. Cook's *Hua-yen Buddhism: The Jewel Net of Indra*.
5. Translated by Wing-tsit Chan in his *Source Book of Chinese Philosophy*.

6. See Manchester's brilliant essay, "The Religious Experience of Time and Eternity," in Armstrong, 1986, pp. 384 ff.
7. Richard Sorabji's *Time, Creation, and the Continuum: Theories in Antiquity and the Early Middle Ages* traces a host of complications of time as entertained in earlier ages, and he shows their sequelae in the modern period.
8. See his *Cur Deus Homo*.
9. The biological sciences are exciting now because of their engineering potential, the manipulation of parts like the tinkering with mechanisms; see Gallistel, 1980.

Chapter 3. The Philosophical Passion for Present Time

1. Whitehead 1929, p. 159. Whitehead's analysis of the subjectivist bias was extremely complex and nuanced. He first divided it into two principles: the "subjectivist principle," namely, "that the datum in the act of experience can be adequately analysed purely in terms of universals" (p. 157); and the "sensationalist principle," namely, "that the primary activity in the act of experience is the bare subjective entertainment of the datum, devoid of any subjective form of reception" (ibid.). He shrewdly criticized Locke, Descartes, Hume, and Kant for the ways they interpreted these two principles, and constructed his own philosophy as a function of "reformed" versions of them.
2. Aquinas said in *De Veritate:* "Truth is 'the conformity of thing and intellect.' But since this conformity can be only in the intellect, truth is only in the intellect. . . . It is clear, therefore, that, as is said in the *Metaphysics* [of Aristotle], natural things from which our intellect gets its scientific knowledge measure our intellect. Yet these things are themselves as measured by the divine intellect, in which are all created things — just as all works of art find their origin in the intellect of an artist. The divine intellect, therefore, measures and is not measured; a natural thing both measures and is measured; but our intellect is measured, and measures only artifacts, not natural things" (1256–1259, pp. 10–11). From this remark of Thomas's I have taken the title of my book, *Recovery of the Measure* (1989), which argues for a theory of interpretation or hermeneutics that reverses the move from the medieval and classical conceptions to the modern conception that experience measures objects.
3. John E. Smith has analyzed the modern theory of experience as a modification of consciousness, which he calls *classical empiricism*, in

distinction from the pragmatic theory of experience. See John E. Smith 1967; 1978, Chapter 3.

4. Immanuel Kant, 1787, B 46–73.
5. The following account summarizes the position of *Process and Reality* (1929).
6. 1929: Part I, Chapter 2.

Chapter 4. No Time without Eternity

1. The essential continuity that distinguishes temporally enduring objects from a succession of discrete though perhaps similar happenings, I have called *discursive individuality* (Neville 1974; 1989). The point is a bone of contention with process philosophy, for which each moment brings a wholly new and complete individual, with the past objectified a second time in the new individual.

2. For Dewey, *enjoyment* was an extremely important term. Its most complete discussion was in his *Art as Experience*. But it was the central notion in his theory of value as expressed in *Human Nature and Conduct, The Quest for Certainty*, and *A Theory of Valuation*. He traced its metaphysical roots in "Peirce's Theory of Quality" in *On Experience, Nature, and Freedom*.

3. The point about engagement addresses what has been a problem for process philosophy. According to process philosophy, present moments are directly connected with their past and future but not with their contemporaries. Connection with contemporaries is only indirect in the sense that they might share a common past and common future. The point made here is that engagement is present but that the present also includes past and future so that direct engagement is possible.

4. The case of the trial for robbery could illustrate the point if there were much consensus on a theory of punishment. If there were a consensus that punishment were for the sake of restoring justice, the date of the future completion of the sentence would be important as future, present, and past. As future, that date is definitive of present moral identity because it can be realized as restored justice only by carrying out and enduring the sentence; should the prisoner escape, the date would pass without guilt absolved or justice restored. As present, the person will on that date change from one who owes a debt to society to one who has paid that debt. As past, that future date will be the condition that ever after restores the person to justice and desert of rights and privileges. On deterrence theories of punishment, or on the medical model that views no one as morally guilty, such an analysis makes no sense. A different example makes the case in the text.

Chapter 5. A Metaphysics of Time and Eternity

1. In an earlier work (Neville 1974, pp. 26–27) I distinguished at some length between metaphysics as the study of determinateness, ontology as the study of being as such, and cosmology as the study of the structures of the cosmos. But in more popular usage, all three studies are comprised within metaphysics.
2. For an extensive study of the idea of experience in ancient, medieval, and modern usages, see John E. Smith 1967.
3. See Whitehead 1929, Part I, Chapter 1, for a discussion of criteria for evaluating metaphysical systems. The list in the text here goes beyond Whitehead; see Neville 1992b.
4. That philosophical theses are themselves hypotheses with more or less plausibility, depending on the cases that can be made for them, is itself an hypothesis that I have defended at length elsewhere (1974, Chapter 1; 1981, Chapter 1; 1989, Chapters 3 and 16; 1992b, Chapter 1). Because speculative philosophy has been condemned roundly by modernist philosophies and that condemnation has been taken at face value by postmodernist philosophies, it is important to understand that the present argument is neither modernist nor postmodernist. See my *The Highroad around Modernism* (1992b). For a quick sketch of the system of which these reflections are a part, see Neville 1987b, pp. 253–273. Readers who wish to leap ahead to direct discussions of the identity of the temporal modes in the next section should feel free to do so. They would miss only the underpinnings of the argument to be made in the next chapter about the reality of the eternal context for temporal differences, an argument that moves from the metaphysics of identity to the ontology of being.
5. The philosophy has been neatly expressed by Harold H. Oliver in *A Relational Metaphysic* (1981) and *Relatedness* (1984).
6. For a more complete analysis of harmony and the misleading ideas often associated with it see Neville, 1992a, Chapters 1–4; and 1989, Chapters 5–8.

Chapter 6. Time's Relations of Otherness

1. See the discussion in Silk 1989, pp. 100–101; Chapter 5 of his book, "Cosmological Models," is an excellent review of alternative Big Bang theories, demonstrating why according to some the universe will expand forever and according to others will collapse back to its original density. The conservation of energy, and strict determinism, are presupposed by all models.

2. Plato himself wrote of his heaven of forms only and explicitly mythically. In the Meno, for instance, reference is made to a realm of pure forms that a soul could see before its birth into the world in order to enable it to recognize forms in things in the world. But if prenatal souls could learn forms by seeing them for the first time in heaven, postnatal souls could learn them in things too. In the Phaedrus the souls fly by the showcase of heavenly forms in chariots, or as chariot teams, to learn about what is valuable; but Socrates' point, which supposes the lesson from the Meno, is to get Phaedrus to learn how to see value and to test it dialectically in the temporal world.

3. See the discussion of this in the still classic *Metaphysical Foundations of Modern Science* by E. A. Burtt.

4. This is the main burden of the extensive argument in *Reconstruction of Thinking* (1981), which was sketched earlier. That book is part of a series called an Axiology of Thinking in which four families of mental activity are shown to be essentially attentive to value: imagination, interpretation, theorizing, and the pursuit of responsibility. Imagination has to do with bringing experiential form to the various stimuli affecting the body, and it is shown that form itself is the norm for achieving value in an integrated plurality. The case is made in part by a discussion of Kant, the toughest customer in the matter.

Chapter 7. Time's Flow

1. Whitehead's thoughts were developed in response to the kinds of problems raised by McTaggart (1927, vol. 2) who distinguished time's flow as a series of before and after moments from a series of past, present, and future moments.

2. They are, respectively, the topics of my *Reconstruction of Thinking*, (1981), and *Recovery of the Measure* (1989).

Chapter 8. Eternal Togetherness of the Temporal Modes

1. See the discussion of the ontological context of mutual relevance in my *God the Creator* (1992a), Chapter 2 and passim.

Chapter 9. Eternity and God's Being

1. A good up-to-date introduction to comparative religions is Ninian Smart's *The World's Religions* (1989). A classic phenomenological study is G. Van Der Leeuw's *Religion in Essence and Manifestation* (1933).

2. See John Cobb, Jr.'s learned and sensitive book, *The Structure of Christian Existence* (1967), that contrasts the Christian structure with that of several other types.
3. This is the thesis of Huston Smith and others who profess the "perennial philosophy." See his *Forgotten Truth* (1976), or Frithjof Schuon's *The Transcendent Unity of Religions* (1984). See also John Hick's *Problems of Religious Pluralism* (1985).
4. Of the many anthropologists dealing with religions' approaches to God, perhaps Emile Durkheim is the most influential; see his *The Elementary Forms of the Religious Life* (1915). A helpful summary of classical anthropological approaches is Annemarie de Waal Malefijt's *Religion and Culture* (1968).
5. My *Behind the Masks of God* (1991a) is a study of methodological questions in comparative theology. The book argues that comparative categories need to be developed carefully by abstracting and purifying motifs from concrete religious traditions and inquiring into how well they can be used to interpret other religions. The comparative categories of creation *ex nihilo* and of personal sanctification or individuation are explored in that book with reference to Christianity and Confucianism, with some reference to Buddhism and Taoism.
6. For a more extensive analysis of Hartshorne's theory, see my *Creativity and God* (1980), where I argue that his model of God's succession of moments is not coherent. Hartshorne's position on time, temporal modes, and eternity has been analyzed in Hahn (1991), Chapter 19.

Chapter 10. Eternal Creation

1. I have made specific objections to its systematic categories in *Creativity and God* (1980). The argument there is that the two main process notions of God, as a single actual entity and as a society of divine occasions, are internally incoherent, that neither the account of God's prehension of the world nor the account of finite being's prehension of God is adequate, that the process distinction between creativity and God cannot be sustained, and that the process conceptions of God are not conceptions of what is ultimately worthy of worship.
2. I have developed this use limited use of Whitehead in *Recovery of the Measure* (1989) and *The Highroad around Modernism* (1992b).
3. The argument to be given in answer to this question was originally and most fully developed in *God the Creator* (1992a), Part I.
4. I have developed this idea of logos in *A Theology Primer* (1991b).

Chapter 11. Creation of All Times

1. These remarks summarize the complex theory and arguments advanced in *The Cosmology of Freedom* (1974), Chapter 3, and *Recovery of the Measure* (1989), chapters 7 and 8. In large measure, the theory derives from points made by Leibniz and Whitehead.
2. Whitehead made the point about the vibratory character of subatomic particles in *Science and the Modern World* (1925). Loye Brad Ashton made the point to me with regard to the present theory of time in personal communications and an unpublished paper.
3. The nature of human freedom is controversial in part because there are many aspects to freedom that are easily confused. At a basic level, appreciated by prisoners, to be free means to be unbound; freedom means also the ability, or practised capability, of acting to fulfill one's intentions; that is different from the freedom to choose what to intend from among open options, which in turn is different from although related to choosing on the basis of standards for which one takes responsibility, as in Kant's sense of freedom. These senses of freedom are all in reference to persons and contrast with freedom as a characteristic of society. Societies are free insofar as they provide opportunities for people, insofar as they allow for a plurality of life-styles or cultural forms of life, insofar as they allow for the public respect for and interaction among persons of different cultures, and insofar as they allow for participation in setting the conditions under which political decisions are made. Metaphysical questions aside, experience has taught that all these senses of freedom exist under certain conditions, have been gained or lost as conditions change, and are usually distributed unequally across society and inside individuals' lives, sometimes being competitive with one another. Freedom itself as a general virtue is perhaps not as important as responsibility or should take its normative shape from what would serve responsibility. See my *The Cosmology of Freedom* (1974), and *The Highroad around Modernism* (1992b).
4. The contribution of divine creativity to the conjunction of future possibilities with present emergence is the topic of careful metaphysical reflection by Lewis S. Ford (1981, 1987, and 1994). He follows process theology, however, in saying that the creativity within an emerging present thing cannot be divine. Therefore he views God's creativity as the process of contracting vague future possibilities down to the nearly specific ones that an emergent thing can grasp; this allows him to hold to a doctrine of providence while still allowing a modicum of external human freedom. The danger in this view is that if God gets too specific human freedom can be shrunk to trivial proportions. And if God offers up immediate

possibilities that allow for serious evil, then God is at least complicit in evil that God could have prevented, which the process view had hoped to avoid.

5. Whitehead called this initial selectivity *subjective unity*, meaning the compatibility of components to be harmonized, allowing that compatibility includes the capacity to exclude some things and change others. Subjective units among the initial data of a happening is to be contrasted with the subjective harmony in the actualized finish, to use Whitehead's language. Saying that the spontaneous creativity in the present selects the components for potentials is a way alternate to Whitehead's of accounting for the separate individuality of present acts of existence. Whitehead's way is to say that God supplies distinct lures for subjective aim to different occasions and does not attempt to account for the particularity in subjective unity. See Whitehead, 1929, Part III, Chapter 1.

Chapter 12. God's Eternal Life

1. Chou's point is made in *An Explanation of the Diagram of the Great Ultimate*, trans. Wing-tsit Chan in his *Source Book of Chinese Philosophy* (1963), Chapter 28.

Chapter 13. The Eternal Identity of Persons

1. This point, expressed in the last two sentences, was made by an anonymous copy editor for SUNY Press, whom I thank.

Chapter 14. The Divine Identity of Persons

1. The concern for immortality is nearly always expressed these days in individualistic terms. The only exception is some of the discussions of why genocide is wrong, and there the claim is that ethnic or socially defined groups have some inalienable right to continue forever; these arguments are not particularly persuasive. Genocide is wrong because of the killing involved.

   The argument in the text briefly treats the ways individuals are involved necessarily in relations with others. I have explored this theme much more extensively in *The Cosmology of Freedom* and *The Puritan Smile*. Persons are also intrinsically involved with a larger nature, a theme developed in *Recovery of the Measure: Interpretation and Nature*. All these studies carry out pragmatic themes developed by Charles Peirce and John Dewey.

2. The phrase "broken covenant" comes from Robert N. Bellah, 1975, but is used here in a far more general sense.

Bibliography

Anselm. 1903. *Cur Deus Homo.* trans. (from the Latin) Sidney Norton Deane. LaSalle, Ill.: Open Court Publishing Company.

Aquinas, Thomas. 1256–1259. *De veritate,* trans. (as *Truth*) Robert W. Mulligan, S.J., vol. 1. Chicago: Henry Regnery Company, 1952.

Armstrong, A. H., editor. 1986. *Classical Mediterranean Spirituality: Egyptian, Greek, Roman.* New York: Crossroad.

Augustine. 398. *Confessions,* trans. and ed. Albert C. Outler. Library of Christian Classics, Vol. 7. Philadelphia: Westminster Press, 1955.

Bellah, Robert N. 1975. *The Broken Covenant: American Civil Religion in Time of Trial.* New York: Crossroad/The Seabury Press.

Bergson, Henri. 1911. *Matter and Memory,* trans. N. M. Paul and W. S. Palmer. London: Allen & Unwin.

———. 1913. *Creative Evolution,* trans. Arthur Mitchell. New York: Henry Holt.

Bradley, Francis Herbert. 1897. *Appearance and Reality,* 2d ed. Oxford: Oxford University Press; 1st ed., 1893.

Browne, Malcolm W. 1992. "Despite New Data, Mysteries of Creation Persist." *The New York Times* (May 12, 1992), pp. C1 f.

Brumbaugh, Robert S. 1984. *Unreality and Time.* Albany: State University of New York Press.

246 *Eternity and Time's Flow*

Buchler, Justus. 1966. *Metaphysics of Natural Complexes.* New York: Columbia University Press.

Burtt, E. A. 1932. *The Metaphysical Foundations of Modern Science,* 2d ed. New York: The Humanities Press.

Chan, Wing-tsit. 1963. *A Source Book in Chinese Philosophy.* Princeton, N.J.: Princeton University Press.

Chang, Garma C. C. 1971. *The Buddhist Teaching of Totality: The Philosophy of Hwa Yen Buddhism.* University Park: Pennsylvania State University Press.

Close, Frank. 1988. *End: Cosmic Catastrophe and the Fate of the Universe.* London: Simon and Schuster.

Cobb, John B., Jr. 1965. *A Christian Natural Theology.* Philadelphia: Westminster Press.

———. 1967. *The Structure of Christian Existence.* Philadelphia: Westminster Press.

———. 1976. *Process Theology: An Introductory Exposition,* with David Ray Griffin. Philadelphia: Westminster Press.

Cook, Francis H. 1977. *Hua-yen Buddhism: The Jewel Net of Indra.* University Park: Pennsylvania State University Press.

Crites, Stephen. 1993. "'The Blissful Security of the Moment': Recollection, Repetition, and Eternal Recurrence." In the *International Kierkegaard Commentary* volume on *Repetition,* forthcoming.

d'Abro, A. 1950, *The Evolution of Scientific Thought from Newton to Einstein,* 2d ed. New York: Dover Books.

Descartes, Rene. 1931. *Philosophical Works of Descartes,* Vol. 1, trans. Elizabeth S. Haldane and G. R. T. Ross. New York: Dover Books reprint, 1955.

———. 1934. *Philosophical Works of Descartes,* Vol. 2, trans. Elizabeth S. Haldane and G. R. T. Ross. New York: Dover Books reprint, 1955.

———. 1956. *Discourse on Method,* trans. Laurence J. Lafleur, 2d ed. New York: Liberal Arts Press.

Dewey, John. 1922. *Human Nature and Conduct: An Introduction to Social Psychology.* New York: Henry Holt.

———. 1925. *Experience and Nature.* In *The Later Works*, Vol. 1, ed. Jo Ann Boydston. Carbondale: Southern Illinois University Press, 1981.

———. 1929. *The Quest for Certainty.* In *The Later Works*, Vol. 4, ed. Jo Ann Boydston, with an introduction by Stephen Toulmin. Carbondale: Southern Illinois University Press, 1984.

———. 1934a. *A Common Faith.* New Haven, Conn.: Yale University Press.

———. 1934b. *Art as Experience.* New York: Putnam's Sons, 1958.

———. 1939. *A Theory of Valuation.* Chicago: University of Chicago Press.

———. 1960. *On Experience, Nature, and Freedom*, ed. Richard J. Bernstein. New York: Liberal Arts Press.

Durkheim, Emile. 1915. *The Elementary Forms of the Religious Life*, trans. Joseph Ward Swain. London: George Allen and Unwin; New York: Free Press, 1965.

Fodor, Jerry A. 1983. *The Modularity of Mind.* Cambridge, Mass.: Massachusetts Institute of Technology Press.

Ford, Lewis S. 1978. *The Lure of God: A Biblical Background for Process Theism.* Philadelphia: Fortress Press.

———. 1981. "The Divine Activity of the Future." *Process Studies* 11/3 (Fall, 1981), 169–179.

———. 1987. "Creativity in a Future Key," in Neville, 1987b, 179–197.

———. 1994. *Transforming Theism: Six Whiteheadian Concepts of God.* Albany: State University of New York Press, forthcoming.

Gallistel, C. R. 1980. *The Organization of Action: A New Synthesis.* Hillsdale, N.J.: Lawrence Erlbaum Associates Publishers.

Griffin, David Ray. 1973. *A Process Christology.* Philadelphia: Westminster Press.

———. 1976. *Process Theology: An Introductory Exposition*, with John B. Cobb, Jr. Philadelphia: Westminster Press.

Hahn, Lewis Edwin, editor. 1991. *The Philosophy of Charles Hartshorne*. Library of Living Philosophers, Vol. 20. LaSalle, Ill.: Open Court Publishing Company.

Harris, Errol E. 1988. *The Reality of Time*. Albany: State University of New York Press.

Hart, Ray L. 1993. "Meister Eckhart: Nothing If Not God; If God, Nothing; If Godhead, Nothingness *Hyper-on*." Forthcoming.

Hartshorne, Charles. 1948. *The Divine Relativity*. New Haven, Conn.: Yale University Press.

———. 1962. *The Logic of Perfection and Other Essays in Neoclassical Metaphysics*. LaSalle, Ill.: Open Court Publishing Company.

———. 1970. *Creative Synthesis and Philosophic Method*. LaSalle, Ill.: Open Court Publishing Company.

———. 1980. "Three Responses to Neville's Creativity and God," with John B. Cobb, Jr., and Lewis S. Ford. *Process Studies* 10, nos. 3–4 (Fall–Winter).

Hawking, Stephen W. 1988. *A Brief History of Time*. New York: Bantam Press.

Hegel, Georg Wilhelm Friedrich. 1807. *Phenomenology of Spirit*, trans. A. V. Miller. Oxford: Oxford University Press, 1977.

———. 1832. *Lectures on the Philosophy of Religion*, trans. and ed. E. B. Speirs and J. Burdon Sanderson, 3 vols. New York: Humanities Press, 1962.

———. 1833. *The Science of Logic*, trans. W. H. Johnston and L. G. Struthers, 2 vols. London: George Allen & Unwin, 1929. The translation is of the 4th ed.; Hegel himself prepared only the 1st and 2nd eds., the latter of which is given as the date here.

———. 1840. *Lectures on the Philosophy of History*, trans. J. Sibree. New York: Dover Books, 1956.

———. 1840a. *Lectures on the History of Philosophy*, translated by E. S. Haldane, 3 vols. London: Kegan Paul, Trench, Trübner, 1892.

Heidegger, Martin. 1927. *Being and Time*, trans. John Macquarrie and Edward Robinson. London: SCM Press, 1962.

——. 1929. *Kant and the Problem of Metaphysics*, trans. James S. Churchill. Bloomington: Indiana University Press.

——. 1954. *The Question Concerning Technology and Other Essays*, trans. William Lovitt. New York: Harper, 1977; 1954 is the original publication date of the title essay.

Hick, John. 1985. *Problems of Religious Pluralism*. New York: St. Martin's Press.

Hoyle, Fred, and Chandra Wickramasinghe. 1988. *Cosmic Life-Force*. London: J. M. Dent & Sons.

Hume, David. 1779. *Dialogues Concerning Natural Religion*. New York: Hafner, 1955.

Husserl, Edmund. 1913. *Ideas: General Introduction to Pure Phenomenology*, trans. W. R. Boyce Gibson. New York: Macmillan, 1931; New York: Collier Books, 1962.

——. 1971. *Phenomology of Internal Time-Consciousness*, ed. Martin Heidegger, trans. James S. Churchill. Bloomington: Indiana University Press.

Jonas, Hans. 1963. *The Gnostic Religion*, 2d ed. Boston: Beacon Press.

Kant, Immanuel. 1787. *The Critique of Pure Reason*, 2d ed., trans. Norman Kemp Smith. New York: Macmillan, 1929.

Kung, Hans. 1986. *Christianity and the World Religions*, with others. Garden City, N.Y.: Doubleday Books.

Lemonick, Michael D. 1992. "Echoes of the Big Bang." *Time* (May 4, 1992), pp. 62–63.

Lucas, George R., Jr. 1983. *The Genesis of Modern Process Thought: A Historical Outline with Bibliography*. Metuchen, N.J.: Scarecrow Press and American Theological Library Association.

——, ed. 1986. *Hegel and Whitehead: Contemporary Perspectives on Systematic Philosophy*. Albany: State University of New York Press.

——. 1989. *The Rehabilitation of Whitehead: An Analytic and Histor-

ical Assessment of Process Philosophy. Albany: State University of New York Press.

McHenry, Leemon B. 1992. *Whitehead and Bradley*. Albany: State University of New York Press.

McTaggart, J.E. 1927. *The Nature of Existence*. Two volumes; Cambridge: Cambridge University Press.

Malefijt, Annemarie de Waal. 1968. *Religion and Culture*. New York: Macmillan.

Neville, Robert Cummings. 1974. *The Cosmology of Freedom*. New Haven, Conn.: Yale University Press.

———. 1978. *Soldier, Sage, Saint*. New York: Fordham University Press.

———. 1980. *Creativity and God*. New York: The Seabury Press.

———. 1981. *Reconstruction of Thinking*. Albany: State University of New York Press.

———. 1982. *The Tao and the Daimon*. Albany: State University of New York Press.

———. 1987a. *The Puritan Smile*. Albany: State University of New York Press.

———. 1987b. *New Essays in Metaphysics*, ed. Robert C. Neville. Albany: State University of New York Press.

———. 1989. *Recovery of the Measure*. Albany: State University of New York Press.

———. 1991a. *Behind the Masks of God*. Albany: State University of New York Press.

———. 1991b. *A Theology Primer*. Albany: State University of New York Press.

———. 1992a. *God the Creator*. Republication, Albany: State University of New York Press. [Original edition Chicago: University of Chicago Press, 1968.]

———. 1992b. *The Highroad around Modernism*. Albany: State University of New York Press.

Nishida Kitaro. 1973. *Art and Morality*, trans. David A. Dilworth and Valdo H. Viglielmo. Honolulu: University Press of Hawaii.

———. 1987. *Intuition and Reflection in Self-Consciousness*, trans. Valdo H. Viglielmo with Takeuchi Toshinori and Joseph S. O'Leary. Albany: State University of New York Press.

Nishitani Keiji. 1982. *Religion and Nothingness*, trans. Jan Van Bragt. Berkeley: University of California Press.

Ogden, Schubert M. 1966. *The Reality of God and Other Essays*. New York: Harper and Row.

———. 1986. *On Theology*. San Francisco: Harper and Row.

Oliver, Harold. 1981. *A Relational Metaphysic*. The Hague: Martinus Nijhoff.

———. 1984. *Relatedness*. Macon, Ga: Mercer University Press.

Origen. 225. *On First Principles*, trans. G. W. Butterworth. New York: Harper, 1966.

Otto, Rudolph. 1917. *The Idea of the Holy*, trans. John Harvey. New York: Oxford University Press, 1926.

Peirce, Charles Sanders. 1931–1935, 1958–1960. *The Collected Papers of Charles Sanders Peirce*, 8 volumes, vols. 1–6 ed. Charles Hartshorne and Paul Weiss, and vols. 7 and 8, ed. Arthur Burks. Citations are to *Collected Papers*, volume, paragraph number (not page number); e.g., CP 6:287–288.

Powell, Corey S. 1992. "The Golden Age of Cosmology." *Scientific American* 267, no. 1 (July), pp. 17–22.

Radhakrishnan, Sarvepalli. 1929. *Indian Philosophy*, 2 vols., 2d ed. London: George Allen & Unwin.

——— and Charles A. Moore, editors. 1957. *A Sourcebook in Indian Philosophy*. Princeton, N.J.: Princeton University Press.

Richardson, William J., S.J. 1963. *Heidegger: Through Phenomenology to Thought*. The Hague: Martinus Nijhoff.

Riordan, Michael, and David N. Schramm. 1991. *The Shadows of Creation: Dark Matter and the Structure of the Universe*. New York: W.H. Freeman & Company.

Schuon, Frithjof. 1984. *The Transcendent Unity of Religions.* Wheaton, Ill.: Theosophical Publishing House.

Searle, John R. 1969. *Speech Acts.* Cambridge: Cambridge University Press.

Sherburne, Donald W. 1961. *A Whiteheadian Aesthetic.* New Haven, Conn.: Yale University Press.

Sherover, Charles M. 1989. *Time, Freedom, and the Common Good.* Albany: State University of New York Press.

Silk, Joseph. 1989. *The Big Bang,* rev. and updated ed. New York: W. H. Freeman.

Smart, Ninian. 1989. *The World's Religions.* London: Cambridge University Press.

——— and Steven Konstantine. 1991. *Christian Systematic Theology in a World Context.* Minneapolis: Fortress Press.

Smith, Huston. 1976. *Forgotten Truth: The Primordial Tradition.* New York: Harper and Row.

Smith, John E. 1967. *Religion and Empiricism.* Milwaukee: Marquette University Press.

———. 1978. *Purpose and Thought: The Meaning of Pragmatism.* New Haven, Conn.: Yale University Press.

Sorabji, Richard. 1983. *Time, Creation, and the Continuum: Theories in Antiquity and the Early Middle Ages.* Ithaca, N.Y.: Cornell University Press.

Stace, W. T. 1952. *Time and Eternity: An Essay in the Philosophy of Religion.* Princeton, N.J.: Princeton University Press.

Suchocki, Marjorie Hewitt. 1986. *God, Christ, Church.* New York: Crossroad.

———. 1988. *The End of Evil: Process Eschatology in Historical Context.* Albany: State University of New York Press.

Tillich, Paul. 1951. *Systematic Theology,* Vol. 1. Chicago: University of Chicago Press.

———. 1952. *The Courage to Be.* New Haven, Conn.: Yale University Press.

———. 1957. *Systematic Theology*, Vol. 2. Chicago: University of Chicago Press.

———. 1959. *Theology of Culture*, ed. Robert C. Kimball. New York: Oxford University Press.

———. 1963. *Systematic Theology*, Vol. 3. Chicago: University of Chicago Press.

Van Der Leeuw, G. 1933. *Religion in Essence and Manifestation*, trans. J. E. Turner with appendices to the Torchbook edition, incorporating the additions of the second German edition, by Hans H. Penner. New York: Harper and Row, 1963.

Vaught, Carl G. 1982. *The Quest for Wholeness*. Albany: State University of New York Press.

Waldenfels, Hans. 1980. *Absolute Nothingness: Foundations for a Buddhist-Christian Dialogue*, trans. J. W. Heisig. New York: Paulist Press.

Weissman, David. 1989. *Hypothesis and the Spiral of Reflection*. Albany: State University of New York Press.

Whitehead, Alfred North. 1925. *Science and the Modern World*. New York: Macmillan.

———. 1926. *Religion in the Making*. New York: Macmillan.

———. 1929. *Process and Reality: An Essay in Cosmology*, corrected ed. David Ray Griffin and Donald W. Sherburne. New York: The Free Press, 1978.

———. 1933. *Adventures of Ideas*. New York: Macmillan.

Wilford, John Noble. 1992. "In the Glow of a Cosmic Discovery, A Physicist Ponders God and Fame." *The New York Times* (May 5, 1992), pp. C1, C9.

Wyschogrod, Edith. 1985. *Spirit in Ashes: Hegel, Heidegger, and Man-Made Mass Death*. New Haven, Conn.: Yale University Press.

Index

69–71; knowledge, 34; philosophy,
31–38
Transformation, 173
Travel, space, 198
Tribal religion, 22
Trinity, immanent versus economic,
141–143
Truth, xi, 194–195, 210; as adequation
of the intellect to the thing, 31–32;
defined by Aquinas, 238; in
metaphysics, 9–10; questions of,
31–32
Two authors, of any action, 166–168

Ultimacy, a concern for Hebrew, not
Greek, religion, 137–138
Ultimate, the, 125–126
Uncanny, the, 202
Unconscious, the, 84, 134; in
Buddhism, 8–10; God as, 203
Unification, in experience, 50–56
Unity, xi; subjective, in Whitehead's
philosophy, 244
Universality, xvi
Universe, expansion or contraction of,
81–82
Unlimited, 132
Unmoved mover, not a good image of
eternity, 130, 132–133
Upanisads, teachers of, 226

Vagueness, 9–10, 236
Value, 87–92, 102–105, 131–132,
161–166, 194–195, 204–207, 241,
239; association with form, 79,
88–91; of different kinds, 164–165;
in past, present, and future, 88–92
Van Der Leeuw, G., 241

Vaught, Carl, xvii-xviii
Vedas, 237
Velocity Map, xxi
Vitalism, 82–83
von Schoenborn, Alexander, xviii

Weiss, Jonathan, xviii
Weiss, Paul, xvii
Weissman, David, xviii, 151
Wells, Rulon, xvii
Wesley, John, 218–219
Western symbols of eternity, 175–176
Whitehead, Alfred North, xiii, xvii,
xiv-xv, 31–32, 37, 39–44, 53–56, 75,
88, 91, 97, 99, 115, 119, 130, 149,
152, 160, 163, 238, 240–244
Wickramasinghe, Chandra, 8–9, 11,
236
Wiebenga, William, xviii
Wilford, John Noble, 235–236
Will, 86
Witness to God, of contingency,
202–203
Work ethic, 26
World, character of reflecting creator,
154–158; created, 140–158; defined,
143–149; "that" and "what",
145–149; philosophically defined,
34–35; representations of, 5–7
Worship, 141–142
Worshipfulness, 150, 242
Wotan, 178
Wyschogrod, Edith, 186

Yahweh, 135–136
Yin and yang, 20, 174–175

Zeno, 104–105